# The Odd Couple

**Allan Behm**

Allan Behm specialises in international and security policy development, political and security risk evaluation, policy analysis and development, and negotiating the policy/ politics interface. Following a career spanning nearly thirty years in the Australian Public Service, he was Chief of Staff to Minister for Climate Change and Industry, Greg Combet (2009–13), and senior advisor to the Shadow Minister for Foreign Affairs, Senator Penny Wong (2017–19). He has a significant publishing record and is a respected commentator in both the electronic and print media. His book *No, Minister* – an insider's account of what happens behind the scenes in Parliament House – was published by Melbourne University Publishing in 2015. It remains a 'go-to' text for those who are interested in leadership, political management, policy development and reform. In March 2022, Upswell published *No Enemies No Friends*, a critical examination of what limits Australia as an actor on the international stage.

# Endorsements for *The Odd Couple*

*The Odd Couple* could not come at a more critical time for Australia's relationship with the United States. As American democracy faces its biggest test in generations, Allan Behm brings a creative and deeply researched approach to the long-term Australia–US relationship, putting it in critical historical and cultural perspective and revealing its true nature. In this captivating read, Behm demonstrates what a genuine partnership with the United States might look like, and how we might build it. Alongside his 2022 book, *No Enemies No Friends*, *The Odd Couple* establishes Behm as one of the most innovative contemporary thinkers on the alliance and Australian foreign and security policy. Working as a colleague at the Australia Institute, I have observed the construction of this empathetic and optimistic study from its beginning. Its logic is as encouraging as it is relentless. *The Odd Couple* is essential reading for those who wish to see Australia and the United States work together in true partnership to build a more peaceful, secure and inclusive world for us all.

DR EMMA SHORTIS,
Senior Researcher in International and Security Affairs at
The Australia Institute
Adjunct Senior Fellow, School of Global, Urban and Social Studies,
RMIT University

The United States and Australia – two countries that are similar in many respects and yet so different, as poignantly set out in this book. Surely, the turn of world events and prospects in critical elections to take place in both our countries should cause us to turn the mirror on our complacent selves and use the reflection to consider proactively what kind of future we want to build.

ADMIRAL CHRIS BARRIE AC, RAN (Ret'd)
College of Asia and the Pacific
Australian National University

This book explores the many dimensions in which America really matters to Australia and in which America's social and political decline would affect us. A must read for those interested in the relationship. This book shines light where too few of us are looking.

ROSS P BUCKLEY
Scientia Professor, Faculty of Law and Justice, UNSW.

Allan Behm

# The Odd Couple

The Australia–America Relationship

**UPSWELL**

First published in Australia in 2024
by Upswell Publishing
Perth, Australia
upswellpublishing.com

This edition prepared for USA distribution.

Upswell operates in the city of Perth, on ancient country of the Whadjuk
people of the Noongar nation who remain the spiritual and cultural
custodians of this beautiful land. We acknowledge their continuing
connection to country and express gratitude to elders past and present for
their strength and creativity ... Always was, always will be, Aboriginal land.

ISBN: 978-0-645-24799-2

A catalogue record for this
book is available from the
NATIONAL LIBRARY OF AUSTRALIA
National Library of Australia

Cover design by Chil3, Fremantle
Typeset in Foundry Origin by Lasertype

*To the memory of Jeane Mildred Nutt (née Grant), born in Brisbane in 1928, married in Brisbane on 4 July 1946, died in Pasadena in 2022, and of Lieutenant Commander Charles Edmund Nutt USN, born in Los Angeles in 1923, died in Pasadena in 2011.*

*My aunt and uncle personified what a great trans-Pacific partnership can be. With love, perseverance and lots of diplomacy, this 'Odd Couple' created a lasting legacy that extends across the United States, and has begun the peaceful resettlement of Great Britain.*

# Contents

# Prologue

The most significant strategic risk facing Australia is the political and social collapse of the United States of America. America's strategic collapse would follow.

While such a collapse would be a disaster for America, it would be a security catastrophe for Australia, leaving the country down-under psychologically and strategically isolated. While Australia frets about the possibility of war with China – a threat that is largely an artefact of Australian insecurity, American strategic ambiguity in the North Pacific and fearmongering by those who should know better – Australians pay no attention to how they might avert or deal with an even more consequential risk: America's collapse.

At least since the visit of the Great White Fleet well over a century ago,[1] Australia has harboured a mawkishly sentimental view of an America seen simultaneously as the inspiration of its hopes and the solution to its problems. The ANZUS Treaty, negotiated in 1951, transformed Australia's security dependence on America to the point that Australia has now upgraded its membership of the ANZUS frequent fighters' club from acquiescent ally to accepting acolyte. In the words of Australia's 2023 Defence Strategic Review, 'The United States will become even more important in coming decades.'[2] Well, maybe it will. But what if it does not?

If Australia does insecurity well, America does exceptionalism very well – just ask any American.

America is blessed – or is it cursed? – with a 'manifest destiny'. It is, in the words of a former secretary of state, indispensable. The world – America's friends, enemies or in between – need America. America does not need the world, however. America is self-sufficient, and its self-sufficiency powers a self-absorption and a self-importance that demand both recognition and acceptance. And in this case, acceptance is premised not on America's natural eminence but on its God-given right to global pre-eminence. America's exceptionalism and manifest destiny confer on it the divine right to lead the world, to decide what is best for everyone simply because it is best for itself. Exceptionalism is not about humility. It is not about pride, either. And it is certainly not about ambition, because the achievement and realisation of ambition is always contested. It is about global dominance, because it is about a state of being, the order of things, the inevitable affirmation of national power that is international in its application and effect.

American confidence was on display from the first days of independence. In 1776, Benjamin Franklin, accompanied initially by John Adams, began a nine-year mission to France, first to win support for America as a sovereign state, and then to represent America at the French court. Thomas Jefferson succeeded him as Minister Plenipotentiary, and for five years advocated America's interests with statesmen, intellectuals, artists and bankers. These representatives were seen not only as equal to the task, but as the intellectual and cultural equals of their hosts. They were exceptional, and exceptionalist. But it was the twenty-nine-year-old Abraham Lincoln who gave domestic resonance to what was already manifest in Europe. Speaking in Springfield, Illinois, in 1838, he began:

> In the great journal of things happening under the sun, we, the American People, find ... ourselves in the peaceful possession, of the fairest portion of the earth, as regards extent of territory, fertility of soil, and salubrity of climate. We find ourselves under the government of a system of political institutions, conducing more essentially to the ends of civil and religious liberty, than any of which the history of former times tells us. We, when mounting the stage of existence, found ourselves the legal inheritors of these fundamental blessings. We toiled not in the acquirement or establishment of them – they are a legacy bequeathed us, by a once hardy, brave, and patriotic, but now lamented and departed race of ancestors. Their's (sic)was

the task (and nobly they performed it) to possess themselves, and through themselves, us, of this goodly land; and to uprear upon its hills and its valleys, a political edifice of liberty and equal rights; 'tis ours only, to transmit these, the former, unprofaned by the foot of an invader; the latter, undecayed by the lapse of time and untorn by usurpation, to the latest generation that fate shall permit the world to know ... All the armies of Europe, Asia and Africa combined, with all the treasure of the earth (our own excepted) in their military chest; with a Buonaparte for a commander, could not by force, take a drink from the Ohio, or make a track on the Blue Ridge, in a trial of a thousand years.[3]

America is the light on the hill. Or, as the poet Emma Lazarus put it, the 'lamp beside the golden door' that beckons the tired and the poor, the 'huddled masses yearning to breathe free'.[4] While that might have been true for the peoples facing persecution and pogroms in nineteenth-century eastern Europe, the beacon now burns no less strongly, but certainly less welcomingly, for the peoples south of the Rio Grande. The light on the hill continues to illuminate, perhaps, but it seems to have lost the power to transform, and even less to create.

Assertions of indispensability notwithstanding, present-day America seems to be significantly constrained in both its action and its effect. The triumphant confidence of the Truman, Eisenhower and Kennedy administrations in the post–World War II years gave way to a more hesitant and querulous America. The 1975 evacuation of the US embassy in Saigon and the ditching overboard of dozens of helicopters (ostensibly the property of the South Vietnamese government, so American property was not being destroyed) was hardly a reflection of Kissinger's "peace with honour". The abortive 1980 mission to rescue the US diplomats held hostage in the embassy in Tehran doomed the Carter administration. Similarly, the failed 1993 peacekeeping mission to Somalia, dramatically commemorated in the movie *Blackhawk Down*, cast a shadow over the Clinton administration. President George W. Bush's Iraq adventure, with its 'shock and awe' bombing of Baghdad on 19 March 2003 and its 'mission accomplished' celebrations aboard USS *Abraham Lincoln* barely six weeks later, ushered in the destruction of Iraq, the repercussions of which continue across the Middle East.

For all its self-confidence and triumphalism, America is displaying symptoms of a deep insecurity that infects both its international over-reach and its internal division. Slowly, but inevitably, it is coming to terms with the fact that, as a relative newcomer among the world's great empires, it is unable to control and transform enduring civilisations like China, India and Russia. Even less is it able to transform the inheritors of more ancient civilisations like Egypt, Iran, Iraq or Israel. Its much-vaunted 'international rules-based order', trumpeted as often by Australia and its other allies as by America itself, is under considerable challenge, and the challengers are getting away with it – not least of all because of its patent hypocrisy. An agreed set of international rules is infinitely preferable to chaos and war. It is imperative that America rediscover its confidence, its 'manifest destiny'. Lincoln continued his Springfield address with this sobering thought: 'If destruction be our lot, we must ourselves be its author and finisher. As a nation of freemen, we must live through all time, or die by suicide.'[5]

America may choose a dystopian future. Thoughtful Americans – and that is most of them – can see that the challenge is to 'live through all time'. The opposite is not unthinkable perhaps, but it is terminal, not only for America but for the global system that it has constructed. It is a system in which its allies, friends and partners are deeply invested.

Australians who were listening to their wireless receivers and crystal sets late in the evening of 3 September 1939 heard Prime Minister Menzies solemnly intone: 'It is my melancholy duty to inform you officially that, in consequence of the persistence of Germany in her invasion of Poland, Great Britain has declared war upon her, and that, as a result, Australia is also at war.'[6] Constitutionally, Menzies was correct. Britain maintained responsibility for the conduct of Australia's foreign and defence policy until the adoption of the *Statute of Westminster (Adoption) Act 1942 (Cth)*. Emotionally and psychologically, Australians were compelled once again to rally around the flag – the Union Jack or the Blue Ensign or the Red Ensign, what did it matter? Australia again signalled its imperial allegiance: the nation's contribution to the land war in the Middle East, the air war in Europe and the Middle East and the maritime war in Europe and the Pacific called itself 'the Second Australian Imperial Force (AIF)'. Australians again bled and died and spent their treasure in support of Britain.

And then, in December 1941, two days after the Japanese navy's attack on Pearl Harbor, Hawaii, the Royal Navy's battleship *Prince of Wales* and the battlecruiser *Repulse* were sunk by Japanese aircraft, precipitating the fall of Singapore. And with the fall of Singapore, Britain's role as Australia's protector and Australia's role as Britain's imperial dependent ended forever. Australia was on its own, insecure and unprotected.

Prime Minister Curtin moved quickly. The replacement protector, itself reeling from a devastating attack, was there for the asking (or begging), and ask (or beg) he did. Within three weeks Curtin was writing in *The Herald*: 'Without any inhibitions of any kind, I make it quite clear that Australia looks to America, free of any pangs as to our traditional links or kinship with the United Kingdom.'[7] And within three months he was appealing directly to the American people. Invoking 'the English-speaking race' and declaring Australia to be 'more than a match for the yellow aggressor', Curtin played the race card with equal facility. His broadcast of 14 March 1942 could not have been more different from Menzies' address to the nation on 3 September 1941. Nor could Curtin have been clearer:

> We never regarded the Pacific as a segment of the great struggle. We did not insist that it was the primary theatre of war, but we did say ... that the loss of the Pacific can be disastrous ... [T]hat is the case. And, realising very swiftly that it would be the case, the Australian Government sought a full and proper recognition of the part the Pacific was playing in the general strategic disposition of the world's warring forces. It was, therefore, but natural that ... we looked to America as the paramount factor on the democracies' side of the Pacific.[8]

Australia has never looked back. It is now emotionally glued to its new protector, its deep insecurity incarnated in a way that its dependency on Britain never was. The creation of the ANZUS myth, affording as it does a security version of the sentimental Anzac myth, has delivered a faith-based strategic platform that subsumes Australia's security interests within America's. When 'interchangeability' replaces 'inter-operability', insecurity morphs into subservience. Signalling the end of any pretence that Australia's strategic agency might include a measure of self-reliance, the defence minister has traded autonomy for the ability to 'operate seamlessly together, at speed'.[9]

This represents a profound repositioning. It is not just a transformation from ally to acolyte, but a realignment of interests as being essentially identical. As Clinton Fernandes has written, 'Australia is a subimperial power: it is subordinate to the imperial centre [America], defends the imperial order known as a rules-based international order, and pro-jects considerable power and influence in its own region.'[10] This raises profound questions about how Australia and America understand themselves and each other. 'Who we are' (our identity), 'what we stand for' (our values) and 'what we want' (our interests) need to be constantly revisited as part of a healthy national conversation. That applies as much to America as it does to Australia. Moreover, these questions need to be part of a healthy bilateral conversation. We need to explain ourselves to each other – which, coincidentally, is part of discovering who we are, what we stand for and what we want as separate national entities. While 'all the way with the USA' may give some Australians a warm feeling of relevance and security, it is an abnegation of responsibility for its own actions and its own future. It is a denial of agency. The AUKUS agreement between Australia, the United Kingdom and the United States on nuclear-propelled subma-rines, to which we shall return later, is emblematic of that.

Australia has felt insecure and in need of protection since European settlement. It will probably continue to do so for decades to come. But it is no more reasonable for Australia to foist itself on America for its long-term protection than it is for America to acquire Australia as a trans-Pacific dependency. A bilateral relationship premised on the demands of a contemporary and confused world necessitates a more nuanced, objective and thoughtful approach to the world and our mutual places in it than can be delivered by a heady cocktail of sycophancy on Australia's part and condescending hauteur on America's. It also demands a deep appreciation of the institutional and structural links between the two, which far transcend the defence and military relationship. The question both need to answer is: 'What matters?' Is there balance and mutuality in the relationship, as might define a long history of interaction not limited simply to military operations? What can we learn from each other, and what can we teach each other? Do Australian and American perspectives converge? And, if they do, how do we exploit that to mutual advantage? Is the relationship doomed to repetitive and largely banal affirmations of mutual admiration and historical derring-do within the framework of confected communiqués issued at the Australia–US Ministerial (AUSMIN) talks? Have we moved on from Prime Minister Harold Holt's fatuous 'all the way with LBJ', as we both found ourselves ever more deeply mired in the pointless war in Vietnam? And if we have not, why not? Were the unthinkable – and totally unnecessary – to happen, and China and the United States found themselves in a war over Taiwan, would it be 'inconceivable that we wouldn't support the US in an action if the US chose to take that action', as Australia's former defence minister Peter Dutton suggested in late 2021?[11] Automaticity is the pathway to annihilation.

International relations commentators talk endlessly about the asymmetrical nature of the relationship between America and Australia – as does everyone else, for that matter. Statements of the obvious are the clearest indication how little such commentators know about international relations, the world at large or much else. All relationships are inherently asymmetrical. Indeed, without asymmetry, diplomacy would lack both substance and purpose. Asymmetry provides the leverage that those who manage international relationships need if mutually beneficial results are to be negotiated. It does not matter that, according to World Bank data,[12] Americans have a lower life expectancy than Australians, are seven times more likely to be murdered, and have a per capita GDP 30 per cent lower than Australia's (in constant local currency). Nor does it matter that America's population is nearly thirteen times bigger than Australia's, or that its government-debt-to-GDP ratio is almost 50 per cent higher than Australia's. It is how quantitative disparities play into qualitative outcomes that counts. This is where institutional and structural compatibility, alignment of national interests and shared cultural, political and social aspirations come into their own. And when the more elusive notion of temperament joins the mix, diplomacy is less a board game than a policy market. It is in that policy market that Australia and America need to operate.

This book is an attempt to explore the character of the emerging policy market, and to argue that partnership trumps dependency every time (pun acknowledged, though not intended). Yet neither side of this critical Pacific relationship seems to appreciate that partnership is less an artefact of mass, power and physical equality than it is of shared objectives, complementarity of effort, compatibility of power and convergence of skills and intellectual resources. Old habits die hard. The beating of the military drum and the blare of the military bugle offer great comfort to those who see the past as the constant guide to the future. But the actions of dead heroes and the history of past deeds no more shape the future than do the gods, tempests, pestilence or earthquakes, as Thucydides was at pains to point out.[13] Like the past, the future is the product of human agency, whether exercised within the framework of enduring institutions and structures, or through their destruction and re-creation.

For Australia and America to shape and weather the massive changes occurring in Asia and the Pacific, they will need to recalibrate the bilateral relationship. A defence relationship is important if mutual defence interests are to be realised. But shaping the future and giving shape to the opportunities that the future will present demand starkly different interventions than defence agreements and force deployments might suppose. Those have some utility in bolstering military relationships. But constructing the regional inter-relationships needed to underpin prosperity and security requires considerably more inter-governmental and inter-agency action and investment. It requires a focus on the strategic benefits of strong economies and strong societies – which are never the results of the death and destruction of war. Yet war is what so many in the Australian and American policy communities continue to contemplate and even advocate. Indeed, they proclaim it to be inevitable.

America and Australia need each other for their own success, and the global community needs both for its success. But America and Australia need to find different ways to achieve different outcomes. This book imagines how to do that using the enormous resources at our disposal. And, more than that, as it contemplates the possibility of an American political and social collapse, it imagines how dependency can transform itself into partnership, in the interests of both parties. The last chapter addresses exactly that possibility.

# 1.
## Beginnings

America and Australia are ill-begotten siblings. Their promiscuous parent – *La Perfide Albion*, as the Marquis de Ximénès described England – dispensed tough love more or less even-handedly. They are the inevitable offspring of Britain's headlong escape from the Middle Ages to the Age of Enlightenment, from insularity to its eventual position as the global economic colossus. The elder sibling, America, rejected the tough love by booting Albion out. The younger, Australia, was effectively abandoned 170 years later as Britain was no longer able to defend her colonial dependents. Of course it was a French aristocrat who declared Albion perfidious, though the description is not wrong on that account. The French are right from time to time, as President Macron was well positioned to affirm. His direct experience of Britain and her former colonies America and Australia as they launched their AUKUS submarine project, while Australia reneged on its Shortfin Barracuda contract, confirmed his view.

The colonial siblings, their births separated by over a century and a half, were long in the gestation. In the late Middle Ages, a massive pandemic, the Black Death, together with a procession of weather calamities and crop failures, heralded seismic social change and political transformation across Europe. These powerful forces disrupted the balance between nations and, perhaps more significantly, between church and state. Rulers replaced covetousness with appropriation as they grabbed the church's enormous wealth, built up over centuries of tithing and manipulation of the faithful's guilt and need for redemption. In combination, these events set the critical preconditions for the Protestant Reformation, beginning in the early sixteenth century, which in turn set in train what was tantamount to a procession of revolutionary changes across Europe, nowhere more profoundly than in England – though with significantly less bloodshed than occurred elsewhere. From the beginning of the seventeenth century, the transformation in British agriculture increased its food production at a much faster rate than its population. Landowners became wealthier. Farm labourers became poorer. Alienation, dispossession and economic insecurity all increased.

Wealth freed imagination, innovation and invention. The result was an explosion in scientific discovery, delivering in turn the industrial revolution that changed the face of the world. It also delivered the climatic forces that currently threaten the globe existentially. But that is another story.

For Britain, there were four extraordinary outcomes that, within a span of 200 years, totally reshaped its economic, political and social contours, and produced its two biggest 'British' colonial offspring. The disruptive forces that reshaped Britain were: a substantial decline in the need for an agricultural workforce, leading to agricultural underemployment and unemployment; a rapid increase in the demand for industrial workers; a consequent drift of the rural population to the new industrial centres; and rapid urbanisation as British towns expanded quickly to accommodate the new industries and their new workforces. The political and social pressures generated by these developments were equally profound, impacting in unpredictable ways on Britain's radical reincarnation as a global power.

In the polity that gave the world the *Magna Carta*, and which, with the exception of the occasional peasants' revolt and food riot, was traditionally law-abiding, one of the more concerning unforeseen consequences of societal transformation was a rapid increase in crime.[1] The most common categories of crime were theft (involving both men and women, many of whom were domestics whose remuneration consisted solely of board and lodging), assault (involving mainly men) and prostitution (involving mainly women). Many of the criminals were children and juveniles, a fact around which Charles Dickens created *Oliver Twist*, his fictional portrait of London street life in the early nineteenth century.

## Convict transportation: A shared heritage

The courts dispensed rough justice.[2] The accused were rarely represented or defended, with the judge and jury (if there was one) conducting interrogation that was at best desultory. Judgement was quickly reached, and sentences were heavy. Death sentences were common, though often commuted to life imprisonment. Prisons were few, brutal, desperately overcrowded and dangerously unhygienic. Cholera, dysentery and typhus were rife, commuting a commutation back into a death sentence. As more people moved to the cities, especially to London, and as the crime rate rose in consequence, the number of prisoners increased, the gaols became more crowded, and prisoners were increasingly accommodated on hulks lined up along the Thames and elsewhere. Something had to give.

War is often a harbinger of transformation, as it is both a cause and a consequence of change. While England pressed on with the subjugation of the Irish and the Scots in the early seventeenth century, the redcoats took prisoners. To solve the problems of imprisonment – cost and the lack of detainment camps – their captors simply sold them as indentured labourers. This introduced a profit motive into the management of prisoners of war that subsequently underpinned the entire British transportation paradigm.[3] Accordingly, enterprising human traffickers complemented their slave trading with the transportation of prisoners of war. In the opening decades of the seventeenth century, prisoners were transported to the new British plantations in the West Indies, and then to America. Britain's export of the victims of its societal revolution was more than balanced by the rapid increase of imports critical to its economic expansion – cotton, sugar, timber, rum, tobacco and, eventually, wool. The indentured labourers more than paid their way, and the plantation owners – often members of the British landed aristocracy – were keen to see the system continue.

Despite considerable scholarship in America and Britain, historical records on transportation to the Americas are nonetheless sketchy.[4] Americans, of course, are more preoccupied with slavery than with their criminal past. Estimates on the numbers of prisoners transported to the Americas vary widely[5] – James Dunmore Lang suggested around 50,000,[6] while Thomas Keneally guessed about 120,000.[7] The main destinations for the transportees were Virginia, Maryland, Delaware, North Carolina, South Carolina, Georgia, New Jersey, New York and Pennsylvania, whence they dispersed across New England and to the west.[8] As these forced immigrants settled into their new environment, and as free settlers combined their religious emancipation with their enterprise and industry, the construction of a new society was underway. Daniel Defoe's *Moll Flanders* offered a somewhat picaresque advocacy of the redemptive character of transportation, a claim strenuously rebutted by Benjamin Franklin, who suggested that the export of rattlesnakes to Britain would be fair recompense for dumping felons in Boston and Baltimore. Unsurprisingly, the War of Independence and America's victory over the British forces in 1783 ended more than 150 years of transportation to North America. Newly independent America's relief became Britain's headache. And so too it became Australia's.

On 22 August 1770, after landing on Possession Island, in the Torres Strait, James Cook claimed New South Wales – the Australian continent (though whether Cook knew that is uncertain) – for the British crown. The fact that his 'possession' of the continent ignored its occupation by peoples who embodied the world's oldest living culture, and had occupied the continent for 65,000 years, was of no consequence. Just as the British 'discoverers' of America and the colonisers who followed them at first ignored and then displaced and 'removed' the original inhabitants, so too Australia's First Peoples were invisible. The Eora peoples living around Botany Bay were quickly introduced to the smell of gunpowder and the sting of birdshot. As Cook recorded in his journal entry for Sunday 29 April 1770:

I order'd the boats to lay upon their Oars, in order to speak to them; but this was to little purpose, for neither us nor Tupia [Cook's Polynesian interpreter] could understand one word they said. We then threw them some nails, beads, etc., a shore, which they took up, and seem'd not ill pleased with, in so much that I thought that they beckon'd to us to come ashore; but in this we were mistaken, for as soon as we put the boat in they again came to oppose us, upon which I fir'd a musquet between the 2, which had no other Effect than to make them retire back, where bundles of their darts lay, and one of them took up a stone and threw at us, which caused my firing a Second Musquet, load with small Shott; and altho' some of the shott struck the man, yet it had no other effect than making him lay hold on a Target. Immediately after this we landed, which we had no sooner done than they throw'd 2 darts at us; this obliged me to fire a third shott, soon after which they both made off.

Like the Māori people upon whom Cook's crew had fired in New Zealand, the Eora people made it perfectly clear that there was no welcoming mat for Cook and his crew. They threw their wooden spears and shouted, 'Go away'. But sticks were no protection against musket balls, and gunfire was a sure conversation stopper. Cook's journal recorded his onward progression along the east coast to Batavia, and then finally to Dover, where he anchored on 13 July 1771. With Cook's return, the Admiralty had a new destination for convicts. Even so, it took over a decade for the British government to reappraise its transportation policy after the American War of Independence terminated the North America option.

From 1775 to 1783, Britain was preoccupied with its rebellious American colony, almost to the point of policy paralysis. Domestically, however, it faced four interrelated and intersecting problems: a rising crime rate; a rising incarceration rate; nowhere to house convicted felons, except for unseaworthy hulks on the Thames; and the newly identified need to assert its strategic position in the antipodes and the Pacific. It examined several options, including Senegal, Gambia and south-west Africa.[9] In 1786 the British prime minister, William Pitt (the Younger), and his cabinet decided, with little more than Cook's reports and Royal Society president Sir Joseph Banks' testimony to a parliamentary committee as evidence, that Botany Bay was to be the new transportation destination. There was certainly no consideration of the interests or wishes of the inhabitant peoples, apart from Banks' throwaway line that 'there would be little probability of any opposition from the natives'. The consequences of this uninformed comment were devastating.

Between 1788 and 1868, over 162,000 persons were transported to Australia. Some, like Mary Wade, who embarked on the *Lady Juliana*, which arrived as part of the Second Fleet in 1790, were as young as thirteen. And at least one female convict, Dorothy Handlyn (alias Grey) was aged eighty-two, according to Arthur Bowes Smyth, ship's surgeon on the *Lady Penrhyn*, which arrived with the First Fleet.[10] With the exception of South Australia, the rest of the colonies accommodated transportees, most of them convicted felons, though some were political detainees who arrived without having been convicted – not that Governor Bligh was dissuaded from sending some of them to Norfolk Island and having them flogged anyway. Hugh Vesty Byrne, for example, who later became a landowner and publican at Campbelltown, New South Wales, was an Irish political rebel who had fought the British in county Wicklow, surrendering in 1803.[11] Although many of the transported prisoners served out their sentences and were eligible for repatriation, most lacked the wherewithal to meet the cost of passage back to England. Generally, they were granted landholdings and settled as farmers and commercial entrepreneurs. They formed the social backbone of early settler Australia, transforming what was essentially an open-air prison into a successful and largely self-supporting colony within sixty years.

## People

As one acerbic American once said, 'Wherever you go in the world, you will find two things: rats and Americans.'[12] This might look like a gratuitously laconic comment on Americans, but it identifies a distinguishing feature that reflects the inquisitive and intrepid aspects of the American character. The world – to infinity and beyond, as Buzz Lightyear readily understood – holds an irresistible attraction for Americans, whether by choice or by force of circumstances. So it is no accident that Americans were present at the very beginnings of Australia's white (and Black, as we shall see) settlement.

One of the key proponents of transportation was James Matra (himself an American), who had been a down-on-his-luck midshipman on Cook's HMB *Endeavour*. With Cook and Banks, Matra was one of the first of the *Endeavour* crew to walk the lands to the north of Botany Bay. The Sydney suburb of Matraville was named after him. Described by Cook as a 'good for nothing', he was a refugee from the American War of Independence, where his wealthy New York family had backed the wrong side and forfeited their property in consequence.[13] Matra presented submissions to parliamentary committees convened under the Portland and Pitt administrations, arguing for both an asylum 'for those unfortunate American loyalists to whom Great Britain is bound by every tie of honour and gratitude' and a settlement for young offenders.[14] He harboured ulterior motives, however. He promoted his case for appointment as governor of the new colony, his hopes delivering little more than a succession of minor diplomatic appointments in the Canary Islands, Constantinople and Tangiers.

Matra was not the only refugee from the War of Independence. Nor was he the only American, at least by birth (they were all British subjects, of course). An ordinary seaman, John Thurman, another New Yorker, was press-ganged by Cook in Madeira on the outward leg of the voyage to the Pacific. He died between Batavia and the Cape of Good Hope on the return leg in 1771.

There were several Americans transported in the First Fleet. Among the twelve convicts of African descent, probably from the West Indies,[15] John Martin, a merchant seaman, and John Randall, a former soldier, were both Americans. Martin was sentenced in 1782 for theft, by 1820 becoming the early colony's poundkeeper.[16] John Randall was sentenced in 1785 for stealing a watch chain.[17] He had been a slave owned by a British army officer, and doubtlessly a reluctant participant in the War of Independence fighting with the British – not that his 'veteran status' provided any extenuating circumstances when it came to sentencing. He eventually joined the New South Wales Corps and was subsequently a constable.[18]

Yet another light-fingered New Yorker and former enslaved man arrived with the Third Fleet in 1801. Convicted of stealing raw sugar, William 'Billy' Blue may have been a freed slave who served with the British Army in the War of Independence.[19] He became a harbour watchman and ferry operator, building a sound business, occasional brushes with the law notwithstanding. Blues Point, with its splendid views of Sydney Harbour, is named after him.

But by far the most influential Third Fleet arrival was the Massachusetts-born captain of the convict ship *William and Ann*, Eber Bunker.[20] A skilled mariner, he established the Australian whaling industry in waters off New Zealand, New South Wales, southern Victoria and south-western Western Australia, as well as undertaking several commercial runs to England and India. He also became a substantial landowner and a close friend of Governor Lachlan Macquarie.

As the early decades of white settlement unfolded, the American presence grew. It was the discovery of gold, however, that led to an explosion in American numbers in the colony. The discovery of gold in California in 1848 initiated the gold rushes that were such a feature of nineteenth-century labour expansion. Between 1848 and 1853, California's population increased over twentyfold, with prospectors from every part of the globe, including Australia, trying their luck.[21] But between 1851 and 1861, Victoria's population grew from about 80,000 to over half a million, with some of the immigrants trading life in California for life on the Victorian goldfields. American miners, in support of the Irish immigrants led by Peter Lalor (whose brothers had emigrated from Ireland to the United States), were among the ringleaders of the Eureka rebellion that changed the industrial landscape in the goldfields. Americans also exploited opportunities for commercial entrepreneurship, establishing Cobb & Co. – a significant transport artefact of the gold rush – and a raft of engineering and manufacturing enterprises. (These themes will re-emerge in Chapter 5.)

Transportation and immigration established the principal early links between America and Australia at Australia's conception. But these two products of Britain's prisons policy were linked in a more sinister way – the repression and destruction of the Indigenous peoples who were expelled from their traditional lands, whose lands were occupied and then expropriated.

## Land theft and Indigenous genocide

Euphemism is so often intended to deceive. It camouflages illegality and wrongdoing in the guise of benevolence towards those who are in fact the victims of rebarbative policy. Words like 'reservation', 'mission', 'reserve' and 'sanctuary' may seem benign, until one appreciates that they are actually synonyms for 'relocation facility', 'concentration camp', 'detention centre' and 'prison'. 'Aboriginal protection', as it was once called in Queensland, 'Indigenous progress' and 'native welfare' sound innocuous until their real meaning – removal, relocation and repression – becomes clear. These expressions mask the grim reality of genocide. The dispossession of Indigenous peoples, whether in America, Canada (where similar expropriation of lands, removal of original inhabitants and extinguishment of traditional land rights occurred) or Australia, was supported by policies and legislation designed to effect their complete disappearance. Confected legal doctrines of *terra nullius* and crown possession were complemented by banishment from ancestral lands, the appropriation and reassignment of land rights, prohibition of the use of Indigenous languages and their eventual extinction, the proscription of cultural activities and practices, and assimilation practices. All these policies were intended to encourage 'social integration', another euphemism for racial extinction. Identity was lost. Alienation, dispossession and deculturation (without any associated acculturation) were the result.

The American approach inadvertently provided the occupation model that Australia followed. British settlement of North America began in earnest in 1587, when Sir Walter Raleigh established a settlement in Roanoke, Virginia – so named in honour of the 'Virgin Queen'. The intrepid settlers disappeared without trace, possibly killed by less-than-welcoming local peoples. Native Americans, like Indigenous peoples in many parts of the world, did not have a sense of land ownership but they could certainly recognise invaders, people who wanted to occupy their lands without belonging there. The Indigenous peoples of the Americas had a strong sense of land use and a deeply spiritual bond with the lands on which they lived. Individual First Nations demarcated their territories, as did the First Peoples of Australia. But, as in Australia, they belonged to the land without a corresponding concept of ownership of or title over the land. This fundamental difference lay at the root of what followed: constant conflict and misunderstanding, fomented by deceit, *mala fides* and treachery on the part of the immigrant communities and the governments they created during the sixteenth and seventeenth centuries. This was racism writ large.

America's modern history is littered with disastrous encounters between the First Nations and immigrant settlers, and even more disastrous agreements and treaties between First Nations and government. History, it has often been said (but not by Winston Churchill), is written by the winners. The history of North America, and the vanquishment of the First Nations, is a cocktail of denial, distortion, half-truths, misunderstanding, mythology, cultural (mis)appropriation, romantic depictions of 'the noble savage' and accusations of barbarism.[22]

James Fenimore Cooper captured both the fatalism of the First Nations people and the inevitability of their extinction in his 1826 novel *The Last of the Mohicans*. Set in the misery of the French and Indian War – the North American dimension of the Seven Years' War between Britain and France – it both legitimises and popularises the disappearance of the Native American peoples and their replacement by a frontier generation of settlers in a new world. Thomas Jefferson's agrarian policies had encouraged expansion of the colonial footprint over Indigenous lands, pushing the First Nations ever westwards in the face of cannons and muskets. *The Last of the Mohicans*, often described as the first 'great American novel', was followed by several other Cooper novels – *The Pioneers*, *The Prairie* and *The Deerslayer* among them – each of which in its own way sanctioned the destruction of the Indigenous peoples as both acceptable and inevitable. Moreover, these novels established the literary trope of the valiant 'white man' and his dutiful 'Indian' sidekick, which, along with the American and Australian myth of the cowboy and the frontiersman, continued to exert a profound cultural influence in both countries. We shall return to the bilateral cultural resonances in Chapter 6.

Longfellow's 1855 epic poem *The Song of Hiawatha*, on the other hand, memorialises the destruction of North America's Indigenous nations in a romanticised and sentimental saga. After a few cantos of mystical scene-setting in a metrical form that imitates tom-toms, Hiawatha eventually appears as a pseudo-Messianic figure who, his tragic love-life notwithstanding, commends conversion to Christianity before sailing off to the happy hunting ground in his birch canoe – but not before prefiguring the Last Day and the Communion of Saints. It is little more than a saccharine misappropriation of Indigenous American language and themes to vindicate the trashing of an ancient culture and the possession of ancient lands. But from Queen Victoria's drawing room to the classrooms in which the Baby Boomer generation imbibed Kipling, Masefield and Longfellow as 'literature', *The Song of Hiawatha* was an iconic distorter and distortion of poetic imagination.[23]

Just occasionally there are some objective facts. The semi-historical, semi-fictionalised accounts of the Native American woman Pocahontas, whose birth name was Amonute and her 'christened' name Rebecca, illustrates the constraints on both historicity and identity. She married a settler, John Rolfe, in 1614 in Jamestown, Virginia. In an episode that curiously prefigures Bennelong's voyage from Sydney Cove to London almost two centuries later, she and Rolfe visited England in 1616, where she died a year later, aged around twenty, at Gravesend, Kent. Her visit to England, along with a group of other Native Americans, was partly to display the Indigenous peoples as curiosities and partly to encourage English investment and settlement. She may have met King James. She certainly had a son, through whom her family line continues in the person of American actor Edward Norton.[24] But whether literary or pseudo-historical, the written record paints a grim picture of genocide in all its dimensions.

For the century and a half following the death of Amonute, the history of the First Nations of North America is one of dispossession, destruction and death, as they were caught up in the colonial wars between the British and French, the Dutch and Spanish, taking sides, changing sides, aligning with each other, abrogating allegiances – all the time caught in the middle of conflicts they did not understand conducted on lands that they could not defend. Their cause was hopeless, as was their future. They were doomed. Whether hunting for bison and other game for food or trapping animals to satisfy the insatiable demand for furs and pelts, the Indigenous people of North America were as much manipulated into acts of genocidal self-harm as they were victims of settler predations and the ravages of disease. With the defeat of the British at the hands of Washington's militia, however, the genocide was about to begin in earnest.

During the next century and a half, the destruction of the Indigenous peoples of America and Australia ran more or less in parallel. While the causal factors differed and governments articulated their policies differently, the outcomes were essentially the same. Treaties were negotiated and signed under duress, and often abrogated before the ink was dry. The first Indian Reservation was established in New Jersey in 1758, which provided a precedent for the US Congress's passage of an ordinance 'for the regulation of Indian affairs' nearly thirty years later.[25] This instrument gave considerable power over the First Nations to the two superintendants (*sic*) who administered the northern district (west of the Hudson River) and the southern district (south of the Ohio River). The purpose of the ordinance was clear: the repression and suppression of the 'Indians'. '[The superintendants] ... shall regularly correspond with the secretary at war ... [and] obey all instructions, which they shall from time to time receive from the said secretary at war.'[26] It was clear that armed force was central to the deal. Hundreds of individual reservation areas followed. A procession of presidents spoke in uplifting terms of the place of the native peoples in the union, only to remove them at will. Here is President James Monroe in his second inaugural speech:

> The care of the Indian tribes within our limits has long been an essential part of our system, but, unfortunately, it has not been executed in a manner to accomplish all the objects intended by it. We have treated them as independent nations without their having any substantial pretension to that rank. The distinction has flattered their pride, retarded their improvement, and, in many instances, paved the way to their destruction. The progress of our settlements westward, supported as they are by a dense population, has constantly driven them back, with almost the total sacrifice of the lands which they have been compelled to abandon. They have claims on the magnanimity, and, I may add, on the justice of this nation, which we must all feel. We should become their real benefactors. We should perform the office of their Great Father, the endearing title which they emphatically give to the Chief Magistrate of our Union. Their sovereignty over vast territories should cease, in lieu of which the right of soil should be secured to each individual, and his posterity, in competent portions, and for the territory thus ceded by each tribe some reasonable equivalent should be granted, to be invested in permanent funds for the support of civil government over them, and for the education of their children, for their instruction in the art of husbandry, and to provide sustenance for them until they could provide it for themselves.[27]

In less than a paragraph, the First Nations people were patronised, dispossessed and left to their own devices. Within months, they were expelled from lands north of the Ohio River.

Eight years later, the slave-owning President Andrew Jackson devoted even less space, though no less sanctimony, to the First Nations:

It will be my sincere and constant desire to observe toward the Indian tribes within our limits a just and liberal policy, and to give that humane and considerate attention to their rights and their wants which is consistent with the habits of our Government and the feelings of our people.[28]

Just over a year later, Jackson persuaded the Congress to pass the *Indian Removal Act*, which forced what remained of the First Nations to leave the Union and settle lands (of other First Nations people) to the west of the Mississippi River.[29] Misleadingly, this act provided that 'nothing in this act contained shall be construed as authorizing or directing the violation of any existing treaty between the United States and any of the Indian tribes' – a provision that did not apply to the Cherokee Nation that was evicted from Georgia. Men, women and children were forced to march the 'Trail of Tears', over a thousand miles (1600 kilometres) to Oklahoma, during which some 4000 people died. Another 10,000 or so First Nations people died as the United States government pursued its land reallocation policies. It too was nothing less than a genocide. And, as Martin Scorsese's brilliant 2023 film *Killers of the Flower Moon* describes with a fatal inevitability, even when exiled to lands deemed worthless, these people were not safe, as the Osage people found with their Oklahoma oil wealth in the years immediately following World War I. The white community murdered them for it and stole their wealth and their rights. And, with the exception of a scapegoat, the white community got away with it.[30]

The removal and death of Indigenous Americans gathered pace over the remainder of the nineteenth century. California's First Nations were pushed out of their homelands in the late 1840s and early 1850s, while the Civil War imposed even greater disruption and suffering on America's First Nations. In 1863 Kit Carson led a Union Army attack on the Navajos in New Mexico, forcing another 'Long Walk' that killed hundreds. Armed conflict between the American government and the First Nations reached its nadir in 1876, when Arapaho, Cheyenne and Lakota fighters annihilated Colonel George Custer's 7th Cavalry Regiment at Little Bighorn in Montana. 'Custer's Last Stand' – a strategic error on Custer's part that served no useful purpose except the violent repression of Indigenous Americans – became the stuff of myth. But it also prompted harsh responses from the US Army and government, and would certainly have been in the minds of those who slaughtered over 300 Lakota people in December 1890 at Wounded Knee in South Dakota.

Both Little Bighorn and Wounded Knee represented much more than 'manifest destiny', contested land rights, racial prejudice, deep disdain for First Nations' cultural practices and First Nations' retaliation against settler supremacists and each other. The destruction of the bison herds, to the point of extinction in many traditional First Nations lands, to make way for broadacre cropping was tantamount to a policy of genocide by starvation. Culturally, materially and nutritionally, the First Nations peoples of the Western Plains were beggared. And once the First Nations peoples had been reduced to impotence and poverty, their cultural, political and spiritual agency destroyed, the 'Indian Wars' could be declared at an end and, in July 1924, President Calvin Coolidge could sign a bill granting First Nations people full citizenship. Of course, the right to vote, a right controlled by the individual states of the union, was not universal until 1948, when the Arizona Supreme Court struck down the disenfranchisement of Native Americans.

George III, King of Great Britain and Ireland, had more to worry about than former American colonies and porphyria. His son George had secretly married a Catholic, and was chafing to exercise royal powers as regent, given his father's increasingly erratic behaviour. So his antipodean possessions did not weigh so heavily on his mind as he signed instructions to Arthur Phillip, his about-to-be governor of New South Wales. After giving instructions regarding animal husbandry and its role in the subsistence of the convicts, he turned his mind to the original inhabitants, helpfully replacing the word 'Savages' (crossed out) with 'Natives'.

> You are to endeavour by every possible means to open an Intercourse with the Natives and to conciliate their affections, enjoining all Our Subjects to live in amity and kindness with them. And if any of Our Subjects shall wantonly destroy them, or give them any unnecessary

Interruption in the exercise of their several occupations, it is Our Will and Pleasure that you do cause such offenders to be brought to punishment according to the degree of the Offence. You will endeavour to procure an account of the Numbers inhabiting the Neighbourhood of the intended settlement and report your opinion to one of our Secretaries of State in what manner Our Intercourse with these people may be turned to the advantage of this country.[31]

Phillip's efforts to maintain the peace notwithstanding – he did, after all, suffer a spear wound to his shoulder – the King's instructions were even less honoured in spirit than they were in practice. For underpinning the entire approach of the early Australian community – and their successors two and a half centuries later, for that matter – was a deep-seated cultural and social racism that relegated non-white people to total 'otherness'.

Like America, Australia finds it difficult to come to terms with its racial history. Anyone who might wish to acknowledge that the past hides confronting evidence of brutality and murder, or who might even wish to explore whether such evidence exists at all, is accused of harbouring a 'black armband' view of the nation's history. The idea that there might be, or might have been, deep-seated exploitation, imperialism, misogyny, predation, racism or rape is anathema to many who are inheritors of a dispensation that thrived on inhumanity and violence. But careful scholarship conducted over the past several decades presents the evidence as incontrovertible. Australia was built as much on the blood, dispossession and death of its First Peoples as it was on natural bounty, good luck or hard work.

And, like America, Australia retreats into euphemism rather than confronts harsh truth. Terms like 'frontier wars' evoke a sense of mutuality, both sides resorting to hostility and violence and both sides sharing guilt, without any accounting for the overwhelming imbalance in power and egregious breaches of natural rights. Euphemism also de-ontologises actions and events by relabelling something that is illegal and/or immoral as a social or national benefit. So police patrols and landholder vigilantes did not 'murder' First Peoples.

Rather, they 'clashed', 'collided', 'confronted', 'dispersed', 'pacified' or 'removed' them.

Like Americans, Australians cannot use the term 'genocide' without descending immediately into sterile nominalism or scholastic logo-daedaly to determine how many murders is enough to justify the term. Yet the historical record speaks for itself: Australia's First Peoples suffered a genocide. It took three major forms: death by communicable diseases, such as smallpox, measles, cholera, influenza, syphilis, typhus and, in the later 'settlements', tuberculosis; death by malnutrition and starvation, when people were expelled from their traditional lands; and death by gunshot, especially following the introduction of breech-loading rifles in the 1870s.

It is clear from early records that disease spread quickly through the groups comprising the Eora nation living around Botany Bay and Sydney Harbour. The effect was catastrophic. As Peter Dowling records, communicable diseases precipitated the greatest human tragedy in the long history of Australia, nearly wiping out Australia's First Peoples.[32] Estimating the numbers of Indigenous people who died from disease or were killed between 1788 and 1988 (arbitrarily chosen) is notoriously difficult. While mass killings were common, they were undocumented, uninvestigated and unprosecuted. As two University of Queensland researchers commented, referring only to Queensland's experience:

> [I]f Aboriginal people had really been treated as other 'British subjects' were, and each massacre site, killing field or individual murder location treated as a conventional crime scene, and evidence to secure convictions assiduously gathered, and the contemporary legal documentation had all managed to survive the test of time, we now might have the kind of evidence that could 'stand up in court'.[33]

Of the currently recorded 430 massacres perpetrated in Australia, only one – the Myall Creek massacre in 1832 – led to the laying of charges and a prosecution, a trial and subsequently the execution of seven of the dozen or so perpetrators by hanging.

The research conducted by Professor Lyndall Ryan and her team at the University of Newcastle was forensic, thorough and compelling.[34] Australia's First Peoples were hunted and killed, with some of the hunter-killers, such as Lieutenant Henry Bunbury, being memorialised by having towns and localities named after them.[35] David Marr, in his compelling and horrifying account of the Uhr brothers, both officers in Queensland's Native Police force, portrays the bloodlust that fuelled the slaughter of Aboriginal people in Queensland.[36] As one reviewer put it, Marr's is the story of a nation without moral foundation.[37] Yet the default position for many Australians is that Australia's settlement was peaceful, and that Australia has achieved its current level of maturity without the civil wars and upheavals that have marked so many other countries, America included.

If, as the University of Queensland researchers suggest, the number of Indigenous people killed in violent encounters is around 60,000, it is reasonable to estimate the death toll from gunshot and armed attacks (such as the sabres used at Myall Creek) as approximately 100,000 – some 12 per cent of the commonly accepted pre-contact Indigenous population estimates of 850,000.[38] And if the deaths due to introduced diseases, epidemics and poisoning (of water sources and bread) are added to the toll, the inescapable conclusion is that Australia hosted a genocide commensurate with others noted in history.

'The truth shall make you free' – perhaps. Settler Australia must come to terms with its past if it to reconcile its history with the continued existence on this continent of the oldest living culture. Perhaps the most symbolic microcosm in which this reconciliation needs to occur is the Australian War Memorial in Canberra, where recognition of the Frontier Wars remains problematic.[39] While slowly, and reluctantly, the War Memorial has come to terms with the fact that Indigenous Australians served in both the world wars, conducting themselves with the bravery and selflessness that is the stuff of the Anzac myth, it has remained resistant to suggestions that the colonial practices of violent suppression of Indigenous peoples should be recognised and properly commemorated. It seems determined to persevere with the spirit of Billy Hughes's outrageous claim registered at the founding of Canberra in 1913. Proposing a toast to the premiers of the states, Australia's attorney-general said:

> We were destined to have our own way from the beginning and America – two nations that have always had their way, for they killed everybody else to get it [sic] ... Here we have a symbol of nationality [Canberra, the national capital] ... The first historic event in the history of the Commonwealth we are engaged in today without the slightest trace of that race we have banished from the face of the earth.[40]

Hubris and racism of that calibre resonates today: it is part of Australia's heritage, as it is part of America's. Hughes was at least correct in that. It has formed our contemporary mindset. How Australia and America might transcend their oppressive and painful beginnings to realise their potential as constructive partners in building a prosperous, safe and secure world is the theme of the following chapters.

# 2.
## Australia

Australia is an idea, founded on hope, clothed (or shrouded?) in myth. It is a country with a sense of humour and a fondness for the absurd. It enjoys mild self-deprecation. But nowadays its appreciation for irony is on the decline. It has become too self-absorbed and too serious for that. And a bit too confused. So it basks in the title 'the lucky country' without any suspicion that Donald Horne was 'having a lend of us' when he wrote the pungent comment that both plays to the nation's insouciance and confirms its complacency:

> Australia is a lucky country run mainly by second-rate people who share its luck. It lives on other people's ideas, and, although its ordinary people are adaptable, most of its leaders (in all fields) so lack curiosity about the events that surround them that they are often taken by surprise.[1]

So far, Australia has avoided Donald Trump's omnibus description of the nations of the African continent, along with Haiti and El Salvador, as 'shitholes', though some of Australia's South-East Asian and Pacific neighbours do employ the term 'arseholes' when describing Australians.[2] Equally, Australia has none of the mystique of Russia, memorably described by Churchill as 'a riddle, wrapped in a mystery, inside an enigma'.[3] The reason Australia fails to plumb the depths of Trumpian dystopia or scale the heights of Churchillian rhetoric is plain: Australia is defiantly ordinary. We love to talk about 'punching above our weight', a continuing tribute to our political leaders' infatuation with delusion. The fact is: Australia punches below its weight. Because we neither appreciate nor understand the nature of our national power (more on that later), we lack the agency to do much punching at all.

In her thought-provoking book *The Idea of Australia*, Julianne Schultz captures this welded-on ordinariness:

> Australia remains an oddly amorphous idea. *What idea?* Some ask. *No idea*, others respond ... The definition of a nation that is more than a place is still a work in progress, denied by those who consider it 'the settler state known as Australia' but celebrated by those whose lives have been transformed by life in a relatively safe, rich and ordered society. The paradox that is Australia is both solid and provisional ... Describing Australia's defining nature beyond the physical – her spirit, her essence – rarely gets beyond worthy but anodyne statements of universal values, pride in democratic institutions, and boastful backslapping about being the most successful multicultural nation in the world.[4]

Hiding behind and within its ordinariness, Australia refrains from making waves. It does not like to draw much attention to itself, to take a high profile or to advocate strongly for change. To the extent that Australia offers any commentary, it is more likely to be 'steady as she goes' or 'she'll be right'. Advocacy is what powerful nations do. Support is what 'middle-ranking' nations like to give. Australia enjoys the company of like-minded nations, gravitating towards the centre, where it is neither singular nor singled-out. At the United Nations, for instance, Australia prefers to be one of the 'others' in the Western European and Others Group, playing it safe, neither leading the pack nor following. Australia is distinct in being indistinct, distinguished in being undistinguishable, noticeable for being unnoticed, outstanding in not standing out. It is not that Australia is supine, or simply reflex. Australia is neither motivated nor ambitious.

Australia's First Peoples had cared for an extraordinary continent, as they had been cared for by it, for some 65,000 years when it suddenly became home to immigrant settlers. The decades immediately following the arrival of the First Fleet were hard. But as the convicted criminals and their guards achieved a rapprochement, melded together, and became self-sufficient and then prosperous, hardship gave way to hope. The replacement of Indigenous land management by cropping and grazing saw the wool industry provide an early and enduring foundation for the Australian economy, as the nation satisfied the insatiable appetite of Britain's 'dark Satanic Mills'.

The gold rush brought massive wealth, such that within a century of the First Fleet's arrival, Australia was the wealthiest country in the world on a per capita basis. The opulent Victorian colonial architecture of Adelaide, Melbourne, Sydney and Brisbane, together with rural centres such as Ballarat, Bendigo, Orange, Bathurst and Wellington, and even Charters Towers with its Stock Exchange, trading the shares of the mining companies at Mount Morgan, bear witness to the economic confidence of the Australian colonies.[5] And with this economic confidence grew the political confidence that enabled the colonies to federate.

For a country whose public self-image is so dominated by the Anzac hero, the charge at Beersheba, the bronzed surfer and the gun shearer, Australia (and New Zealand it must be said) established an early reputation as an international pace-setter on gender equity issues. The colony of South Australia enacted legislation in 1894 that recognised the rights of women, First Peoples women included, both to vote and to stand for parliament. Women's suffrage was contentious in the constitutional conventions of the 1890s. South Australia's insistence on the retention of women's suffrage as a condition of its joining the federation ensured universal suffrage for women across Australia. Disgracefully, though not unexpectedly, Indigenous suffrage was denied, and remained so for another sixty years. Immediate post-Federation Australia was a laboratory for political and social innovation. At this distance, Australia's early reputation for feminism, equality and social inclusion is too often overlooked, especially by male historians. But Australian advances on women's political rights (particularly women's suffrage), the secret ballot, industrial arbitration, the minimum wage, aged pensions, maternity allowances and children's courts

– just a few examples – inspired American progressives. The first International Women's Suffrage Alliance conference, held in Washington DC in February 1902, was a major stage for Vida Goldstein, an electrifying speaker and compelling advocate for women's suffrage. President Teddy Roosevelt felt compelled to meet this Australian dynamo who validated his personal commitment to women's equality. When she returned to Melbourne in August that year, she was met with the news that the Commonwealth Franchise Act had been signed into law. But it took another eighteen years for her American sisters to win the right to vote. In her fascinating essay on women's suffrage, Clare Wright commented:

> It is clear that Americans recognised the Australasian accomplishment regarding women's rights … But it was not always a relationship of mutual admiration. Goldstein was critical of her host country. 'Most of us regard America as the most democratic and advanced country politically in the world,' she told Australian audiences. 'Instead, it's as conservative a country as a country can well be. As democratic form of government does not necessarily mean that the people rule.' Goldstein offered an analysis of the root cause of the hypocrisy: '[America's] written and hidebound constitution [has] played directly into the hands of moneyed and unscrupulous politicians.'[6]

The nineteenth amendment to the US constitution notwithstanding, America dragged the chain. But sadly, in the racially-charged atmosphere of the White Australia policy and the entrenched disenfranchisement of African Americans, such progressive aspirations were widely seen on both sides of the Pacific as the white people's prerogative. As Marilyn Lake has pointed out in her monumental study *Progressive New World*, racial exclusion and the further marginalisation of Indigenous peoples was a mostly unintended consequence.[7] Nonetheless, racial inequality became entrenched in both America and Australia. Lake captures this point well: 'Like colonization, progressivism rested on the division of the world into advanced and backward peoples".[8] In Australia, as in America, much work remains to be done to entrench both gender and racial equality.

Somewhat surprisingly, by 1901 Australia was already one of the most urbanised countries in the world. With a national population of around 3.75 million people, Melbourne and Sydney, each with about half a million people, were much higher on the list of big international cities than they are now. And four of Australia's top ten cities were inland cities. Now only Canberra fits that bill. Australia's population lives predominantly on the nation's coastal fringe, in the temperate zones well south of the Tropic of Capricorn. Yet Australia's self-image remains anchored in the 'bush', where almost none of its people have ever lived, and where few Australians have family roots.

The myth of the frontier and outback roots of the nation was given currency by the ballads 'Clancy of the Overflow', 'Saltbush Bill', 'The Man from Snowy River' and, of course, 'Waltzing Matilda' – each glorifying the male bush larrikin. And each was written by a city-slicker Sydney solicitor who moonlighted as a freelance journalist. A.B. 'Banjo' Paterson was born on a sheep run near Orange, in rural New South Wales, and was a skilled horseman. He attended Sydney Grammar School, becoming a law clerk and eventually a war correspondent during the Boer War and World War I. He and Henry Lawson did much to create the mythical Aussie bushman, who successfully morphed into the Anzac digger of World War I and the infantry soldier of World War II. With their R.M. Williams boots and Akubra hats, a bourgeois nation of suburbanites congests the kerbed and guttered streets in their sports utility vehicles (SUVs) and recreational all-terrain vehicles (RAVs), four-wheel drives and twin-cab utility vehicles (utes). The closest most come to back roads or open terrains are the shopping centre car parks of Balmain, Balmoral and Bellevue Hill, or Bentleigh, Brighton and Brunswick.

Australians are inveterate mythmakers. The National Party of Australia has been riding on the back of the 'farmer as national hero' myth for over a century. Once upon a time, its politicians were farmers and graziers. Nowadays, they are more likely to be country accountants or stock-and-station agents. The party's founder, Dr Earle Page, claimed that the nation owed a special debt to the farmer, a debt that needed to be repaid through special consideration for people living in 'the bush'. This special consideration was underpinned by a form of agrarian socialism that reinforced the idea of 'country-mindedness' and consolidated the claim that Australians depended on farmers and graziers for their high standard of living. A key constant on which the 'people in the bush' myth depended for its continued resonance was the claim that farmers 'forged the core elements of the national character by taming the environment, making it productive, and creating a home'.[9] Of course, this failed to take account of the fact that 'taming the environment' was a key contributor to 'settler-colonial violence and the dispossession of Indigenous Australians' land and foodways'.[10]

The mining industry amplifies the frontier and outback myth, with its photographs of immense ore trains and muscled miners wielding shovels and driving massive excavators. It constantly advertises the fiction that it is a major national employer and that the national economy is dependent on the wealth it generates and the taxes it pays. The truth is completely different. The mining workforce accounts for just over 2 per cent of the national labour force,[11] while tourism accounts for 4.6 per cent, manufacturing for 6.5 per cent and the health sector 15.6 per cent. As the Polish-American mathematician Alfred Korzybski observed, the map is not the territory.[12] Similarly, economic statistics are not the economy. Just as a road map highlights entirely different features of a city to a topographic map, different economic statistics highlight entirely different features of an economy. So the Australian mining industry exploits people's confusion over the difference between gross domestic product (GDP) and gross national product (GNP), just as it exploits Australia's coal, iron and copper for its own profit and at the Australian community's cost.

GDP sounds the same as GNP, but they map vastly different terrain. GDP includes the value of all goods and services produced within a country's national borders, while GNP covers the value of production attributable to entities and people resident in Australia. Such statistical hair-splitting is usually irrelevant – except for a country like Australia. Its biggest industries almost entirely foreign-owned. Put simply, while the mining industry accounts for around 15 per cent of the value of all the goods and services produced in Australia (contributing significantly to GDP), its contribution to national income is quite small because mining is around 85 per cent foreign-owned. The vast majority of the industry's profits flow to the United States, the United Kingdom and Switzerland. As the Reserve Bank of Australia has noted, 'a large share' of mining profits are 'remitted to foreign shareholders' and so never touch the national accounts.[13] To add insult to injury, Australia does a poor job of taxing its resources sector. For example, Australia and Qatar produce comparable amounts of oil and gas, yet Qatar collects almost six times more revenue.

If agriculture and mining translate the frontier myth into a contemporary language, board riding and surfing provide the coastal tonality. Max Dupain's iconic photograph *Sunbaker 1937* (actually shot in 1934) created an indelible image of the bronzed surfer that continues to sustain both Australia's self-image and its reputation for laid-back hedonism. It is 'one of those emblematic images by which a nation comes to identify itself ... a focus for what it means to be Australian', wrote the art critic Miriam Cosic. 'The image, taken by a man, has homoerotic force.'[14]

But it is the heroic Anzac – male, fearless, tough and valiant – that is the apotheosis of the Australian myth. He plays into the narrative that nations are forged in war, and that what finally gave Australia its character was the courage, endurance, egalitarianism and mateship that defined the 'digger'. The facts that he was terrified in battle, suffered catastrophic injuries and died in appalling conditions are ignored, as is the fact that many of those who returned were broken in body and mind.

Nor does the national myth include nursing sisters like Elsie Rose Grant and the other women who also served in Egypt, France and England, many of whom succumbed, like the soldiers, to what is now identified as post-traumatic stress disorder. Matron Grant tended to the wounded and the dying in Cairo, Armentières, Ypres and London from 1915 to 1918. She committed suicide in 1927. She was the paternal aunt of the woman to whom this book is dedicated. She is not part of the national mythology.[15]

For better or worse, myths are inevitably part of the creation of the national character, and icons inevitably represent the national character. They provide the aural and visual metaphors that signal values while sanctioning taboos. They both create and reflect the emotional and volitional dynamic of national decision-making, nourishing the national subconscious – or at least the national herd instinct. For Australia's First Peoples, the complex systems of myths that form the Dreaming provide the cultural context within which the relationship between 'mob' and 'country' is defined. More importantly, they provide the spiritual foundation that gives meaning to personal and communal existence.

At this stage in its historical development, Australia's myths are a work in progress, largely transactional rather than transformative, descriptive rather than explanatory. In many respects, they tend to legitimise the white settler view of the nation: exclusionary, unconnected, dominant and dismissive of 'the other'. The 'white picket fence' view of Australia was nowhere more clearly symbolised than in the legislative canonisation of the cricketer Don Bradman in the pantheon of national heroes. In 2000, Prime Minister John Howard described Bradman as 'a man representing many of the values, much of the character of his countrymen'. He continued:

> Even now, in another century, in a world scarcely recognisable to that in which he played, the name Bradman resonates with meaning – talent, determination, commitment, fair play, honour. What then does this say about Bradman and what does it say about Australians that Bradman was so elevated to the honoured status that he now occupies in the national psyche?[16]

What indeed – a question posed totally without irony! Howard then proceeded to amend the *Corporations Act* to protect the name 'Bradman' in the same way that the names of the King, members of the Royal Family, ex-servicemen's organisations, Mary MacKillop (Saint Mary of the Cross), the police, the RSL and Anzac are protected.[17] Not too many nations have something with the redolence of Don Bradman or the Anzac biscuit to substantiate their national iconography.

## Identity

Myths are important in establishing identity. The ongoing problem for Australia, however, is that the national myths are too thin to support a robust identity. We do not really know who we are, which is perhaps one of the principal reasons for our deep-seated insecurity. We do not even know who we are not. Canadians often define themselves as 'not Americans', the Irish as 'not British', and New Zealanders as 'not Australians'. All, especially the Irish, are further down the path of self-identification than are Australians, while Canadians and New Zealanders continue to make progress in harmonising their settler and Indigenous histories, employing ethnic and linguistic identifiers in their respective pursuits of identity. Alone among the community of nations, only Australia and America define any departure from groupthink and conformity as 'un-Australian' and 'un-American'.

Identity is much more than homogeneity: it is multidimensional and multi-layered, embracing difference and diversity as it pursues unity around shared objectives and common values. To create a national identity, no one has to give up anything. Rather, everyone has to accept something that broadens their perspectives and enriches their sense of belonging to an enterprise much greater than themselves. Yet so often identity is portrayed as a lowest common factor, a minimalist affirmation of or attachment to something more symbolic than substantial.

Always a skilled purveyor of jejune reductionism, former prime minister Tony Abbott posed the question: 'Is there something other than mere geography that explains the affinity that almost every Australian has for nearly any other Australian whenever we happen to meet in some corner of the globe?' To contextualise his question, Abbott trotted out the standard conservative binary that the 'wonderful Australian commitment' to a fair go for all should be tempered by 'that equally wonderful injunction' to have a go. And not one to readily eschew the trivial, he answered his question with a few other questions:

Is it the 'fair go/have a go' instinct; is it some concept of mateship that transcends wealth, background, neighbourhood or gender; or is it a subconscious shaping by an 'up yours' larrikin culture starting with convicts and Aborigines and extending through Number 96 to Crocodile Dundee?[18]

If, during the COVID-19 pandemic, this sort of nonsense could be seen as an authoritative contribution to the necessary conversation on national identity, Australia is in trouble. A mishmash of tired and tawdry tropes offers no basis for a serious consideration of identity. To add *Number 96* (a groan-worthy risqué sitcom of which most Australians are ignorant or cannot remember) and *Crocodile Dundee* to the white picket fence, Don Bradman and Anzac biscuits is to depict Australia's identity as white, male, British, superficial and stupid.

Australia is better than that, however. The fact that the First Peoples of Australia could propose a set of concepts as majestic as those contained in the Uluru Statement from the Heart suggests an approach to identity factored around inclusion, a shared idea of belonging as the basis of sovereignty (the various domains of which are mutually convergent) and truth telling. And that these ideas were so emphatically rejected by the majority of Australian voters – except in the Australian Capital Territory and the remote polling booths of northern Australia – reinforces the possibility that Australia's national identity has changed little since the White Australia policy began its inglorious life during the gold rushes of the 1850s.

Because of the deep discomfort many or most Australians have with ideas of race, identity remains a constant problem. Across the world, the search for national identity tends to suppress the identities of Indigenous peoples. But identity is central to any modern polity that is inclusive and resilient, because identity is ultimately constructed upon the intrinsic value of each individual member of the community, each individual citizen who comprises the nation. As Francis Fukuyama has argued, the tension (or perhaps the contradiction) between the individual and society is not resolved by obliterating individuality and forcing the individual to conform to society's rules, but by society accepting and welcoming individual difference.[19]

## Values

If Australia's national myths are a work in progress, the identification of a set of national values has barely begun. The reason for this is as clear as it is disheartening: there is considerable confusion around what values are, especially when politicians attempt to exploit the term 'values' as part of the currency of diplomatic dialogue and inter-national relationship management. They beaver about trying to find the elusive things that Australia might have in common with other countries, before they even attempt to work out what Australians have in common with each other. So Australia has comprehensive strategic partnerships with countries as diverse as China and Japan, India, Indonesia, Malaysia, Singapore, ASEAN (as an association) and Papua New Guinea, and enhanced (what is the difference?) strategic partnerships with France and Germany. Australia shares values with America, India and Japan. Shared values – openness, diversity, trust, transparency, security, interoperability and resilience – authenticate the Quad defence consultative arrangement, for instance.[20] And with ASEAN, 'Australia is committed to the promotion of common values such as peace, harmony, intercultural understanding, the rule of law, good governance, respect, trust, tolerance, inclusiveness, moderation, social responsibility and diversity'.[21]

These lists consist of a mishmash of ideas and hopes, all of which may be 'valued' in various ways. Sloppy language is always a sign of sloppy thinking, nowhere more so than in political and diplomatic discourse where ambiguity, imprecision and vagueness serve to deliver a level of confidence that is ultimately undeliverable. It is difficult to identify and map out common ground around things as important as deeply shared principles and unbreakable rules. So in the world of a more superficial and transactional diplomacy, 'shared values' is an expres-sion that often validates diplomatic sludge as an acceptable substitute for meaning, precision and truth. Former Australian prime minister

Scott Morrison delivered a masterclass in linguistic looseness when he said that Australia and India enjoy a relationship where they are aligned in 'the things that matter and the values that we hold and we both seem to champion those values together in our region and independently as very proud sovereign nations and very vibrant liberal democracies as well and I think we hold that flag up very proudly, each of us'.[22] COVID-19 was in full swing at the time, but whew!

The term 'values' is increasingly weaponised in the domestic discourse that surrounds any attempt to codify national values. Dominant elites work constantly to extend their control over the body politic, while marginalising those who speak with a different voice or simply do not belong. Just as it would be difficult to imagine that Don Bradman or Saint Mary of the Cross could contribute much to a consolidated idea of national identity for Australia's First Peoples or immigrants from non-Anglo and non-Christian backgrounds, so it would be difficult to imagine that 'Christian' values could define the core values of an Australia that includes adherents to other faiths, agnostics and atheists. An insistence on faith-based values may, inadvertently or intentionally, constrain diversity rather than foster cohesion and inclusion.

There is little doubt that religious faith can inspire ethical behaviour. Equally, it can inspire intolerance, as historical examples in countries professing the Christian, Hindu or Islamic faiths have demonstrated over the centuries. The Spanish Inquisition had no respect for freedom of religion or individual conscience, while the pogroms of Eastern Europe legitimised and normalised the oppression of Jewish communities to the point of genocide. The exclusion and intolerance that drives religious persecution is just as much 'values-driven' as the imposition of atheism and the abolition of all religions (as was the case in Albania until its collapse in 1990). Saudi Arabia no more welcomes the practice of Christianity and Judaism than Modi's India welcomes the practice of Islam, or China welcomes the practice of any religion at all. What in the West is seen as intolerance reflects a widely shared national value and a cornerstone of national identity – in these instances, Islam, Hinduism and communist atheism.

It is all very well to ascribe value to the things we might hold dear: freedom, peace and tranquillity, for instance. We might also attach value to legal principles such as the rule of law or political practices such as democracy. They are certainly important. But they are not values. Values determine and drive the ethical and moral behaviours that impact on people, communities and societies. They are the abstract forces that inform action. And, for that reason, they are not necessarily 'good'. Greed and cruelty can unite groups and inspire action just as readily as generosity and kindness. And if values inspire behaviour – 'values-as-ethics', as some academic commentators term it – values also inform identity – the 'values-as-identity' concept that appears in more contemporary literature. This becomes problematic when they are postulated as alternative approaches to the consideration of values. The fact is, of course, that they are complementary ways of addressing the infinitely variable permutations of the relationship between values and identity.

Symbols – flags, badges, costumes, icons – are important focal points for establishing identity. So too are languages. And so too are values. In pluralistic societies such as Australia's and America's, it is important that citizens enjoy a commonly accepted set of values (such as mutual respect, inclusion, compassion, equality), just as it is important that they coalesce around commonly accepted elements of identity – shared political practices, respect for national institutions, basic freedoms of expression, association and belief, respect for the rule of law and acceptance of diversity.

Australia's politicians generally shy away from any extended or thoughtful discussion of values. But one who does show characteristic determination to talk about values and their place in validating Australia's agency on the international stage is Penny Wong, the present Minister for Foreign Affairs.

> Our values give coherence and strength to all dimensions of public policy, just as they inform both the content and the conduct of our foreign policy ... Values define who we are. Values guide our behaviour as individuals and as nations, determining the moral compass

that is as necessary for national leaders as it is for the individual ... Values are what drive action. Values motivate the pursuit of interests. If interests describe the reasons for action, values describe the motives for action. Hence values inform our interests and how we seek to advance and secure them.[23]

Never one to baulk at saying what she thinks, Wong is able to identify explicitly the values that lie at the core of Australia's national identity: a strong adherence to a fair go for everyone; a live-and-let-live approach to the beliefs and views that people might hold dear; a wish to help people who are doing it tough; and pride in the fact that we are a tolerant and inclusive community.

Some pundits proclaim that values and interests are in some kind of binary relationship, and that, when it comes to the crunch, values will always be traded away to protect interests. This is cynical nonsense. Interests must be founded on values and informed by them if they are to enjoy popular support and resonate in the broader international community. They are simply not separable. And as a lapidary expression of Australia's national values, Wong's equity, tolerance, compassion and inclusion are compelling – except, unfortunately, when it comes to driving national behaviours.

## The national interest and national interests

There are probably no two phrases in common political parlance more abused than 'the national interest' (singular noun) and 'national interests' (plural noun), especially when the two phrases are conflated and the singular noun 'interest' is substituted for the plural. Even a political scientist of Joseph Nye's eminence conflates the two expressions.[24] In 1997, the Howard government released a foreign policy white paper titled *In the National Interest*.[25] Six years later, it published a foreign policy white paper titled *Advancing the National Interest*.[26] In neither case was the term 'the national interest' defined. More recently, the Albanese government refused Qatar Airlines' request for additional flights between Dubai and Australia because it was 'not in the national interest'. In a television interview, the Minister for Transport, Catherine King, said:

> But in terms of the request that was before me, which was for doubling of the Qatar flights under their bilateral International Aviation Services Agreement, four times more than has ever been granted before, I did take the view that it was not in the national interest. Now, we don't routinely go into all of the factors that are part of the national interest.[27]

She might have said that no one routinely goes into *any* of the factors that are part of the national interest. The phrase is used as a conversation stopper: nothing else can be said, principally because nobody knows what they are talking about. 'The national interest' remained unexplained, though one might have been forgiven for imagining that 'the national interest' and Qantas's profitability were the same thing.

Spin and obfuscation are part of the political discourse. As Humpty Dumpty said in rather a scornful tone, 'When I use a word it means just what I choose it to mean – neither more nor less.' But when it comes to understanding what a nation stands for, how it articulates its key goals and what gives it agency, precision is important.

Between them, Jeremy Bentham, the English philosopher, and Hans Morgenthau, the American doyen of international relations theorists, explained the difference. Bentham was fascinated by political reform and the principles that underpinned it. He wrote, 'The interest of the community is one of the most general expressions that can occur in the phraseology of morals: no wonder that the meaning of it is often lost.'[28] He then glossed this enigmatic remark as follows: 'Interest is one of those words which ... cannot in the ordinary way be defined.'[29] Bentham's principal preoccupation was the link between individual and public good, 'the happiness of the party whose interest is in question' – not just of the private citizen but of 'every measure of government'.[30] Today, that interest would be described as national wellbeing.

Morgenthau was a legal theorist whose research on international jurisprudence established the realist school of international relations. For him, the defining preoccupation of the nation-state, and the defining determinant of the relations between nation-states, was power, pure and simple. 'The main signpost that helps political realism to find its way through the landscape of international politics is the concept of interest defined in terms of power,' he argued.[31] Before addressing the nature of national power and the factors that constitute national power, it is important to deconflict the terms 'interest' and 'interests'.

The *national interest* concerns identity and power, conferring legitimacy and authority on all aspects of national policy and providing it with its energy and purpose. The national interest is substantive, because it is about the nation as a whole – its agency, its prosperity, its security in the broadest sense, and its wellbeing.

The *national interests*, on the other hand, are purposive. They are the reasons for which the nation exercises its agency – why we do what we do. National interests evolve over time. In Australia's case, they have remained quite stable over the past several decades, reflecting Australia's comparative political stability as much as Australia's relative lack of ambition on the international stage. Successive governments have coalesced around four principal national interests:

- The security of the nation and its citizens;
- The prosperity of the nation and its citizens;
- The security and prosperity of the region (South-East Asia and the Pacific) and its peoples; and
- Playing a constructive role in international affairs – good international citizenship.

A constant problem in Australia's pursuit of its national interests is the inability of most foreign ministers, and their Department of Foreign Affairs and Trade, to distinguish between the transactional dynamic of diplomacy – the day-to-day grind – and the transformational dimension – building a better world. The mantra of most Australian foreign ministers, and the standard by which they measure themselves, is the claim that they 'deal with the world as it is, not as one might wish it to be'. So what is the point? A foreign policy that lacks ambition, and a foreign minister who lacks energy and imagination, invests simply in the status quo, going through the motions of international engagement without ever attempting to control (or contribute to) the nature and pace of change. When 'laissez-faire' becomes a synonym for laziness and role subordination to more senior (and more dominant) prime ministers and defence ministers, the national interest is sacrificed on the altar of short-term political expediency.

This is the story of almost three decades of Australia's non-pursuit of its national interests. Its international policies have been characteristically defensive and deferential to the interests of others. The plangent invocation of the 'international rules-based order' and the constant genuflection to the AUSMIN talks as the nation's principal investment in 'strategic equilibrium' are symptomatic of a nation that lacks both power and agency. 'The balance of power' and 'strategic equilibrium' are buzzwords that trumpet Australia's inability to imagine a world that is preferable to the one in which it lives, and its inability to carve out a constructive role that pursues – and perhaps even achieves – the kind of regional and global environment that better represents our national interests. This is a matter to which we shall return in the last chapter of this book.

## National impotence and national power

As Morgenthau's work makes clear, however, the concept of power is not itself univocal. Over a period of some two decades, Joseph Nye identified three principal streams of national power: soft power (essentially, the power of persuasion), hard power (essentially, the power of coercion) and smart power (essentially, investment in global public goods to help nations attain what they are unable to realise alone).[32] Much of the contemporary discussion about global affairs, however, is fixated on military power and the ability to terminate conventional warfare with nuclear weapons – the ultimate expression of hard power. So 'strategic power' has become largely synonymous with possession of a nuclear deterrent than could destroy humankind.

That so-called strategic planners could contemplate the annihilation of the citizens of a belligerent country and their own destruction in response is the epitome of cynicism. It also defies the fundamental logic of survival: the optimism that, regardless of the problems that might confront a community or a nation, human ingenuity can fashion a solution. And part of the reason that human ingenuity can resolve seemingly insoluble problems is that power presents itself in so many forms, and the various types of power interact with each other in many and surprising ways. And the forms of power are themselves manifold: cultural power, diplomatic power, economic power, ideological power, intellectual (persuasive) power, physical (coercive) power, political power and social power, to identify but a few.

An enduring problem for Australia is its national impotence – its reluctance to recognise and employ its power. This is the fatal weakness of most of Australia's political leaders. There are many reasons for this, but foremost among them are a lack of self-confidence; a deep sense of insecurity, which leads to psychological dependency on a 'great and powerful friend'; a sense of inferiority, which displays itself in a form of boisterous overconfidence; and an incapacity for self-affirmation, which finds expression in the 'cultural cringe'. And, of course, it is impossible for a nation to exercise its national power when it does not know what constitutes national power.

Morgenthau identifies eight main elements of national power, four quantitative and four qualitative. The size of the landmass, natural resource wealth, industrial capacity and military strength make up the quantitative elements. And population, national character (things like endurance and resilience), national morale (a nation's determination to support its government in peace and war) and the quality of a nation's diplomacy constitute the qualitative elements. Morgenthau's comments on diplomacy are especially pertinent:

Of all the factors which make for the power of a nation, the most important, and of the more unstable, is the quality of diplomacy. All the other factors which determine national power are, as it were, the raw material out of which the power of a nation is fashioned. The quality of a nation's diplomacy combines those different factors into an integrated whole, gives them direction and weight, and awakens their slumbering potentialities by giving them the breath of actual power ... Diplomacy, one might say, is the brains of national power, as national morale is its soul.[33]

The implications of Morgenthau's observations for Australia are profound. By any measure, excepting the size of its population and the quality of its diplomacy, Australia has considerable power. The indicators of Australia's national power are many: it boasts the twelfth-largest economy;[34] nine of its universities rank in the world's top 100;[35] four of its cities rank in the top twelve of the Economist Intelligence Unit's *Global Liveability Index*;[36] and for a nation of sport lovers, Australia averages eighth position on the Olympic medal tally. Our principal deficiencies are clear, however. With a population of 25 million, Australia is comparatively underpopulated, lacking the population mass for a fully self-sustaining economy, large industrial workforce or large military forces. This, as Michael Fullilove pointed out in his 2015 Boyer Lectures, is a strategic vulnerability.[37]

Australia seriously undercooks its diplomacy. Back in the day, prime ministers Whitlam, Fraser and Hawke brought originality to the way Australia conducted itself internationally. Normalising relations with China, taking a stand on apartheid, developing more open international trading systems – these took energy and perseverance. Their foreign ministers, particularly the late Andrew Peacock and Gareth Evans, took Australia to new levels of bilateral and multilateral engagement. Importantly, the Department of Foreign Affairs had both the capability and capacity to support them. But since the mid-1990s, Australia's diplomatic efforts have been placed in cold storage. Four major factors have combined to eviscerate Australia's diplomacy: budget cuts; the politicisation of foreign policy issues for domestic political purposes; the transformation of diplomacy into a stage for celebrity performance instead of sustained negotiation; and the constant triumph of the immediate over the important. These have rendered Australia's diplomacy almost totally transactional.

The hollowing-out of DFAT's operating budget has been well documented elsewhere.[38] Suffice it to say that Australia's international footprint and performance is near the bottom of the thirty OECD nations, and has continued to decline in real terms. Our diplomatic missions are overstretched and underfunded. Moreover, the profession of diplomacy continues to be amateurised, as successive governments continue to appoint former politicians – who generally lack language skills, international negotiating experience or any particular subject matter expertise – to key diplomatic posts. More worrying is the growing practice of reducing critical foreign and security policy issues, whether their focus is the bilateral relationship with China or the security connection with the United States, to bit roles on the stage of domestic politics. Mindless tests of manhood on the floor of the parliament are no substitute for the patient grind of sustained diplomacy.

This is exacerbated by the emerging trend towards reducing complexity to artificial linear binaries, so that the negotiation of mutual accommodation between conflicting objectives, for instance, is labelled 'appeasement'. As more photographs of prime ministers, ministers, assistant ministers and parliamentary secretaries are hung from the walls of Australia's embassies and missions abroad, one might be forgiven for assuming that modern diplomacy is more about representing the government of the day than it is about securing the nation's enduring interests. The politician becomes the celebrity and the 'fixer', while the diplomat is the faceless and risk-averse courtier who sets the stage for the arrival of the celebrity, and then dances attendance on the fly-in-fly-out virtuoso.

The erosion of diplomatic capacity has one final debilitating consequence – the immediacy of unanticipated events trumps the importance of sustained investment in building real international influence. It is, of course, important that Australia responds effectively and generously to natural disasters, provides quality consular assistance to Australians in distress and facilitates the day-to-day business of managing complex bilateral relationships. Such activities are time-consuming, however, and – the competencies of our diplomats notwithstanding – there is little capacity left for creating the long-term public good that is the result of an effective diplomacy.

Without an effective diplomacy, effective national power remains a chimera.

If, as this book proposes, Australia's long-term security – in the more profound sense of its long-term prosperity and wellbeing – is intimately bound up with that of America, it is important that we now think about America, what it is and where it is going. Every odd couple needs to understand how each other works.

# 3.
## America

The comfortable, narrow and somewhat make-believe world that Australia and America have created for themselves is consistent with the complacency that infects the bilateral policy settings informing the dialogue between Canberra and Washington. It is all very Panglossian, at least as represented in the gushing remarks delivered by Australian prime ministers at state dinners in the White House and on the floor of the US House of Representatives, and in the condescending comments made by American presidents in the Australian Parliament. But America's motto, *E pluribus unum* – 'One from many' – suggests complexity and depth that are at once a source of strength and weakness. That is the paradox of America – as it is of Indonesia, which boasts the similar motto *Bhinneka tunggal eka* – 'Diverse but one'. It is that paradox and the inherent divisions that underpin it to which we now turn.

America's post–World War II greatness is receding from view, faster perhaps than most people appreciate. In a trenchant summary of America's decline, Nick Bryant charts the shifts that have signposted America's slide into political and social atrophy. It is a dismal list. At any point, leadership and sound policy design could have combined at least to arrest the decline, and possibly to reverse it. But the task is now enormous. He writes:

> Shifts over time, more than singular events, are the key to understanding the country's downward spiral: the widening wealth gap; the widening influence gap, compounded by the Citizens United

Supreme Court ruling, which enabled the super-rich to flood US politics with so much unregulated money; the weakening of once trusted institutions, such as Congress and the overly politicised courts; the ideological clustering of the Big Sort, and the political distancing it has wrought; the decline of reason; the discord between a knowledge-based economy and a knowledge-free polity; the shift in values from community-oriented ideals to extreme individualism; the primacy of the internet, which has helped turn politics, and society more broadly, into such a rage-filled ruckus.[1]

America's collapse is a clear and present danger. Confusion and self-doubt are cancers at America's core, constantly manipulated by Russian and Chinese interference with America's pervasive social media – enemies exploiting internal social division. The riots that occurred at the Capitol in Washington on 6 January 2021 shook the fabric and the foundations of US democracy and American society more broadly. Those events continue to reverberate through the political and social structures of the United States. The very idea that a US president could even contemplate a popular insurrection that was tantamount to an attempted coup – and that a US vice president could be manipulated and manoeuvred into entertaining an act of treason (which he rejected), that the Congressional suite of the Speaker of the House of Representatives could be invaded and trashed, that senior office-holders could be threatened with death, that armed citizens could run amok in the Congress, and that law-enforcement officers could be killed in defending the Capitol – was seen as impossible and unbelievable. Key instigators have been sentenced to long periods in prison, but the restoration of broad American confidence and trust in the nation's political system will take much more time than the judges have imposed on the organisers and perpetrators. And Donald Trump may not only escape sanction: he may also return to the White House.

The editorial board of *The New York Times* offered a bleak warning when it wrote: 'The American public is gradually and alarmingly becoming inured to the presence of this violence, but it is the duty of our lawmakers to take this threat seriously and to use the tools they have to stop it.'[2] Sadly, the US Congress has yet to address this task.

The lawmakers are too busy building their power bases, holding onto office and saving their own skins. After themselves and their party, their local communities are an afterthought, and the nation comes a distant fourth.

The resentments simmering deep within the American polity, especially among alienated males who feel themselves dispossessed and powerless, exploded with the provocation of President Trump's electoral defeat. Through the skilful use of social media and the manipulation of public anger fomented by his distortions and lies, President Trump authorised and empowered a disaffected mob to 'take back control' and to 'make America great again'. Noting the rise in threats against American institutions and office holders, *Time* commented in late 2022:

> Most of these threats are not made by deranged individuals or habitual criminals. They're made by ordinary Americans acting in an environment in which the political discourse has been coarsened to the point that threats of violence have become commonplace ... About one in three Americans now say they believe violence against the government can sometimes be justified, including 40% of Republicans and 23% of Democrats, according to a Washington Post–University of Maryland poll earlier this year [2022].[3]

There are emerging signs that America's democracy is being devoured from within. The symptoms manifest themselves right across the union, as the same issue of *Time* chronicled, not just in the poor rural areas. It makes for alarming and depressing reading. In its analysis of America's democracy crisis, *The Guardian* is equally sobering. It quotes the political scientist Barbara Walter's grim forecast that a second civil war would look nothing like the first: 'If a second civil war breaks out in the US, it will be a guerrilla war fought by multiple small militias spread around the country'.[4] The ensuing turmoil would destroy what passes for law and order and, more fundamentally and existentially, the rule of law on which it is founded.

And in a country where massacres and mass murders have become commonplace, where there are more guns than people, and where the National Rifle Association is both permitted and encouraged to peddle its malevolence, lawlessness is increasingly normalised and tolerated. Is it any surprise that Americans take a dim view of their nation's future? Research undertaken by the Pew Research Center in early 2023 tracks a dismal decline in national optimism: 'Americans are in a negative mood about the current state of the country, with large majorities expressing dissatisfaction with the economy and overall national conditions. And when they look toward the not-too-distant future, they see a country that in many respects will be worse than it is today.'[5]

Across the political spectrum, as across age groups and the ethnic communities, despondency is on the rise. While it might be expected that older Americans have a rosier view of the past than do the young, the alarming fact is that young Americans hold a less positive view of the future than their parents. At this point, America has replaced the ebullient self-confidence of the post–World War II years with a profound uncertainty about who it is and what it stands for. The conservative–liberal divide has become more polarised and more destructive than any of the previous contests of ideas that have been, to a large extent, the source of America's strength, at least in the world of ideas and policy. The fault lines are well captured by Charles King in his essay 'The Antiliberal Revolution': 'There is a growing intuition that the problem with liberal democracy is not just the adjective. It is also the noun.'[6]

The vitriol in the current debate reflects an anger that is the enemy of reason. In King's opinion, it is an engulfing anger that is 'by turns elegiac, evangelising, and blusterous, delivered with the self-assurance of a college sophomore conversant with all of human history'.[7]

America is a deeply divided nation. Its cultural, economic, political and social fault lines generate a kaleidoscope of conflicting and potentially devastating possibilities. In January 2021, *Time*'s editor-at-large wrote: 'There is no advanced industrial democracy in the world more politically divided, or politically dysfunctional, than the United States today.'[8] Ian Bremmer went on to identify three principal features of contemporary American society: the enduring legacy of race, the changing nature of capitalism, and the fracturing of the collective media landscape.

As America's internal divisions become more entrenched and as America's political landscape becomes even more treacherous and ideological, additional features of America's division and dysfunction have begun to emerge. Besides race, neoliberalism and the emergence of new and highly competitive forms of media influence, five additional and equally disturbing dynamics are at play: profound political partisanship; massive disagreement regarding identity; the emergence of ideology (political and religious) as a tool for social exclusion; deep structural misogyny; and, as both cause and consequence of misogyny and racism, structural inequality in educational and employment opportunity, attainment and consequent social status. And all these dimensions of division and dysfunction are in turn riven with currents and eddies and countervailing forces that further exacerbate disharmony and amplify imbalance.

Of course, Australia and other democracies also confront these centrifugal and destructive internal forces, though none of them to the extent that America does. We are, all of us, tossed about on an ocean of discontent.

## Toxic racism

Race and racial inequality remain a fundamental rip in America's social fabric. At the most superficial level, the Black–white divide is emblematic of American disharmony, harking back to entrenched slavery before the Civil War of the 1860s and the Jim Crow laws and racial segregation that followed it.[9] In an October 2022 report, the US Government Accountability Office (GAO) reviewed its work on race in America dating back several decades.[10] The report was sobering. Whether in education, voting rights, equal employment, representation in the census, racial profiling, access to capital and housing, health care or treatment in the US military, the situation of Black people and Hispanics had gone backwards.

This is not, however, simply a Black versus white or a Hispanic versus white and Black phenomenon: just as there are enduring class and economic divisions within the white communities, so within the Black and Hispanic communities there are deep social divisions. These were visible in the formative years of the civil rights movement, and were the subject of a series of watershed essays edited by Booker T. Washington in *The Negro Problem*, published in 1903.[11] The leading Black intellectual and scholar W.E.B. Du Bois argued for the rapid development of an African-American leadership cadre to pave the way for a progressive improvement in the lot of Black Americans. At the end of 'The Talented Tenth', his contribution to Booker Washington's opus, Du Bois implored all Americans in a way that resonates today, its gendered language notwithstanding:

> Men of America, the problem is plain before you. Here is a race transplanted through the criminal foolishness of your fathers. Whether you like it or not the millions are here, and here they will remain. If you do not lift them up, they will pull you down. Education and work are the levers to uplift a people. Work alone will not do it unless inspired by the right ideals and guided by intelligence. Education must not simply teach work – it must teach Life. The Talented Tenth of the Negro race must be made leaders of thought and missionaries of culture among their people. No others can do this work and Negro colleges must train men for it. The Negro race, like all other races, is going to be saved by its exceptional men.[12]

Almost fifty years later, Du Bois conceded that his dream had foundered on the rocks of individual self-interest, with a new and more insidious class divide holding back the Black American community.[13] As the Black Lives Matter movement is discovering, there are two nations within Black America – the haves and the have-nots. The haves seek to consolidate their gains and their social position, while the have-nots are either doggedly aspirational or resignedly alienated.

And among the alienated communities, some are desperately passive, while others resort to criminality and violence. The toxicity of two centuries of white police oppression of Black Americans has infected relations among Black Americans themselves. The death in January 2023 of Tyre Nichols at the hands of five Black police officers in Memphis, Tennessee, is indicative of the problem of Black people oppressing Blacks.[14]

The drift in Hispanic votes to Trump's camp during the 2020 election surprised many US political commentators, who had long seen the Latino vote as a single glued-on Democratic bloc. The reality, however, is considerably more complex. The large migrations of Mexicans to California and the Southwest, and the settlement of many Puerto Ricans in New York and Cubans in Florida, initiated the formation of political alliances on the east coast quite distinct from the more iden-tifiably Democratic-aligned Mexican enclaves on the west coast. But for at least five decades, the Democrats and Republicans have sought to divide and conquer the Hispanic community by exploiting differ-ences in both aspiration and occupation. Republicans in particular have successfully exploited the deep Roman Catholic allegiances and anti-communist pathologies of the Cuban community.

Disparity and division in the Hispanic communities will endure. Ben-jamin Francis-Fallon captured the significance of this development in the wash-up to the 2020 election:

> Party leaders will continue to try to influence – and manipulate – [the] discussion [about a 'Latino vote'], to be sure. But so will a growing number of independent and grass-roots organizations committed to mobilizing Latino/a voters on their own terms. Demog-raphy may not be destiny. But with Latinos proving critical for both candidates in a variety of states, it is obvious that their diverse array of experiences and identities have already transformed American democracy.[15]

The horizontal and vertical fractions that complicate and divide America's Black and Hispanic communities are amplified within and between the white communities, where community (rural/urban), economic, ethnic, geographic (north/south and east/west), religious and social divisions play out in surprising and often destructive ways. The Civil War, for instance – in which over 600,000 men, most of them white, died and millions were wounded or injured – was essentially a contest between the northern Union and southern Confederacy whites. Lee's surrender to Grant on 9 April 1865 notwithstanding, many of the deep political and social issues that led to the Civil War are still in place, and their resolution seems as distant now as it ever was. The Civil War might have ended slavery. It did not end racism and Black segregation.

The adoption of the battle flag of the Confederacy by white suprem-acist groups remains, like the white robes and hoods of the Ku Klux Klan, a provocation both to the Black community and to white moder-ates. While the confederate flag enjoys official use only in Mississippi, it continues as a rallying point for white grievance, particularly among low-educated, poor and unemployed rural males. And it was certainly carried as a direct challenge to the legitimacy of the Stars and Stripes during the Washington riots in January 2021. These were elements of a deeply divided white community challenging both the legality of Joe Biden's electoral victory over President Trump and the very legitimacy of the United States' government institutions themselves. In America, as in Australia, racism is hidden in denial and expanded and legitimised in acceptance and practice: nobody will admit to being racist, yet everybody – almost – turns a blind eye to it in practice.

## Neoliberalism and the destruction of value

Like all transient economic theologies, neoliberalism – the 1930s brainchild of Friedrich Hayek, conceived, improbably, at the same time as John Maynard Keynes was developing his *General Theory of Employment, Interest and Money* – would probably have disappeared had it not been given political life by President Ronald Reagan and his acolyte British prime minister Margaret Thatcher. And were it not for its adoption by both President Clinton and Prime Minister Tony

Blair as a political philosophy that both justified and legitimised the subordination of the state and its institutions to 'the market', neoliberalism might have died an early and natural death as an ideology that reduces politics to little more than a price mechanism.

By placing the market at the centre of reality, and positing it as both the source and purpose of personal and political existence, neoliberalism is fundamentally anti-humanist. Human dignity and value, happiness and wellbeing, achievement and contentment are nothing more than opinion, meaningless unless they can be priced. Of course, once the price has been established, who cares about value? Reagan's genius was to transform abstraction and theory into one-liners and soundbites that appeared to restore some kind of political sense to the self-destructive forces that had emerged in America during the Vietnam War. Government was the problem, not the solution. Regulation was its dead hand, taxes little more than its theft of the workers' hopes for a decent life, and trade barriers its way of protecting communism at the expense of an unconstrained capitalism. Small government would make way for the big American dream.

And then President Clinton discovered globalisation.

At the centre of Reagan's and Clinton's massive reorientation towards an anomic and amoral market-based politics was the re-legitimation and restoration of racism and racial inequality. This was hammered into place by far-reaching law-and-order campaigns that both expanded and militarised police departments, focused anti-drug campaigns on Black communities, and constructed more prisons while at the same time reducing social safety nets and welfare programs. Assets in public ownership were privatised, while the industrial economy gave way to the world of ticket-clipping through high-tech innovations, high finance and high-end real estate. Instead of creating a world where the market self-regulated, rewarding efficiency and penalising waste, it legitimised greed and replaced long-term investment with short-term 'shareholder value'. And when the world of greed-driven and out-of-control lending fell into a chaotic mess of loan defaults, the losses were socialised – 'restored' by taxpayers – while 'performance bonuses' (where 'performance' was code for larceny in many instances) continued to be paid to the high-net-wealth individuals leading failed financial institutions. Government bailed out investors while mortgagees were bankrupted. The 'best' prospered while the 'rest' became fertile ground for what was to follow.

Into America's world of declining wages, rising unemployment and increasing prices strode Donald Trump. He railed against the elites, doubled down on protectionism and implicitly advocated a return to race-based nationalism. President Biden has managed to restore a measure of normalcy to the US body politic, though the continuing ructions within the Republican Party do not bode well for 'the land of the free and the home of the brave'. Far from draining the swamp, President Trump managed to introduce even more alligators, reptiles awaiting his return in 2025 with enthusiasm and exuberance. America's immediate prospects do appear bleak.

Yet the Nobel Prize–winning economist Joseph Stiglitz discerns signs of a more progressive agenda for America, where 'every individual has the opportunity to live up fully to his or her potential'.[16] Stiglitz continues:

> In this progressive agenda, government plays a central role, both in ensuring that markets work as they are supposed to, and in promoting the general welfare in ways that individuals on their own, or markets on their own, can't ... The view that government is the problem, not the solution, is simply wrong. To the contrary, many if not most of our society's problems, from excesses of pollution to financial instability and economic inequality, have been created by markets and the private sector.[17]

As Gary Gerstle observed in an insightful essay in mid-2021, America needs to return to the Rooseveltian policy framework of 1932:

> Roosevelt himself broke with free market dogmas, insisting that the federal government had to manage capitalism in the public interest. He undertook major projects of infrastructural improvement,

understanding their importance both for economic growth and for demonstrating in visually dramatic ways the Democratic party's ability to transform for the better the everyday world in which Americans lived and worked. He opened his Democratic party to the left, believing that such an alliance would enhance, rather than imperil, the chances of reform. He understood the need to reinvigorate democracy in the US at a time when it was on the defensive in most of the rest of world.[18]

## The curse of the new media

New media influencers have completely restructured the traditional media landscape. The balanced broadsheets and the titillating tabloids, along with their masthead-owned radio and TV newsrooms with journalists beavering away to establish 'the facts', have given way to a shimmering miasma of competing media forms. When Marshall McLuhan argued that 'the medium is the message' in the early 1960s, he could not have imagined how the work of Tim Berners-Lee and engineers at CERN (*Conseil Européen pour la Recherche Nucléaire*, or the European Organization for Nuclear Research), Stanford and other universities would explode into the world wide web, creating an information universe and linking virtually every human being within it.

As the US Census Bureau has reported, 'the rise of digital media and technology … [has] had a devastating impact on print publishing industries'.[19] Between 2002 and 2020, newspaper revenue dropped by over 50 per cent, while circulation fell by almost 60 per cent. The millions of servers that support the world wide web place unlimited data and information resources at the fingertips of anyone who wants to use them. Many of these resources lack certification or validation, existing in a world where 'truth is always relative' – itself an extraordinarily absolute statement. Channelling Dr Who, we now live in a 'wibbly wobbly, timey-wimey' world of factoids, data points, part truths and deliberate falsehoods intended to deceive. The problem of data reliability is exacerbated by the unconscious or intended bias of the data users, whose selective use of information and data can easily prejudice balance and objectivity. Citizens are left to their own devices, in every sense, to validate competing claims – to 'do your own research', in internet-speak.

Balance and objectivity are rendered even more problematic by the ubiquity of algorithms that match data users with their preferences. Twitter, for instance, actively invites users to 'follow' individuals and associations with similar interests and tastes, simultaneously broadening the field of acceptability and conformity of opinion while narrowing the availability and impact of contrary opinion. In this world of vast variety, fluidity, endless noise and ever-changing truth horizons, chaos and confusion are the only constants. In the Elon Musk era of X, where the sacking of content moderators accompanies his personal descent into white supremacy, chaos nurtures immorality. Left with few options but self-guidance, citizens make choices that are largely determined by what their peer groups, social and professional associations, friends and family members are doing.

Chaos and confusion are fertile breeding grounds for conspiracy theories, 'fake news', foreign interference, language manipulation (where tropes of various kinds exist, such as 'Canberra' or 'Washington' being shorthand for incompetence or corruption) and memes that glorify and/or denigrate – sometimes simultaneously – prominent political actors. Chaos and confusion feed individual insecurities. Personal anxiety and community alienation work in combination to build mistrust in government and group solidarity with people who are similarly affected.

No one in recent memory has been more adept at media manipulation than the former (and maybe future) US president Donald Trump, whose subversion of Fox News created a megaphone for his disinformation, megalomania and paranoia. Fox News was an early Trump backer: it amplified his 'birther' campaign against President Barack Obama, and he then used Fox News' reporting of his lies as evidence of their truth – a self-validating feedback loop. It became the mirror by which ugliness was transformed into beauty, in the eyes of some beholders at least. Fox News became, as Ruth Ben-Ghiat commented on NBC's *Think* page, a risk to America's democracy by assuming a role normally occupied by state media in strongman regimes.[20] It was alarming to see CNN follow suit by televising Trump's primetime 'town hall' rally in May 2023. What was intended as an attempt to win back disaffected Republican voters with a newsworthy 'broadcast it as it is' approach was transformed by Trump into an exercise in demagoguery. There appears to be no way out of this impasse.

This form of media radicalism depends on the reinforcement of preference and prejudice by making acceptability and popularity (the number of 'hits' or 'likes') the basis of authority and validity. Argument and evidence are no longer the determinants of truth. News becomes propaganda. 'Fake' (as in 'fake news') replaces 'fact'. When President Trump's press advisor Sean Spicer claimed that record numbers of people had attended Trump's swearing-in ceremony in January 2017, senior White House aide Kellyanne Conway identified 'alternative facts' as the basis for a more convenient truth.[21]

This phenomenon is one of the leading indicators of the emergence of totalitarianism. And the concentration of media ownership – whereby print, radio and television outlets are merged under sole editorial and proprietorial control – appears to be both a necessary and sufficient precursor. News Corporation holds a dominant media position in America, Australia and the United Kingdom. The alarm bells are certainly ringing when a former director of US national intelligence, James Clapper, supports calls by former Australian prime ministers Kevin Rudd and Malcolm Turnbull for a royal commission into the Murdoch media to prevent further slippage into 'truth decay'.[22]

But if race, neoliberalism and a disruptive media have combined to transform America's political landscape, a set of additional pathologies have combined to embed this transformation.

## Political partisanship

Religious sectarianism as a principal source of structural division in America has long since retreated into history, replaced by political partisanship. For several decades, the Pew Research Center has tracked the increasing distortion of American society. Its findings are disturbing. A decade ago, Pew commented that Americans engaged in the nation's political processes were even less tolerant of their political opponents than they had been in earlier times:

> Partisan animosity has increased substantially … In each party, the share with a highly negative view of the opposing party has more than doubled since 1994. Most of these intense partisans believe the opposing party's policies 'are so misguided that they threaten the nation's well-being'.[23]

Partisan hostility has continued to grow, and to deepen. Alarmingly, the basis of such hostility has moved from disagreement on policy issues to a focus on personal qualities. In 2022, Pew noted:

> Partisan polarization has long been a fact of political life in the United States. But increasingly, Republicans and Democrats view not just the opposing party but also the *people* in that party in a negative light. Growing shares in each party now describe those in the other party as more closed-minded, dishonest, immoral and unintelligent than other Americans.

> Perhaps the most striking change is the extent to which partisans view those in the opposing party as immoral …

> Large majorities in both parties also describe those in the other party as more closed-minded than other Americans (83% of Democrats and 69% of Republicans say this), and this sentiment also has increased in recent years.

> Yet there is one negative trait that Republicans are far more likely than Democrats to link to their political opponents. A 62% majority

of Republicans say Democrats are 'more lazy' than other Americans, up from 46% in previous studies in 2019 and 2016. Only about a quarter of Democrats (26%) say Republicans are lazier than others, and this has changed only modestly since 2016.[24]

The dynamics behind this political implosion have been long in the making. Both parties have become more ideologically cohesive, with moderates, especially among Republicans, in sharp decline. At the same time, they have both moved away from the ideological centre, with the Democrats becoming more liberal and the Republicans more conservative. And, tellingly, the geographic and demographic make-up of both parties has changed dramatically. Almost half of Republicans come from the southern states, while nearly half of Democrats are Black, Hispanic or Asian/Pacific islander.[25]

Racial diversity is, of course, a welcome development in the US Congress. It has, however, reflected and amplified the same divisions within and between America's ethnic communities that have affected the country's social stability. And these divisions have both influenced and consolidated a national political polarisation that is only intensifying. It is not restricted to America: it is a global phenomenon, not least of all in the Western world. But America is the outlier. No other advanced Western democracy has experienced such intense polarisation over such an extended period. As scholars at The Carnegie Endowment for International Peace have observed, 'the United States is in uncharted and very dangerous territory'.[26] The risks are profound.

Multiple factors entrench America's political self-destruction. Identity politics has come to define America's political imagination. This may well be irreversible, due to the demographic decline in the majority status of the white communities and the resultant insecurities that have caused them to regard their historical domination as threatened. These insecurities are exacerbated by the inflexible institutional characteristics of the American political system, where a rigid two-party system consolidates binary divisions within society. Whereas comparable democracies witness the rise (and fall) of minor parties, the American system both constrains and then penalises such aberrations. And, uniquely, America's strong majoritarian electoral system is checked and balanced by its strong minoritarian institutions.

The structure and practices of the US Senate, in particular, reinforce the political polarisation of the Congress. California's population is around 40 million, as compared with Wyoming's population of around 600,000. Yet each state has two senators. Individual senators can single-handedly delay nominations and debates on legislation, while the filibuster rule enables minority parties to prevent consideration of legislation that would garner a majority. Disproportionality in Senate representation drives disproportionality in the Electoral College, where the voter majority is regularly overturned by the imbalance in Electoral College votes. These factors are exacerbated by the established practice of partisan sorting, whereby the major parties reinforce racial–ethnic, religious–secular and urban–rural divides, rather than consolidate cross-cutting compromises. The cross-party coalitions of the past are increasingly rare.

In this, America is once again exceptional. To quote the Carnegie Foundation, 'The United States is quite alone among the ranks of perniciously polarized democracies in terms of its wealth and democratic experience.'[27] The situation is not hopeless, though, especially if America is able to learn from its friends and model some of the political innovations that both protect and secure their democratic independence and robustness. That will, however, demand the humility and imagination that political polarisation so strenuously suppresses.

## Identity

Identity is the core and perhaps the determining factor in contemporary political discourse. At least since the rise of globalisation as a key driver of worldwide economic, political and social change, individual identity has sought validation and reinforcement in social identity, and social identity in turn has sought legitimacy in political identity. This has occurred in a world where competitive forces have created both dominant and displaced groups that constantly search for narrower and more disaggregated avenues for defining their separateness. This, in turn, constitutes a major disincentive to consensus and collective action by governments in the interests of the whole community.

As Francis Fukuyama observed in 2018:

> [G]roups have come to believe that their identities – whether national, religious, ethnic, sexual, gender, or otherwise – are not receiving adequate recognition. Identity politics is no longer a minor phenomenon, playing out only in the rarified [sic] confines of university campuses or providing a backdrop to low-stakes skirmishes in 'culture wars' promoted by the mass media. Instead, identity politics has become a master concept that explains much of what is going on in global affairs.[28]

In the America of both Trump and Biden, racism and sexism flourish. African-Americans continue to suffer discrimination. They continue to experience police brutality, including from Black police officers. Black incarceration rates continue to climb. Educational opportunities for Black Americans continue to lag, and Black unemployment levels remain stubbornly high. And as we shall see shortly, discrimination against women remains a chronic indicator of inequality in American society due to structural misogyny. But in a society where white supremacy was once assumed, white nationalism has now shifted from the rural fringe to the urban mainstream. The appearance of 'white lives matter' white supremacist groups in response to the Black Lives Matter movement is yet another example of the normalisation of identity politics in America's national political discourse. But it is a dangerous development, since it creates a moral equivalence between Black disadvantage and white radicalism.

Identity is nonetheless a critical element in constructing a polity that is inclusive and diverse, that accepts difference while building community, that can answer the questions 'Who am I?' and 'Who are we?' through agreement on values and behaviours rather than by reference to race, religion or political affiliation.

## Ideology

Ideology seems to die frequently, only to resurrect itself as if to demonstrate that nature abhors a vacuum. The United Nations Charter was in some senses a celebration of the death of the ideological contest that fuelled World War II. The détente forged by President Richard Nixon and Secretary Leonid Brezhnev was widely seen as resolution, in part at least, of the ideological tension that sustained the Cold War. The fall of the Berlin Wall in 1989, and the collapse of the Soviet Union in 1991, were also seen as the transmutation of ideological swords into irenic ploughshares, with peace dividends available to all. Yet, according to President Biden at least, we are currently caught in a war between competing ideologies, as democracy and autocracy fight it out in Taiwan, Ukraine and wherever else America's supremacy is contested.[29] Like the poor in Deuteronomy, it seems that ideology is with us always.

The political partisanship that inflames much of America's contemporary political discourse is driven by deeply held and deeply contested ideological beliefs. These coalesce around religion, race, identity (including gender), political creed, property rights, social entitlement, historical grievance and many other factors that have become rallying points for disaffected groups. These ideologies share a common feature that is difficult to contest or manage: a fixed and immovable faith that is not susceptible to the tests of evidence or logic. For many, ideology is the basis of their political affiliation, a critical element of what unites them with their co-adherents and separates them from their competitors.

The emotional and psychological dimensions of ideology become especially potent when demagogues and populists manipulate the adherents of ideologies to generate and sustain mass movements. Very often, ideologically driven popular movements are fuelled by strongly shared senses of disadvantage, discrimination and injustice. President Trump was skilful in coalescing the support of disparate white supremacist elements across Middle America to legitimise neo-fascist groups such as the Proud Boys[30] and the even more dystopian adherents of QAnon, who believe the world is run by a cabal of Satan-worshipping paedophiles.[31] As with many such groups, conflicting ideological elements are conflated and rationalised through a focus on revolutionary and violent forms of political action. In America's case (and, for similar reasons, in countries like Colombia, Haiti and Venezuela), guns play a crucial, even totemic role.

Writing in *The Atlantic* in 2020, David Brooks described America's current flirtation with ideology as a symptom of moral convulsion, a pathology that Samuel Huntingdon averred struck the nation every sixty years or so.[32] It has struck with a vengeance. The retreat into ideology and the mindless sloganeering that so often distinguishes ideology from other forms of group membership and social belonging delivers a sense of security. And in a time of moral convulsion, security is exactly what people crave – and what they do not find. It is not just a pointless search: it is a self-defeating one.

As in all systems where evidence and reason play no part in the assertion of truth, ideology is no more than a massive political confidence trick. Its adherents gain a false sense of security and belonging that, when it collapses, leaves behind individual isolation, social fragmentation and a moral vacuum. Its ultimate consequences are chaotic.

## Structural misogyny

Like 'structural inequality', 'structural misogyny' is a somewhat moralising term that masks rather than illuminates chronic discrimination against women. It is deeply ingrained in American economic, industrial, political and social practice, as it is in Australia. What it describes is a practice whereby women, even when they are as well (or better) equipped and qualified than men to perform substantial roles in the real economy, the professions, the arts and politics (to identify just some domains), continue to miss out because of the inherent and usually unacknowledged (by men at least) biases emblematic of a world that works to the advantages of men, on the basis of rules designed by and for men.

In her cool and understated way, the late justice of the Supreme Court of the United States of America, Ruth Bader Ginsburg, wrote in 2016:

> Most people in poverty in the United States and the world over are women and children, women's earnings here and abroad trail the earnings of men with comparable education and experience, our workplaces do not adequately accommodate the demands of child-bearing and child rearing, and we have yet to devise effective ways to ward off sexual harassment at work and domestic violence in our homes.[33]

She spent her long and distinguished judicial career attacking and seeking to change those structures. It remains a work in progress. It is a catastrophic irony that Justice Ginsberg's death opened the door for Justice Amy Coney Barrett to advocate and entrench the denial of women's control of their reproductive rights – a signal victory for intolerance and intransigence, and the entrenchment of structural misogyny.

On at least three principal indicators – political representation, executive representation and economic participation (income) – America remains stuck in systemic gender inequality. In its 2022 *Global Gender Gap Report*, the World Economic Forum ranks countries according to the rates at which equality gaps are closing rather than in absolute terms. That leads to surprising (and perhaps misleading) results. America as 27th overall, a modest improvement on the previous year, trailing New Zealand (4th), Nicaragua (7th), Namibia (8th) and Canada (25th), but ahead of the Netherlands (28th) and Australia (43rd).[34] In terms of economic participation, America ranks 22nd (Australia 38th); and in terms of political empowerment, America ranks 38th (Australia 50th). There are always lies, damned lies and statistics. But here the sampling method is mischievous.

National-based studies paint a different picture. When it comes to political representation, women in America continue to face significant structural disadvantage. The first woman was elected to the US Congress in 1916, while the first woman senator was appointed to fill a vacant seat in 1922, though she served for only one day. Things have improved, though hardly at breakneck speed. As the Pew Research Center reports:

> Counting both the House of Representatives and the Senate, women account for 153 of 540 voting and nonvoting members of Congress. That represents a 59% increase from the 96 women who were serving in the 112th Congress a decade ago, though it remains far below women's share of the overall U.S. population [50.5 per cent].[35]

In the current Congress, women Democrats outnumber Republicans by more than two to one, though historically that figure drops to just below two to one. California and New York are the states most likely to elect women to Congress; Vermont has yet to elect its first woman representative or senator. It is noteworthy that, of the 153 women presently in the US Congress, only ten identify their ethnicity as other than white.[36]

On the gender pay gap, Pew finds that there has been no appreciable change in two decades, with women earning around 82 per cent of average male earnings.[37] When questioned about the reasons for the gap, half of those surveyed point to 'women being treated differently by employers', suggesting structural forces at play. In particular, women are pressured to manage responsibilities at home. In professional qualifications (accounting, dentistry, engineering, financial services, law, medicine) and in the number of doctorates awarded, women continue to trail men, although women now hold more bachelor's and master's degrees than men.[38] These improvements in educational attainment, however, have not been matched by a reduction in the gender pay gap – again an indicator of structural disadvantage.

Donald Trump established a new standard in representing structural misogyny in America with his blatantly sexist language and behaviour. But in language reminiscent of Julia Gillard's famous misogyny speech in the Australian Parliament in 2012,[39] the very articulate congresswoman Alexandria Ocasio-Cortez (widely known as 'AOC'), identified the entrenched nature of political misogyny in America in a powerful speech in the US Congress on 23 July 2020:

> This [misogyny] issue is not about one incident. It is cultural. It is a culture of lack of impunity, of accepting of violence and violent language against women, an entire structure of power that supports men, because not only have I been spoken to disrespectfully, particularly by members of the Republican Party and elected officials in the Republican Party, not just here, but the President of the United States last year told me to 'go home to another country', with the implication that I don't even belong in America. The Governor of Florida, Governor DeSantis, before I even was sworn in, called me a 'whatever-that-is'. Dehumanising language is not new. And what we are seeing is that incidents like these are happening in a pattern. This is a pattern of an attitude towards women and dehumanisation of others.[40]

During the COVID-19 pandemic, Governor DeSantis also recommended that America sever its diplomatic relations with Australia, since the quarantine restrictions and border controls imposed by state premiers had turned Australia into the biggest gaol in the world. But, as the Iowa caucuses in January 2024 made plain, even Republicans in that state were not much interested in what DeSantis thought. Perhaps AOC has somewhat less to worry about.

## A gloomy prospect

The 2024 primaries, however, offered little else to encourage optimism about America's political future. Donald Trump personifies both the depth of America's political and social structural fracture lines and the continuing threat of even greater division following the November 2024 presidential election. This chapter has shown that America's longstanding claim to leadership of the 'free world' is not without consequences, chief among them its own responsibility to model democratic practice and the values upon which democracy ultimately rests. Equally, the 'leader of the free world' needs to demonstrate that moral compass on which global security and the peace that is the precondition for prosperity ultimately depend. That is all at risk.

Bruce Stokes opens his disturbing essay 'The Decline of the City Upon a Hill' with this warning:

> American global leadership faces a crisis – not of economic vitality, diplomatic prowess, or military strength but of legitimacy. Around the world, polls and interviews show that publics and elites in countries that consider themselves U.S. allies harbor doubts about the state and direction of American democracy. They no longer see it as a model, and they worry whether the American political system can still produce trustworthy outcomes.[41]

Far from being resolved by a second Trump presidency, this crisis may well be exacerbated as the president plays to his domestic political base, itself consumed by doubt, uncertainty and a deep conviction that domestic and international powerbrokers have 'screwed' them. And because those who vote for Trump doubt the reliability of the global system, they see no reason for America itself to be reliable. Social policy issues are central to this malaise, with income inequality, discrimination against minorities and the treatment of immigrants and refugees topping the list.[42]

As Stokes concludes his essay, '[T]hose who care about U.S. stature and influence in the world must engage in strengthening American democracy at home.'[43]

# 4.
## Law

America quickly followed up its declaration of independence with a constitution. Drafted in secrecy in 1787, agreed in 1788 and becoming operative the next year, the Constitution of the United States was a massive political achievement. More than that, it provided a blueprint for constitutional and democratic government that has endured. Its birth, however, was fraught. It depended on the legal and political skills of key individuals, their diplomatic skill in garnering support from major European powers, especially France, and their organisational skill in coalescing divergent interests and views to generate the military force and sustained effort needed to defeat Britain. The Founding Fathers (and they were all men) were brilliant, bringing together some of the foremost intellects and leaders of their age. Their legacy is enormous and the world is beholden to them. It is important, however, to have at least a passing acquaintance with the circumstances from which American constitutionality emerged.

The dewy-eyed view that independence and constitutionality came easily and naturally, with Americans deeply aligned in pushing the British out and thereby setting the stage for America's consequent exceptionalism, is far from the truth. America was no more exceptional in the mid-eighteenth century than it is now. The first steps towards colonial unification (as distinct from political independence) were a somewhat panicky response to the raids and insurgency conducted by the Mohawk and Iroquois Nations as they sought, with French assistance, to defend their traditional homelands and push back settler incursions. Representatives of seven colonial legislatures convened in Albany, New York, in 1754 to consider Benjamin Franklin's 'Plan of Union', whereby eleven colonies would unite under a president appointed by the British Crown. While the representatives supported the plan, their legislatures rejected it. Narrow self-interest prevailed, as so often it does. Curiously, self-interest fostered an unanticipated consequence: independence from Britain.

Just over a decade later came the opening moves towards self-determination. An initial continental congress (also known as the Stamp Act Congress) met in New York in 1765. Nine of the eighteen eligible American colonies convened to protest Westminster's revenue-raising imposition of a stamp tax on the colonies. The protest took the form of a declaration of loyalty to the Crown and a boycott of British goods, whereupon the attendees all went home and the congress dissolved. The British government repealed the stamp duties legislation, replacing it with tariffs on a variety of goods imported from the Americas and other measures to penalise the pesky colonialists.

As the protest over duties and taxes gathered momentum and economic malaise turned into political dissent, marked by sporadic outbursts of violence, the First Continental Congress – this time involving delegates from twelve of the colonial legislatures – met in Philadelphia in late 1774. New York and Boston had become hotbeds of discontent, New York specialising in confrontations with the British military – the Red Coats – and Boston preferring 'on water' activities around Boston Harbour. And as the Bostonians stepped up their agitation – they had landed casks of wine without paying duty in 1768, and now, more dramatically, dumped several hundred chests of British East India Company tea in Boston Harbour (the Boston Tea Party) in 1775, the mercantile protest morphed into a fully fledged armed political revolution.

As the Revolutionary War gathered momentum, the colonial governments had little option but to combine their resistance to British rule, particularly in the face of considerable internal support for the status quo, and the colonial government's tactic of divide and rule. In late 1775, the Second Continental Congress brought together twelve of the colonies to decide how they would conduct and support the revolutionary war, the appointment of diplomats and emissaries, the drafting of petitions and declarations and eventually, on 4 July 1776, a declaration of independence from Britain.

British intransigence served to coalesce American resolve, but only just. Americans were in fact deeply divided. It has been estimated that fewer than half the colonists supported the struggle against Britain and the War of Independence, and that more than a third of the colonists fought *with*, not against, the Red Coats. Nor were the forces opposing Britain aligned regionally, as they would be during the Civil War a century later. Rather, the War of Independence divided families, pitting sibling against sibling, neighbour against neighbour, village against village. Americans (or some of them) did not just fight against Britain. They fought each other, which led to a per-capita death rate that was higher than in any subsequent war involving America, even the disastrous Civil War.

One of the great ironies of the American revolutionary war is that, initially at least, Americans sought a form of self-government within Britain's broader imperial rule, whereas Britain regarded self-rule within the empire as tantamount to independence. But even as the political positions of the protagonists hardened and dialogue gave way to disruption, allegiances within the opposing sides wavered. As success ebbed and flowed depending on who was winning or losing, so too did support.

In the midst of all this conflict, confusion and contumely, America's civic leaders were thinking through what form of government might best suit the particular circumstances of an emerging national polity. While the creation of some form of political union in revolutionary America was a no-brainer, it was certainly not an inevitability. The precise form of the union, and the nature of its powers over each of the state legislatures, was highly contested. Those with vested interests disagreed, but nevertheless dominated discussion of the distribution of powers and rights. The rights of individual citizens, to the extent they were considered at all, came a distant second to the powers and rights of government itself, with each of the constituent governments opting for substantially different and often contradictory approaches to states' rights and individuals' rights.

The delegates to the continental congresses were ordinary men – some might say very ordinary men. As the spiritual inheritors of the Calvinists, Dissenters, Protestants, Puritans and Quakers who had initially settled the eastern seaboard, the delegates shared a generally astringent view of their fellow citizens. People, they thought, were naturally selfish, barely rational, untrusting and untrustworthy, inconsistent and impulsive, and their leaders devious, self-interested and unreliable. And, as their experiences during the congresses demonstrated, they were right. So the challenge was to design political institutions that countered, or at least mitigated, these malign influences.

But who had the authority, backed by insight or persuasive power, to argue for a centralisation of political authority to counter the forces of narrow self-interest at the state level that so limited America's commercial and economic prospects and so undermined its diplomatic efforts to align the support of the European powers against Britain? Who could transform the bold brilliance of the Declaration of Independence into a constitution?

George Washington, elected unanimously as president in January 1789, was not a signatory to the Declaration of Independence. Among those who did sign it, John Adams (the second elected president), Thomas Jefferson (the third) and Benjamin Franklin were certainly capable of bringing their skills to the task, though their complicated interpersonal relationships might not have brought it to fruition. That was left to three truly remarkable political thinkers and statesmen who, between them, argued for and articulated the principles on which the US Constitution was eventually settled. Alexander Hamilton, John Jay (the first Chief Justice of the United States) and James Madison (the fourth president) assembled the critical philosophical insights that brought the US Constitution into being and established its enduring authority.

### The Federalist Papers

The eighty-five essays by these three men, collected and published as *The Federalist* (they are now known as *The Federalist Papers*), remain a bedrock of both constitutional argument and constitutional compromise. The brilliance of the three authors' work was to create a governmental system with sufficient power to operate nationally and consolidate the union but without so much power that the basic rights of the constituent states and their citizens were threatened or diminished. This was achieved through the separation of government power into three branches – the Congress, the executive and the judiciary – and then by the application of checks and balances designed to ensure that no single branch could gain ascendency over the other two.

Of course, the authors did not think and write in a vacuum. The *Magna Carta*, the Elizabethan jurist Edward Coke, and the writings of John Locke, David Hume, Montesquieu and the contemporary English jurist William Blackstone were all powerful influences on the contemporary thinking that created the US Constitution. This distillation of continuing and mainstream European thought into a set of accessible and compelling constitutional principles has continued to offer a persuasive model for subsequent federal constitutions, including Australia's. By examining the roles of the House of Representatives (Federalist 52 to Federalist 61), the Senate (Federalist 62 to Federalist 66), the executive (Federalist 67 to Federalist 77) and the court (Federalist 78 to Federalist 83), and the principles that sustain the separation of powers, *The Federalist Papers* provide a blueprint for a federal constitution that grounds both America, and by association Australia, as enduring democracies.

One of the pivotal papers, written by Madison under the *nom de plume* 'Publius', effectively resolves a core tension at the centre of the compromise that is democracy. Titled 'The Union as a Safeguard Against Domestic Faction and Insurrection', Federalist 10 is an elegant and persuasive argument for cultural, economic, political and social pluralism as the defence against and solution to majority (or mob) rule. The key to managing the complex intersections between the many categories of interests and views and the people who entertain them is to establish compromise and conciliation as the pathway to the agreement that legitimises any democratic majority. Against the more commonly held contemporary view that effective government was possible only in small states defined by their narrowness of interests and identity of purpose, Madison argued that the more numerous and heterogeneous the population was, the more likely it was that the majority position would represent and protect the interests of the majority of the citizens:

> The smaller the society, the fewer probably will be the distinct parties and interests composing it; the fewer the distinct parties and interests, the more frequently will a majority be found of the same party; and the smaller the number of individuals composing a majority, and the smaller the compass within which they are placed, the more easily will they concert and execute their plans of oppression. Extend the sphere, and you take in a greater variety of parties and interests; you make it less probable that a majority of the whole will have a common motive to invade the rights of other citizens; or if such a common motive exists, it will be more difficult for all who feel it to discover their own strength, and to act in unison with each other.[1]

Majority rule was not an end in itself, but the optimal means of delivering justice and protecting liberty. The individual *Federalist Papers* deal with the specifics of a democratic constitution to establish a federation of states unequal in population and wealth. Critical to the distribution of powers both between the national and the state legislatures, and within the branches of the national legislature, is the place of the courts, particularly the Supreme Court. As Hamilton determined with great clarity, the judiciary had to be above politics. But, more than that, it could only function credibly to the extent that it had no direct control over functions of the executive.

Federalist 78 is a lapidary example of jurisprudential writing. Hamilton, also writing as 'Publius', establishes a set of basic principles that argue the role of an unbounded judiciary in defending democratic government:

> Whoever attentively considers the different departments of power must perceive, that, in a government in which they are separated from each other, the judiciary, from the nature of its functions, will always be the least dangerous to the political rights of the Constitution; because it will be least in a capacity to annoy or injure them. The Executive not only dispenses the honors, but holds the sword of the community. The legislature not only commands the purse, but prescribes the rules by which the duties and rights of every citizen are to be regulated. The judiciary, on the contrary, has no influence over either the sword or the purse; no direction either of the strength or of the wealth of the society; and can take no active resolution whatever. It may truly be said to have neither FORCE nor WILL, but merely judgment; and must ultimately depend upon the aid of the executive arm even for the efficacy of its judgments.

> This simple view of the matter suggests several important consequences. It proves incontestably, that the judiciary is beyond comparison the weakest of the three departments of power; that it can never attack with success either of the other two; and that all possible care is requisite to enable it to defend itself against their attacks. It equally proves, that though individual oppression may now and then proceed from the courts of justice, the general liberty of the people can never be endangered from that quarter; I mean so long as the judiciary remains truly distinct from both the legislature and the Executive ... And it proves, in the last place, that as liberty can have nothing to fear from the judiciary alone, but would have every thing to fear from its union with either of the other departments; that as all the effects of such a union must ensue from a dependence of the former on the latter, notwithstanding a nominal and apparent separation; that as, from the natural feebleness of the judiciary, it is in continual jeopardy of being overpowered, awed, or influenced by its co-ordinate branches; and that as nothing can contribute so much to its firmness and independence as permanency in office, this quality may therefore be justly regarded as an

indispensable ingredient in its constitution, and, in a great measure, as the citadel of the public justice and the public security.[2]

## The Australian connection

Australians do not reflect much on the profound debt they owe to America's founders, if indeed they recognise the debt at all. America fought a revolutionary war at a time when revolution was in the air, at least in France. The American armed revolution was generated as much by an unsympathetic and unthinking British monarchy incapable of delivering the rights of *Magna Carta* while maintaining the allegiance of its colonial citizens as it was by demands for independence. Intransigence always has a price. And the British monarchy was itself autocratic, about which the House of Commons became increasingly restive until, by the time of Queen Victoria's death and the accession of George V to the throne, Britain had transformed itself into a constitutional monarchy.

Australia, coming later to constitutional self-government, was the beneficiary of America's bloodshed and Britain's much less bloody reforms. As a model for Australia's constitution, however, the US Constitution has no peer. The former clerk of the House of Representatives, Harry Evans, has written:

> It is well known that the framers of the Australian Constitution drew extensively upon the United States constitution for many aspects of their creation. This is best demonstrated by the impressive list of the characteristics of the Australian Constitution drawn directly from the American model: the employment of special procedures, different from those applying to normal legislation, for consulting the people in establishing the Constitution and for amending it; the special legal status thereby given to the written constitution; the division of powers between the central and state governments; the prescription of the powers of the national government in the written constitution; the establishment of a constitutional court to interpret and enforce the constitution; the delegation of national

legislative power to two elected houses of parliament of virtually equal competence, each representing the electors voting in different electorates and reflecting the geographically pluralistic character of the country.[3]

This is not to suggest that the Australian Constitution is some kind of lazy transcription of the US Constitution to fit late-nineteenth-century Australian conditions. The Australian Constitution and the legal system that supports its operation were developed in quite different circumstances from its American counterpart; the cultural, historical and social conditions in which both were crafted also differed substantially. The horrors of the Civil War profoundly influenced American constitutional and political thinking, and must have concentrated the minds of Australia's fledgling constitutionalists. More significant, perhaps, was the looming influence of the Colonial Office in London, second-guessing the preferences of Australia's constitution framers in a manner that Lord North and the Earl of Shelburne were unable to do in the 1780s as Americans were designing theirs.

What is suggested is that the US Constitution and its antecedents are in the DNA of the Australian Constitution, and that the different but complementary constitutional experiences of America and Australia resonate deeply in their democratic and federal practices and preoccupations. There is little direct evidence in the records of the Australian constitutional conventions of the 1890s that *The Federalist Papers* was much read or quoted. It is clear, however, that Samuel Griffith was familiar with at least two of the papers (Federalist 15 and Federalist 43), and it is not unreasonable to imagine that he was at least aware of Federalist 10, cited above.

*The Federalist Papers* was certainly part of the discussion at the 1890 Melbourne Convention and at the 1891 Sydney Convention.[4] What was even more part of the discussion at the constitutional conventions was James Bryce's three-volume study *American Commonwealth*, published in 1888. As James Warden has remarked, 'The framers of the Australian Constitution adopted the American theory of federalism which was derived from *The Federalist* but mediated through Bryce's *American Commonwealth*.'[5]

In his illuminating review of Bryce's contribution to the framing of the Australian Constitution, Stephen Gageler, Chief Justice of the High Court of Australia, pointed out that, besides interpreting the US Constitution for Americans and anyone else who might have been interested (all three volumes were bestsellers), Bryce connected the American constitutional model to the mainstream of British constitutional practice. As Chief Justice Gageler commented, the 'crimson thread of kinship' – the metaphor coined by Sir Henry Parkes at the 1890 Melbourne Conference – rendered the American experience not only accessible but also familiar:

> The utility of Bryce to the framers of the Australian Constitution lay in the fact that The American Commonwealth was not a work of philosophy or history, and that it was not merely a study of the blueprint of the American Constitution, but was instead a warts-and-all description of the contemporary practical operation of the United States Constitution. The book presented an honest assessment of what worked and what didn't … Bryce's unquestioned knowledge and integrity, the detail of his exposition, the ease of his prose, the evident balance of his presentation, and his lack of overt editorialisation, meant that *The American Commonwealth* was able be treated by the framers of the Australian Constitution as an authoritative repository of objective information: profitably to be mined for the purpose of examining any important topic on which there was something to be gained from a consideration of the experience of the United States, and available to be deployed by any side in debate if and when any topic of that nature became contentious.[6]

While the American constitutional experiment might be deep in the DNA of the Australian constitution, the latter boasts a number of features that were simply unimaginable to Hamilton, Jay, Madison and their fellow representatives. In a federation, the balance between the people's house and the states' house is of critical importance. Conflict between the two chambers, and the deadlock that may ensue, can be politically transfixing. But it does little for community wellbeing or public confidence in the governing institutions. America, for instance, finds itself in governmental paralysis not infrequently. The executive, quite separate from the Congress, has few powers of intervention and so must simply plead and then wait – a practice that would be impossible were the president and the executive creatures of the Congress. So Australia created a constitutional novelty – the double dissolution and subsequent joint sitting of both houses of parliament as a device to resolve (and sanction) any deadlock that might occur.

It is significant, too, that the passage of time between 1787 and the 1890s afforded the Australian constitutional drafters opportunities to reflect on the critical developments in American, British and European political theory and constitutional practice. This had a particular impact on the constitutional framers' consideration of the role of the High Court and its judicial review function. The Australian High Court is far less activist or politically interventionist than its American Supreme Court counterpart tends to be.

The American constitutional model was perhaps of greatest influence in Australia's consideration of its residual links to Britain, particularly regarding the vexed issue of appeals to the Privy Council. For its part, the Colonial Office sought to keep a leash around the throat of the nascent Australian federation by retaining the role as the final arbiter on matters of constitutional and legal interpretation. And, for their part, the framers of the Australian Constitution bridled at the thought that they lacked the authority to interpret their own constitutional text and an informed understanding of the circumstances in which that interpretation might be needed. So they looked to American practice. Chief Justice Gageler approvingly quotes the views of Alfred Deakin, speaking as attorney-general in 1902 on the proposed Judiciary Bill:

> The organ of the national life which preserving the union is yet able from time to time to transfuse into it the fresh blood of the living present, is the Judiciary[:] the High Court of Australia or Supreme Court in the United States. It is one of the organs of Government which enables the Constitution to grow and to be adapted to the

changeful necessities and circumstances of generation after generation that the High Court operates.[7]

A year later, speaking in support of the same bill, Senator Richard
O'Connor – shortly to become one of the inaugural judges of the High
Court – provided additional heft to this view (and an even more gen-
erous acknowledgement of the American model):

> There can be no question that if it had not been for the establishment
> of the United States Supreme Court, and the position which that
> court has always occupied in the working out of their system of gov-
> ernment, the history of the United States to-day would have been
> very different indeed. As has been explained by some of her writers,
> one of the most remarkable qualities of the American Constitution
> seems to have been its wonderful adaptability to the changing condi-
> tions which have gone on in the country during the last 112 years. It
> is the universal testimony of writers and historians that that adapt-
> ability to changing conditions has been made possible only by the
> power invested in the Supreme Court of the United States, and the
> way in which that power has been exercised.[8]

Former High Court justice Robert French amplified this view in a pen-
etrating 2018 essay, 'United States Influence on the Australian Legal
System'. Addressing Australia's constitutional 'borrowing' from the
United States, he wrote:

> Important elements of the United States Constitution were reflected
> in the Australian Constitution. A major coauthor of the Australian
> document was Andrew Inglis Clark, the Attorney-General for the
> Colony of Tasmania … He believed in the natural or rational rights
> of man as a counter to what he called 'the tyranny of the majority,
> whose unrestricted rule is so often and so erroneously regarded
> as the essence and distinctive principle of democracy.' He was a
> believer in judicial control of official power. The Supreme Court of
> the United States was a model which he admired. It could 'restrain
> and annul' any folly that the ignorance or anger of a majority of the

Congress or the people might at any time attempt to do in contravention of the Constitution.[9]

It is easy to view the law as an amalgam of interconnected institutions – the parliament enacting laws; the courts interpreting them, dispensing justice between litigant parties and ensuring the proper administration of the law as it affects people's day-to-day lives; the bar representing people in the courts; and solicitors providing the extended range of legal services that enable a democratic society to function efficiently and, more importantly, justly. The law sits at the centre of the social contract between the governed and their government. But, more than that, it defines the structures that enable a society and a nation to operate – its behaviours and practices. The law sits at the centre of the ongoing and evolving relationship between citizens themselves. As Justice French argued, the evolution of the law is a human phenomenon, not just a national one: 'Major legal traditions and principles have historically resisted confinement to national silos.'[10]

The common law of England exerted a major influence on the development of American law, as it did for Australia. And American civil and constitutional law influenced the development of the Australian legal system, and continues to do so. The links are both institutional and structural – the institutional expressions of the law are modelled, reimagined, repurposed and restyled, while the structural expressions of the law guide both practice and behaviour. The legal resonances between America and Australia are not accidental. They are vital expressions of the nature of things. But like the nervous and vascular systems in the human body, the significance of the law as a bond between nations goes unremarked until something goes terribly wrong.

Both America and Australia fret about the rise of China, worrying that its accumulation of economic and military power constitutes a threat to the national security of both countries and significantly increases the probability of armed conflict. But there are internal threats that, like cancer, can remain unseen while internal pathologies erode national confidence, good order and wellbeing. Some of those threats have materialised in America, as we saw in Chapter 2. And America faces associated risks that are perhaps yet to manifest themselves: risks of deep urban economic and social alienation, for example, leading to even more frequent and more pronounced acts of civil disobedience and violence. Australia is not immune from such risks, especially if racism were to take on even more virulent forms. This is where the deep legal infrastructures that link Australia and America come into their own, not as threat remedies but as risk mitigations. They have to be identified and exercised, however. And more importantly, they have to be discussed and become a critical element in the bilateral conversation.

## The rule of law

For both America and Australia, the rule of law is central to both the maintenance of jurisprudence (how the rules are crafted) and the dispensation of justice (how the rules are applied). 'The rule of law' is a shorthand (or symbolic?) expression of a principle that is foundational to both rights and obligations in a democratic society. It found early expression, in English law, in the *Magna Carta*, where the individual's freedom – or at least the individual's protection from legal oppression – was proclaimed:

> No freeman is to be taken or imprisoned or disseised of his free tenement or of his liberties or free customs, or outlawed or exiled or in any way ruined, nor will we go against such a man or send against him save by lawful judgement of his peers or by the law of the land. To no-one will we sell or deny o[r] delay right or justice.[11]

The rule of law has continued to define the relationship between the citizen and the state. It is the foundation of democracy. More fundamentally, it is the ultimate guarantor of liberty. And, as liberty's guarantor, it is the cornerstone on which the various constructs that deliver security at the personal, community and national levels rest.

In an important 2017 speech, Justice French provided a comprehensive description of the role that the rule of law plays in a democratic society:

> The rule of law provides a kind of societal infrastructure. It creates and maintains the space within which we can enjoy our freedoms, exercise our rights, develop our capacities, find opportunities, take risks and generally pursue life goals. It is that infrastructure, strengthened by efficient and impartial and independent courts and tribunals, which encourages the investment of capital from domestic and offshore sources. It might also be thought, because it supports a society with respect for the human rights and freedoms of its members, to attract human capital in the form of people coming from other places to live and work here and contribute to the common good. It gives shape and definition to Australia as a particular kind of society in the global community of nations.[12]

As America continues to wrestle with deep internal divisions, and as Australia also confronts its racial demons,[13] it is imperative that both nations recognise and affirm the centrality of the rule of law in maintaining their national integrity.

But what is the rule of law anyway? As Justice French commented in the same speech, 'the meaning of the term "rule of law" is much debated'.[14] Understandably, most legal commentators see the term through the lens of the law itself: how the law is expressed and how the law is practised. They understand 'the rule of law' in terms of the rules by which it applies to behaviours and relationships. It is commonly articulated as 'nobody – private citizen, public official or government – is above the law' or 'everybody is equal before the law'.

So, from the perspective of the law, the rule of law has seven main aspects. First, state power is codified in laws enacted under the national constitution or under the constitutions of the nation's component states. Second, laws cannot be enacted on the run and applied retrospectively. Third, state power is limited by and to those laws. Fourth, people are equal before the law, and justice must be dispensed equally. Fifth, laws must be applied legally and in a manner that meets the demands of due process. Sixth, it is the job of the courts to determine disputes. And, finally, government is bound by the same laws as the governed, and disputes are determined in the same way – through the courts.

Of course, these aspects are all very well in theory. In practice, they are tricky to implement, especially where equality before the law is concerned. It is a sad and shameful fact that Australia's First Peoples, like America's First Nations and Black Americans, are not treated equally before the law, as conviction and incarceration rates so clearly show.

That lawyers concentrate on the expression and operation of the law is all very understandable. But the rule of law depends on an even more fundamental and subtle principle, one that goes to what it means to be a human being. It is a principle that underpins the values that form the 'glue' holding democratic societies together, and that grounds both their legal and political systems. The wellspring of the rule of law is recognition of the fact that all human beings have dignity and value by virtue of their shared humanity. This principle found expression in the preamble to the United Nations Charter, drafted in the immediate aftermath of the calamities that were World War II: 'We the peoples of the United Nations determined ... to reaffirm faith in ... the dignity and worth of the human person, in the equal rights of men and women and of nations large and small.'[15] Foreign Minister Penny Wong summed this up in a speech delivered at Griffith University, Brisbane, in 2017:

> What distinguishes the values system in democratic societies is the fact that the various specific values that we might identify come to a focus in what we term the rule of law ... At the core of the values to which we as Australians adhere is the intrinsic worth and dignity of each person by virtue of their basic humanity – their fundamental right to exist, to live a life of worth and fulfilment, to chart their own course through life and to pursue happiness. Far from being a sentimental, romantic or even a religious notion, the idea of the intrinsic worth of each individual was the gift that the Age of Enlightenment

conferred on the framers of the US Declaration of Independence [who] gave the idea political force when they wrote: 'We hold these truths to be self-evident, that all men are created equal, that they are endowed by their Creator with certain unalienable Rights, that among these are Life, Liberty and the pursuit of Happiness.'[16]

It would be a singular contribution to the balance, security and well-being of both nations were Australian and American politicians and jurists to remind themselves and their polities frequently of the force of Penny Wong's remarks. Recognition of human dignity and worth provides the energy that drives constructive national and international development policies. Along with the transformational change that makes the world a better place, it redefines security as a goal that unites rather than divides at both the national and international levels. It replaces the negative and limited concentration on fear and threat with an emphasis on collaboration and cooperation to deliver contentment, harmony and prosperity to the global community. Risks abide, of course – risks from natural and anthropogenic sources, such as global warming, and risks arising from human miscalculation and the poor exercise of political agency. But the best way to mitigate those risks is constantly to reaffirm the critical significance of the rule of law in both the national and international domains.

## A bill of rights

Australia does not have a bill of rights. Neither in the constitution nor in subordinate legislation are the basic rights of Australian citizens specified. That is not to suggest that Australians lack rights. It is to suggest, however, that Australians do not know what their rights are and, as a result, whether their rights are protected or ignored. Just as the Australian Constitution was adopted without a bill of rights, so was the American Constitution. This led George Mason, a key delegate to the 1787 Constitutional Convention from Virginia, to refuse to sign the text, instead releasing his own draft bill of rights. His fellow delegate from Virginia, James Madison, had in fact strongly opposed suggestions that the American Constitution was incomplete without legislated rights. Madison's position was similar to that of Australian constitutional purists, who also argue against the need for a bill of rights: government can only exercise the powers accorded to it by the constitution. Popular opinion was on Mason's side, however, and Madison was quick to change his position, especially when public support for the constitution increasingly depended on the inclusion of clearly articulated rights. If Americans learned one thing from their dealings with Westminster, it was that rights must be legislated to be acknowledged. Interestingly, the British people learned the same lesson from their own civil war, Cromwell's protectorate and the restoration of the Stuart monarchy: Westminster legislated its bill of rights in 1689. The pity is that, a century later, Westminster could not see its relevance to its North American colonies.

Madison was quick to follow up on his change of heart. He introduced a raft of constitutional amendments in June 1789. The Senate reduced the House of Representatives list of seventeen amendments to twelve, and by the end of 1791 three-quarters of the state legislatures had confirmed ten of the amendments, which became known as the Bill of Rights. It is a powerful statement of the fundamental rights of all Americans, and in view of the growth in the power of the executive, especially the office of the president, one can only wonder whether the Supreme Court could have constrained the power of the president or the Congress in its absence. While some of the amendments that comprise the Bill of Rights have been problematic from time to time – as the Second Amendment (the right to bear arms) continues to be – taken together, they are much more than a line in the sand. Rather than simply representing a set of political values that defined a moment in America's constitutional history, the Bill of Rights expresses the fundamental freedoms that define America's democracy. The fact that Americans are such constant advocates for their form of democratic politics is emblematic of the power and efficacy of the constitutional recognition of basic rights.

Australia's constitution, on the other hand, is testament to a trouble-free journey from foreign settlement in 1788 to constitutional independence, albeit subject to the British monarch. And the absence of a bill of rights to guarantee fundamental freedoms is equally a testament to the Australian preference to let sleeping dogs lie. America had to fight for its independence. Australia negotiated its independence with the UK parliament. While some freedoms are explicit – the right to vote, the acquisition of property on just terms (the nub of the cult film *The Castle*), trial by jury (at least for some offences) and freedom of religious practice – others are simply implied.

The assumed freedom of speech is a case in point. Australia's defamation laws vary across jurisdictions, and in the absence of an express right to free speech, defamation remains a highly contested area of the law and a highly lucrative domain of legal practice. The High Court of Australia has determined that there is an implied freedom of political communication, without which voters would be unable to exercise their electoral rights in a free and informed manner. While that High Court judgment constrains the ability to resort to defamation proceedings in some instances by granting qualified privilege to journalists and publishers, it has not found a positive right that would afford public interest immunity to the publication of materials that might otherwise offer a defence in defamation proceedings. As one leading constitutional expert, Professor Anne Twomey, has noted, freedom of political communication remains problematic at both the federal and state levels.[17] And the relationship between a right to free speech and defamation remains even more contested.

Australians do enjoy rights under international law. As party to the seven main international human rights treaties, Australia explicitly acknowledges Civil and Political Rights; Economic, Social and Cultural Rights; the Elimination of All Forms of Racial Discrimination; the Elimination of All Forms of Discrimination against Women; the Prohibition on Torture and Other Cruel, Inhuman or Degrading Treatment or Punishment; the Rights of the Child; and the Rights of Persons with Disabilities. These rights are unenforceable, however, as are rights conferred under the Refugees Convention, for instance. So Australian governments have enacted legislation to give such conventions domestic force: the *Sex Discrimination Act* (1984); the *Racial*

*Discrimination Act* (1986); the *Disability Discrimination Act* (1992) and the *Age Discrimination Act* (2004).

Whether Australia needs a bill of rights remains a matter of contention. Justice French, quoted earlier in this chapter, displays his signature discretion in his commentary on rights and freedoms as they are practised in Australia. While refraining from adopting a position one way or the other, he could not be accused of sitting on the fence. His words are instructive:

> The words 'rights' and 'freedoms' echo through our history and our civil and political discourse. They attach, in our ordinary speech, to individual men and women. The usage reflects the idea in international law of human rights and freedoms as aspects of the dignity and equality of every human being. The Constitution does not provide expressly or by implication general guarantees of human rights and freedoms. There are, however, several provisions of the Australian Constitution which incorporate guarantees of rights and freedoms ... The rule of law ... is perhaps the most important protections [sic] of our rights and freedoms. In the end, however consistently with the rule of law, statutes can be enacted by parliaments driven by short-term political imperatives which erode although perhaps only in a piecemeal way elements of those rights and freedoms. Over time, and cumulatively, this can be a process of death by a thousand cuts ... In the end the rule of law provides the framework within which we can protect and enjoy our rights and freedoms. It does not guarantee them.[18]

While Justice French sounds a caution, Professor George Williams provides an answer.[19] Acknowledging the challenges, he mounts a persuasive case for a bill of rights legislated by the Australian Parliament rather than delivered by way of constitutional amendment. Australia would do well to emulate America's preference for a clear statement of where citizens stand with respect to each other and with respect to their parliament, he argues. The healing that is necessary at so many levels within America would be impossible were it not for a clearly articulated and widely accepted bill of rights. Australia, too, faces a deep need for healing, reconciliation and tolerance that would be similarly facilitated by a bill of rights. The simple fact is that Australians no longer trust their governments. Nor do they trust one another. To address this, Australians would do well to look to the American example and institute a 'long overdue dialogue between parliament, the courts and the people'.[20]

And, because it goes to the core of what the rule of law is all about, Australia and America would do well to embark on a serious bilateral conversation in the mutual national interest.

# 5.
## Money

Few Australians, and even fewer Americans, appreciate the extent or depth of the two nations' bilateral economic relationship. Australians in general think little about the underlying strength of the Australian economy, instead preferring comfortable myths about the nation riding on the sheep's back and the export of energy and minerals. For their part, and to the extent that they think of it at all, Americans continue to see Australia as an outpost of the US Pacific Fleet and a safe place for cheap holidays.

America and Australia are deeply invested in each other's economies, however. Tens of thousands of Australians live and work in the United States, as tens of thousands of Americans live and work in Australia. Two-way investment is significant, and – largely as a consequence of Australia's compulsory superannuation funds – Australian foreign direct investment in America is growing quickly. The 2005 Australia United States Free Trade Agreement (AUSFTA) gave both countries preferential access to each other's markets. In gross terms, the economic relationship, valued at $2.2 trillion, is comparable with Australia's annual GDP of $2.5 trillion.[1]

Given the historical and political links between America and Australia, it is unsurprising that the economic links go back to the very beginnings of colonial settlement in Australia. After 1801, whaling expanded during the next thirty years as American and British vessels from Fremantle to the east coast of Australia hunted down their prey. Disastrously, whaling also exacerbated the dispossession and genocide of the First Peoples of Australia, as they came into contact with whalers in southern Victoria and south-western Western Australia.[2] By the 1840s, there were more than a hundred American vessels plying their trade.[3] So began an active and profitable two-way trading link, whereby American vessels, 'welcomed as the sole link with the outside world', provided 'both a significant export market [for Western Australian products] and an important source of manufactured items and otherwise unavailable consumer goods', such as tinware and tobacco.[4] This trade relationship was so lucrative that many American whalers stocked their vessels according to the needs of West Australian ports, both generating a market and undercutting British rivals. The explorer George Grey – later Governor of South Australia, New Zealand and the Cape Colony – stated that the bartering between American vessels and West Australian settlers was 'so profitable to both parties that it would be impossible to prevent it'.[5]

## The gold rushes

Edward Hargreaves did not discover gold and begin the Australian gold rush. Like many an entrepreneur before and since, he commercialised a discovery made by others. He was, in effect, a conman. The hapless brothers William and James Tom and their friend John Lister entrusted their discoveries to Hargreaves, who promptly hot-footed it to Sydney, won the support of the colonial secretary and claimed the honour and the reward.[6]

The rest, as the saying goes, is history. Just as the discovery of gold at Ophir, New South Wales, in 1851 transformed the colonial economy and set Australia onto the path of becoming a mining superpower, so it transformed the economic relationship between pre–Civil War America and the Australian colonies. As devotees of the American TV series *Deadwood* would know, the American gold rushes attracted adventurers from all corners of the globe, including Australia, most of them unskilled men seeking to make their fortunes, and most of them failing to do so. Within five years, California's population grew fifteen-fold, with excess fortune-seekers moving from California to Alaska, South Dakota and anywhere else that gold was discovered.

The Australian goldfields reversed the emigration flow as the American goldfields were exhausted. And with the waves of immigrants came trade: between 1851 and 1853 the value of imports into Victoria alone rose from less than £3 million to almost £15 million.[7] But gold was only a trigger for more substantial economic development and links between Australia and America. While the miners were panning for gold, engineers were constructing the infrastructure necessary for mining, crushing and processing, bringing and developing skills that spread across the industrial and manufacturing landscape of Australia. And as for the natural landscape? As they placed their mullock-heaps indiscriminately across despoiled fields and polluted rivers, Australian and American colonisers reinforced mutual lessons on the link between economic development and wanton environmental destruction.

An early American gold rush entrepreneur was Freeman Cobb, who with his partners established the eponymous Cobb & Co., Australia's earliest networked transport company, in 1853. Cobb found that transporting miners, mining equipment, bullion and the mail was a much more lucrative business than mining itself. With horse-changing stations every twenty kilometres or so, and hostelries every seventy kilometres or so, Cobb & Co. played a pioneering role in opening up Australia's transport infrastructure. Consistent with its American origins, Cobb & Co. also introduced one of the largest commercial horse-drawn coaches in the world, the sixteen-horse, sixty-passenger Leviathan. With its elaborately painted side panels featuring an American eagle and the Stars and Stripes, the opportunity for jingoism was not missed.[8]

As the gold that Cobb & Co. transported from the goldfields to the major cities found its way into the global financial system, Australia's colonial capitals expanded and Australia itself grew in confidence. Mining and the workforce immigration it attracted enabled commerce and investment, particularly investment in urban and industrial infrastructure, which in turn fostered prodigious economic growth. The Melbourne International Exhibition of 1880, for example, was an industrial 'demonstrator' that, among other things, initiated the introduction of tramways modelled on Boston and San Francisco. The first tram began operation in 1889 between the Box Hill Post Office and Doncaster, on the eastern edge of Melbourne.[9]

With nascent industrialisation of its economy, Australia began to look more like America: rapid urban growth and the establishment of factories, and the associated urban industrial employment, changed the face of both the countryside and the political institutions. The colonies quickly transformed themselves from communities built around landowners and rural labour to suburbs built around capitalists, an industrial workforce and expanding service industries employing white-collar workers.

Illustrative of how Australia and America were forging separate but parallel industrial identities was the employment of a young Stanford graduate by Berwick, Moreing & Co. to oversee the Sons of Gwalia mine in Coolgardie in 1898. Herbert Hoover, subsequently America's thirty-first president, quickly introduced radical employment changes to cut costs and increase production. In an episode that has a curiously contemporary ring in both America and Australia, for gig economy workers at least, he increased the hours, introduced single-handed work, changed shifts at the ore face rather than above ground, and cut double time on Sundays and bonuses for working in the wet. He employed contract labourers willing to work for lower wages, causing industrial action by the Miners' Union.[10] By 1904, Sons of Gwalia was responsible for almost half of Western Australia's gold production, and employed around 20 per cent of the mining workforce – productivity on steroids.

After a mere six months working with Sons of Gwalia, Hoover transferred to China to continue his stellar career as a mining engineer and investor, amassing substantial wealth on the way. He returned to America at the end of World War I, having managed complex multi-partite negotiations between Europe's warring nations on behalf of President Woodrow Wilson's international relief operations until America's declaration of war on Germany in 1917. Elected president in 1928, Hoover assumed office with a melange of progressive labour policies – who knows, perhaps influenced by Justice H.B. Higgins's 1907 Commonwealth Court of Conciliation and Arbitration *Sunshine Harvester* decision, which enshrined the principle that Australian workers should be paid a living wage – and decidedly conservative social policies, such as his support for prohibition. His presidency was overshadowed by the perfect storm of the Great Depression and his total blindness to America's deep-seated racial problems. If America were ever considered a 'lucky country', to recall Donald Horne's ironic description of Australia, Hoover would surely be counted as one of the second-rate people who shared in its luck.

## World wars and economic transformation

America and Australia entered the twentieth century vastly different in size but interestingly similar in the shape of their economies. Their societies shared similarities too. America had weathered the recessions in the late 1880s and late 1890s, while Australia had survived the collapse of the land boom and the bank crashes of the 1890s. Both entered the new century as buoyant, confident and resilient societies, with economies to match.

These parallels notwithstanding, however, the two-way economic relationship was far from 'sweetness and light'. In the years after Federation, tariffs were regarded as a revenue source. But gradually tariffs, along with quotas, were seen as protection instruments. So both the Australian and American economies began to hide behind tariff walls, with protectionism and feather-bedding of domestic producers taking precedence over any form of bilateral preferential or free trade agreements that might have flow-on effects for other international trade arrangements. Multilateral trade arrangements remained a very distant prospect.

Australia, of course, remained firmly locked into the sterling area arrangements, a fact clearly reflected in Australia's investment and trade dependence on Britain. The imperial alignment was signalled even more dramatically in August 1914, when Australia, effectively without any independent choice of its own, committed its support – and its youth – to the defence of Britain and its empire. Of those who departed Australia for the 'Great War' with a spring in their step, so many returned four years later on crutches, broken in body and mind. Australia, and New Zealand, paid a horrendous price for the intransigence of European political leaders. As Professor Joan Beaumont narrates in her magisterial account of Australia's emergence from World War I, the Anzacs returned to two decades of desolation and despair: pre-war optimism gave way to post-war depression that changed the Australian character.[11] America, for its part, also incurred terrible losses on the Western Front, though its late entry into the war substantially limited the social and economic effects on the American population.

In the first half of the twentieth century, mining continued to grow in economic importance, but Australia remained principally an agricultural products exporter. Wool and wheat exports to Britain, along with dairy, meat and fruit, accounted for over 50 per cent of Australia's GDP before World War I. They fell sharply during the war, then recovered to pre-war levels in the early 1920s, fuelled by the wool boom.[12] The Great Depression smashed Australia's trade with Britain, which fell to 20 per cent of GDP before rising steadily again through World War II to pre–World War I levels during the Korean War.

The United States, on the other hand, with its protectionist trade policy, remained a tough market for Australian exports. Even the relaxation on the import of Australian wool during World War II had little material effect on Australia's export performance, which struggled to reach 20 per cent of GDP by the mid-1970s (Britain accounted for over 55 per cent of GDP). The imperial overhang left the former colony with an enduring hangover. Although Australia celebrates itself as a trading nation, exports today account for only 27 per cent of GDP (2022–23 figures).

World War II triggered a profound reset in Australia's understanding of its place in the world and the nature of its central international relationships. As we have seen, Britain's inability to retain its strategic toeholds in Hong Kong and Singapore, or to come to Australia's defence against Japan in any material way, persuaded Prime Minister Curtin to embark upon a strategic reorientation towards America. The aberration of AUKUS and its completely unscoped and uncosted relationship with the British nuclear submarine program notwithstanding, that remains the case to the present day.

During the years immediately following Japan's December 1941 attack on Pearl Harbor, the significance of that strategic reset was perhaps best demonstrated in the Lend-Lease arrangements entered into by America and Australia. These allowed Australia to access the American manufacturing colossus, in parallel with Britain, Canada, New Zealand and the other World War II allies, helping it to acquire the vast volumes of defence matériel it needed to conduct successful wars against both Germany and Japan. Generating the largest foreign debt ever incurred to that point by Australia – over \$2 billion worth of aircraft, ships, armaments and other military equipment – Lend-Lease facilitated Australia's delivery into the warm embrace of the emerging American military-industrial complex. Once captured, it was difficult for the recipients to extract themselves without acrimony and ill-feeling. As Mark Clayton has written in a perceptive essay:

> Approved by Congress in 1941, the US Lend-Lease aid programme was ... extended to [Britain and] dozens of other allied nations [including Australia]. Congressional architects of the Lend-Lease (1941) and subsequent Surplus Property (1944) Acts, however, had made no effective post-war provision for acquitting these Lend-Lease obligations beyond reasserting America's title interest, and reminding lessee-nations that those aid supplies neither 'destroyed, lost, or consumed' were to be returned to the United States 'at the end of the present emergency.'[13]

As an instrument for supporting the Allied war effort, Lend-Lease was critical, essentially determining the outcome of the war (the Soviet

Union was a principal beneficiary, though it refused at war's end to pay any charges or debts) and establishing the capability preconditions for the Cold War. As a complex system to be terminated on equitable terms in the aftermath of World War II that saw America emerge as the dominant global power, however, Lend-Lease was a nightmare.

Consistent with its entrepreneurial spirit, and its policy of using Lend-Lease and the redemption of other loans to shape the post–World War II global economic environment, America drove a hard bargain. Despite early presidential assurances that America did not expect restitution from its Lend-Lease debtors, Congress (as is so often the case) had other ideas. Deeply resentful of the financial settlement reached with Britain, Senate Republicans simply did not care whether the deals struck with other Lend-Lease recipients precipitated budgetary hardship or constraints on currency reserves. Negotiations were testy. As Mark Clayton has observed: 'Collectively these [US attempts to undermine Australia's ability to make independent procurement decisions] made for an extremely difficult negotiating environment, with Australian politicians and negotiators being repeatedly shocked and dismayed by the apparent dishonesty, fickleness, hypocrisy, callousness, and at times small-mindedness displayed by their US counterparts'.[14]

While sustained access to the American war machine proved to be considerably more difficult than initial acquisitions, World War II did transform the Australian economy, and with it the country's economic relationship with America. The import of manufactured goods and manufacturing technology – most notably in the car industry, following the entry of Ford and General Motors in the late 1940s – continued to climb.

**Economic emancipation and expansion**

World War II transformed Australia. The introspection and lament that marked the immediate post-World War I years, made even more bitter by the Great Depression and the draconian demands of the Bank of England's Sir Otto Niemeyer, gave way to a measure of optimism as prime ministers Curtin and Chifley led Australia through the war with Japan into a period of remarkable growth.

As happens frequently in Australia, Labor innovation prompts conservative implementation. The long prime ministership of Robert Menzies brought a political stability that consolidated the two great economic innovations of the Chifley government: immigration and industrialisation, especially the motor vehicle industry. The most obvious shift in the Australian economy was in the mining and services sectors, facilitated by increased American direct investment and the arrival in Australia of major American (or at least American-owned) mining companies. At the end of World War II, coal and iron ore declined as key exports. Sixty years later, they were the top two exports. In 1998, Australia exported over half a million kilograms of gold, compared with 96,000 kilograms at the peak of Victoria's gold rush, in 1856.[15] Further, the service industries (such as health, finance, and tourism) more than doubled as a share of GDP from around 22.5 per cent in 1951 to just under 50 per cent in 2001. About two-thirds of Australia's services trade in 2000 was with the United States.[16]

The domestic economic liberalisation reforms of the Whitlam, Hawke and Keating governments completely reoriented the Australian economy through the 1970s and 1980s. In combination, the removal of exchange rate controls that tied the Australian currency to the British pound, the floating of the Australian dollar, labour reforms and the wages accord opened the doors to substantial growth in foreign (especially American) investment in Australia and set the stage for three decades of economic growth.

The figures are impressive. Between 1949 and 1970, 'the annual inflow of [net] foreign direct investment increased from $100 million to $900 million'.[17] The American share of foreign investment in Australia, driven initially by mineral exports, doubled from 16 per cent of total foreign investment in Australia in 1949 to 32 per cent in 1999. During the same period, Australian investment in the United States increased from 1 per cent to an astonishing 41 per cent of total Australian foreign investment. As we shall see, the Keating government's creation of a national superannuation scheme and the accumulation of funds to support it played a major role in this remarkable development.

The spillover effects of economic development and economic growth often pass unnoticed. Negative spillover effects, however, tend to become all too obvious, as they did when the US stock market crashed in 1929, bringing down the global economy with it. Governments have become adept at containing the negative spillover effects of economic crises – the Asian financial crisis of 1997 and the collapse of Lehman Brothers and the ensuing global financial crisis (GFC) of 2008 provide compelling examples. The Rudd government worked tirelessly with the Australian financial regulators on contingency planning, and with the international banking community. But it was the consultation with the American political and economic leadership, and the bilateral efforts to act in close coordination, that made the difference between make and break. As Kevin Rudd put it:

> Immediately following the Lehman's collapse, I travelled to New York for meetings with US President George Bush and the president of the New York Federal Reserve, Tim Geithner. I had earlier spent time with US Federal Reserve chairman Ben Bernanke and the US Treasury Secretary Hank Paulson on their own contingency plans. *Whatever we did in Australia would be useless unless we could anticipate the timing and content of US sovereign interventions in the crisis* [my emphasis], particularly the Targeted Asset Recovery Plan (TARP). I also lobbied President Bush on bailing out the global insurance giant AIG once I discovered the scale of AIG's presence in the Australian insurance market. Had AIG failed, the consequences for us would have been catastrophic.[18]

In this context, it is critical to note that the combination of tireless application, energy and foresight enabled both governments to weather an existential threat to both economies – a threat that imperilled the lives and wellbeing of the citizens more profoundly than any credible threat of armed attack. There is a delicious irony in the fact that the Australian government was able to head off the potentially negative effects of the GFC by leveraging the positive spill-over deriving from the deep institutional and structural links between the American and Australian economies built up over the previous half-century.

There is a powerful and long-term message for both Australia and America in this. The positive spillover effects of the expansion of the Australia–US economic relationship have been profound, particularly for Australia, and particularly in the services (educational, financial, medical and tourism) sectors. Both innovation and productivity have benefited enormously from the deep interaction between the Australian and American economies at virtually all levels. To take a single example: gifted Australian students pursue their higher degrees at American universities (and, increasingly, vice versa), returning home with advanced skills that further expand the economy while adding depth to Australia's academic and intellectual culture.

## Protection against protection: The Australia–United States Free Trade Agreement

America's constitutional compact necessarily enshrined state-based protectionism in the national economic DNA. The condition on which most of the states joined the union was protection of local enterprise and industry against competition from neighbours, and against competition from abroad. That protection extended to the protection of local economic interests more broadly and, unsurprisingly, of the personal economic interests of the legislators. Then as now, self-interest was a strong motivator. And just as self-interest defined the neutrality and non-interventionism characteristic of American foreign policy in the nineteenth and early twentieth centuries, so protectionism defined America's approach to trade. It still does.

The combination of neutrality, non-interventionism and protectionism served America well, allowing it to grow its economic and military power during the nineteenth century. While the Monroe doctrine, which sought to constrain European colonial expansion in the Western

Hemisphere, was initially disregarded by the European powers, by the end of World War I it had become the defining principle of American grand strategy and its so-called statecraft. American intervention came late in the Great War. But America emerged from the Paris Peace Conference as the pre-eminent global power, and President Woodrow Wilson as the pre-eminent global leader. Their idealism notwithstanding – or perhaps because of their idealism – the Fourteen Points articulated by President Wilson in his speech to the US Congress on 8 January 1918 became the foundation of the 'international rules-based order', which has effectively remained the cornerstone American foreign policy and the driver of American dominance ever since.[19] As it has evolved over more than a century, the *Pax Americana* remains the fundamental authority on which the international rules-based order rests, and the wellspring of its legitimacy. And as Australia and America continue to advocate for the international rules-based order as their preferred determinant of global security and stability, both need to recognise that it is essentially an artefact of American policy.

America is powerful. It has the power and authority to encourage others to adopt courses of action that it has no intention of pursuing itself. Whether it is in negotiating arms control and disarmament measures, the Law of the Sea convention, international legal arbitral institutions such as the International Criminal Court, or the dispute resolution mechanisms of the World Trade Organization (WTO), America is always able to blame its non-membership on difficulties in the US Congress. Or it simply affirms that it is not prepared to accept what it might describe as gratuitous external pressure, as it has from time to time in the International Labour Organization (ILO) or the United Nations Educational, Scientific and Cultural Organization (UNESCO). And its power is such that it is generally not prepared to accept the constraints entailed by agreements where the other members expect more than America is prepared to give. As America defaults to its traditional protectionism, lowest-common-denominator multilateral agreements become the norm. So what do other nations do? Generally, they seek to improve particular elements of trade agreements by negotiating separate bilateral free trade agreements with America to obtain special access to the US market in return for specific concessions. They seek protection against American protectionism.

It is against this background that the AUSFTA should be evaluated. It was, of course, an important development in the bilateral Australia–America bilateral relationship. But it was also a response to the limitations imposed by America on multilateral economic and trade agreements that caused problems for US agricultural, industrial and service businesses leading to lowest-common-denominator outcomes. Often, America's trading partners (Canada is a good example) seek refuge in bilateral arrangements, where they hope to broker most favoured nation (MFN) arrangements in return for concessions to American interests. In Australia's case, a preferential trade agreement with America had the added attraction of satisfying the political interests of the then prime minister, John Howard, who saw a free trade agreement with the United States as a logical extension of Australia's bilateral security relationship. Locked into the unnecessary (and almost certainly illegal) war in Iraq, Howard saw such an agreement as an appropriate reward for Australia's military support. The reward went substantially to America's advantage.

Nonetheless, the AUSFTA was a key moment in the development of the bilateral economic and investment relationship in the early twenty-first century. Negotiated in 2003 and 2004, the agreement came into force on 1 January 2005. Basically, it secures preferential access to each other's markets by ensuring free transfer of capital and profits, creating a MFN clause, removing performance requirements for investment approval, and increasing the Australian Foreign Investment Review Board's (FIRB) threshold for general US foreign direct investment (FDI) review from $50 million to $800 million (which is indexed for inflation and is now over $1.2 billion).[20]

Commentaries on the AUSFTA issued by government departments and agencies such as the Department of Foreign Affairs and Trade and by US-funded bodies such as the United States Study Centre are full-throated in their advocacy for the agreement and trumpet its successes. Other commentators have been more critical, however. In a study prepared for the Australian Parliament before the agreement entered into force, Philippa Dee wrote:

> It is often claimed that preferential trade agreements can achieve faster progress than multilateral negotiation in the difficult areas. This appears not to be the case with AUSFTA. On a strict cost-benefit calculation, the agreement is of marginal benefit to Australia, and possibly of negative benefit given some of the pernicious but unquantifiable elements in the intellectual property chapter. Australia will continue to be subject to US bilateral opportunism, whether or not it signs AUSFTA, unless it can persuade the United States and all its future bilateral partners to multilateralise all future concessions, not just those in services and investment. And while Australia need not fear major retaliation from third parties if it were to sign AUSFTA, this is only because Australia has failed to achieve as much as some of our other trading partners have in their bilateral negotiations with the United States. In particular, Australia has achieved less than others in the difficult area of agriculture.[21]

As Dee noted, the US stance was understandable. It reserved its major sugar concessions, for instance, to benefit less developed countries in its immediate geopolitical neighbourhood. The only avenue open to Australia, if it were to make headway on agriculture, would be in a multilateral forum. And that did not happen. Negotiations on the agreement were conducted at breakneck speed to meet Howard's political agenda, and the result was not nearly as advantageous to Australia as Australian companies and enterprises had hoped.

This assessment was strongly supported in two trenchant contemporary analyses. In *All the Way with the USA: Australia, the US and Free Trade*, Ann Capling argued that Australia's approach to the AUSFTA was not only naive, but undermined both Australia's long-term insistence on multilateralism to improve its trade performance and consigned Australia to economic client status to powerful American business interests.[22] For their part, Linda Weiss, Elizabeth Thurbon and John Mathews were excoriating in their assessment that the Howard government took Australia to a do-it-yourself execution in its enthusiasm to subordinate itself to the US in some kind of extension to the bilateral security relationship. *How to Kill a Country: Australia's Devastating Trade Deal with the United States* paints a dismal picture of how the bilateral expansion of a trade relationship can have the perverse effect of reducing broader and more economically beneficial expansion in multilateral trade.[23]

Writing a decade later, Shiro Armstrong commented:

> The critics were right. Ten years after the Australia–United States free trade agreement (AUSFTA) came into force, new analysis of the data shows that the agreement diverted trade away from the lowest cost sources. Australia and the United States have reduced their trade by US$53 billion with rest of the world and are worse off than they would have been without the agreement ... Deals that are struck in haste for primarily political reasons carry risk of substantial economic damage. The question then is whether the economic costs of such policies are worth whatever the political gain, and indeed, how the balance of properly calculated political gains and costs might look.[24]

And that was almost ten years ago. The difference between bilateral trade benefits and multilateral trade costs has doubtless grown.

But if the two-way trade relationship has stifled expansion in multilateral trade, bilateral investment has flourished. A few statistics make the point. When the AUSFTA came into force in 2005, US investment in Australia was $334 billion ($75 billion of which was FDI), and Australian investment in the US was $303 billion ($114 billion of which was FDI) – valuing the two-way investment relationship at $637 billion. By 2022, US investment in Australia had reached over $1 trillion ($184 billion of which was FDI), and Australian investment in the US also exceeded $1 trillion ($193 billion of which was FDI) – a two-way investment relationship of over $2.165 trillion.[25] Further, between 2015 and 2020, US investment in Australia grew by 25 per cent, while Australian investment in the US grew by 27 per cent. Moreover,

'Australia captures 18% of US investment in the Asia-Pacific region, although [Australia] represents only 5% of regional GDP'.[26]

Comparisons bring home the point. With about a quarter of all foreign investment, America is the largest foreign investor in Australia. It is also Australia's top destination for foreign investment, accounting for about 30 per cent of all Australian foreign investment abroad.[27] For all the worry that Australians harbour about China's penetration of the Australian economy, most of them ill-founded, American investment is some thirteen times greater than that of China, which remains Australia's largest trading partner. And as for Australian direct investment in the United States, that is on an inevitable growth trajectory. The reason is clear. By 2019, at over $2.7 trillion, Australia had the world's fourth-largest – and growing – pool of pension (superannuation) funds, of which over 20 per cent was invested in the US, the top destination for Australian international portfolio investment. This was more than five times the pre-AUSFTA amount of just over $100 billion – a tribute as much to the Hawke/Keating governments' enactment of compulsory superannuation saving legislation as to the bilateral investment climate. And for its part, America's holdings of Australian securities are almost double the amount of the second-largest holder, the UK.

This shared access to capital markets, facilitated by the AUSFTA and backed by strong legal and financial institutions, makes raising funds, repaying debt and financing companies easier, cheaper and less risky. As Joey Herlihy has commented, that the bilateral investment relationship is 'significant' is an understatement.[28] And underpinning this deep and extensive investment relationship is the strength of the economic institutions and investment structures, together with political stability and strong relationships at the decision-making level. Taken together, these institutional and structural linkages generate the confidence needed to commit to long-term investment decisions.

It is the absence of such confidence that limits Australia's (and America's) willingness to invest in some Asian economies. It is not simply concerns about graft and corruption, but the often precarious relationship between governments and the national courts, the absence of reliable and impartially administered legal frameworks (such as corporations law, real property law, intellectual property law, insolvency law, taxation law and industrial law) and the variability of government policies that heighten investment risk. For Australia and America, high credit ratings, business certainty, skilled workforce, low entry barriers, and harmonised legal, corporate and regulatory frameworks make for attractive mutual investment destinations.

The validity of these principles is demonstrated in practice. As of 2021, there are over 420 Australian parent companies with over 1,500 entities in the US, employing over 150,000 people at an average annual salary above $130,000.[29] Further, US trade with Australia supports around 300,000 American jobs, and over 12,000 Australian companies export to the US. On the flip side, there are around 1,100 US majority-owned companies employing around 323,000 people in Australia, with an average salary above $100,000.[30]

## Constraints and prospects

Like the curate's egg, the AUSFTA is good in parts. While it has cemented an economic relationship of considerable moment, it has failed to deliver on its promise, at least as advocated by Prime Minister Howard. As an adjunct to a longstanding though overhyped security relationship, it provides some political substance to a strategic partnership, though just how 'substantial' that substance might be is moot.[31] As noted earlier, the 'free trade agreement' is not truly about free trade. It is about preferential trade as a workaround to resolve the restrictive consequences of America's protectionist instincts. That has some sectoral utility, though overall the benefits in specific sectors are more or less cancelled out by the constraints in others. There is little doubt that Australia made significant concessions during the 2004 negotiations, concessions that were politically mandated rather than struck in the *quid pro quo* world of the negotiating forum.

There are three principal domains in which the AUSFTA constrains Australia's agency and economic independence: a retreat from multilateralism; a major imposition on and limitation of the Pharmaceutical Benefits Scheme (PBS), a cornerstone of Australia's public health system; and the subordination of Australian policy development and consequent legislation to US economic, legislative and policy preferences. This last constraint is best seen in the powers afforded to American companies to constrain Australia's political sovereignty by securing the right to participate in Australian policy consideration of matters that might affect American commercial and economic interests, even if that falls short of the right to sue the Australian government for damages, losses and reduced profits deemed to result from government social policies (such as legislated controls on the sale of tobacco products on health grounds). To his credit, Prime Minister Howard resisted attempts to introduce what are euphemistically described as Investor–State Dispute Settlement (ISDS) processes into the AUSFTA – a position similarly adopted by the Gillard government in 2011.[32] Attempts to extend mandatory ISDS processes into the management of the Australia–America economic relationship were little more than a brazen (and ultimately unsuccessful) attempt to protect American interests at the expense of the health and amenity interest of Australian citizens.[33] Nonetheless, America continues to assert strong intellectual property protections across the entire American industrial spectrum, extending from drugs to information technology to film and the creative arts. IP protection is tantamount to monopoly power, which fits awkwardly with the advocacy of free trade.

The retreat from multilateralism was a major change in Australia's economic and trade policy, worthy of much greater parliamentary, peak body and academic consideration than it has received. Australia has a distinguished record in multilateral trade negotiations and in the establishment of international institutions that both establish the rules and settle disputes. The Uruguay Round, which concluded in 1993 after seven years of complex negotiation, was something of a triumph for Australia. It was imaginative, 'big-picture' and broad-sweeping in its ambition for both an equitable global trading system and a distinctively Australian role in it, particularly in Asia. But it is important to understand that one of the reasons that the negotiations took so long was that America got cold feet and was sorely tempted to retreat into bilateral trade agreements and the protection-ism that inspired its traditional divide-and-rule approach. America's sentiment was infectious, giving comfort to the Howard government's rejection of multilateralism and clearly stated preference for bilateral agreements.

This has long been another divide between the two major sides of Aus-tralian politics, and as the Howard government rolled in, delivering a major electoral defeat to the Keating government, it circled its wagons and embarked on the 'culture wars' – essentially sold as the difference between a 'little Australia' and an over-reaching Australia. So the Howard government marched to its own drum, the AUSFTA signalling a swift arrival. Whereas the Uruguay Round took over seven years to negotiate, Howard's trade agreement with America took one. But was it worth it?

In its 2010 report *Bilateral and Regional Trade Agreements*, the Productivity Commission found that there was little evidence to sup-port the view that preferential agreements have provided significant commercial benefits, and that the modest benefits that did accrue were in fact overstated.[34] But the costs of the AUSFTA to Australia were a small price to pay, at least in Prime Minister Howard's view, for the political and security benefits that it might deliver. And in this view, he was playing right into America's hands – no real extension of America's security obligations (such as they are) but more control over Australia's agency and independence. As an Australian Senate committee commented:

> Australia's pursuit of a free trade agreement with America has as much, if not more, to do with Australia's broader foreign policy objectives as it does with pure trade and investment goals. Certainly for the United States administration, free trade agreements can only be situated within a particular foreign policy setting. This was made clear in a widely reported speech (May 2003) to the Institute for International Economics by USTR Zoellick: ... countries that seek free-trade agreements with the United States must pass muster on more than trade and economic criteria in order to be eligible. At a

minimum, these countries must cooperate with the United States on its foreign policy and national security goals. The U.S. seeks 'cooperation – or better – on foreign policy and security issues,' Zoellick said, given that the U.S. has international interests beyond trade, 'why not try to urge people to support our overall policies?' Zoellick said that he uses a set of 13 criteria to evaluate potential negotiating partners, but he insisted that there are no formal rules for the selection or any guarantees. 'It's not automatic,' Zoellick said. Negotiating an FTA with the U.S. 'is not something one has a right to. It's a privilege.'[35]

Put in the starkest terms, the Americans could see the antipodean hayseeds coming, and gulled them for all they were worth. Why not? It is what Australia likes to do to its 'Pacific family' and its neighbours in South-East Asia, where it can – just like America, it talks long and delivers short. And, of course, there is not the slightest indication that the AUSFTA made Australia safer or more secure. It was just another step in the ANZUS long con.

One of the few examples of a national public policy mandated by a national referendum, the PBS has long delivered cheaper and subsidised prescription drugs to Australian citizens. Basically, it reimburses pharmaceutical companies for the innovation and patent value of their drug research. Central to the operation and pricing of the PBS is the principle that drugs with identical or similar effects should have similar prices, a principle known as 'reference pricing'. The drug companies make little money out of 'generics'. But drugs that remain subject to patent are seen by the drug companies as a golden opportunity for rent-seeking. And given that many of the major drug companies are American, or have major American investors, reference pricing is a true *bête noir*.

Initially, the AUSFTA was not to include any rules on pharmaceuticals. But it ended up in an annex that applied obligations to Australia without any reciprocal obligations on America. This provided a valuable Trojan horse for American pharma, which has exploited the Australian model in its negotiations with other nations. As Thomas Faunce has remarked:

Allowing the US to alter the basic processes of Australia's PBS represented an inexcusable surrender of Australia's democratic sovereignty. It represents just how compromised the state has become as a representative of citizens' interest in the face of corporate power. It also provides salutary lessons as Australian citizens attempt to prevent their government surrendering democratic sovereignty on an even greater scale by agreeing to investor-state dispute settlement in the US-led Trans-Pacific Partnership Agreement.[36]

It is understandable that America would seek to protect its pharmaceutical industry and maximise the benefits of its medical investment. But the global experience with the COVID-19 vaccines dramatically demonstrates the difference between ROI (return on investment) and predatory pricing. The Oxford University–developed AstraZeneca vaccine sold for approximately US$2.15 per dose, compared with Pfizer's price ranging between US$22 and US$37.[37] Clearly, in the world of free trade agreements, there is no room for sentiment or community service obligation.

There is little to be said in favour of ISDS regimes where national political sovereignty becomes subject to foreign corporations. It is capitalism and neoliberalism gone awry: the wellbeing of the citizens – surely the primary responsibility of any government – is rendered subject to the continued and growing profitability of foreign investors. There are many grounds for both supporting and objecting to ISDS regimes, and these have been amply covered by the Australian Parliament in its report *Comprehensive and Progressive Agreement for Trans-Pacific Partnership*.[38] In the context of the Australia–America relationship, the basic objection to ISDS regimes lies in the discriminatory effects on domestic economic and financial entities when compared with international entities of a similar nature. In her submission to the Joint Standing Committee on Treaties, Dr Elizabeth Thurbon wrote:

> ISDS provisions violate the principle of National Treatment and Non-Discrimination enshrined in Australia's WTO obligations (and indeed in the obligations of its other [trade agreements]). They do

so by discriminating against local firms. Specifically, ISDS provisions give foreign investors more rights than local firms by extending the right to sue national governments for 'indirect expropriation' to foreign firms alone.[39]

As rule-of-law nations with complementary and robust legal institutions and structures, America and Australia both have courts and other mechanisms to protect citizens and corporations against the arbitrary use of state power. Third-party arbitration derogates from the authority and responsibilities of the judiciary. But, more than that, it questions and diminishes the agency and sovereignty of government.

The prospects for a broader and deeper economic relationship between Australia and America are excellent. To that end, a bit of jostling in the relationship, as distinct from Australia's customary deference, would be a welcome development. The Australian economy may be dwarfed by America's, though given America's massive debt overhang that may be less significant than it once was. Australia is still the thirteenth-largest global economy, a major energy and minerals exporter, a major supplier of agricultural commodities, a stable recipient of FDI and an increasingly active source of FDI in America and Europe. It would certainly be in America's interests to see Australia as something more than a reliable (not to say subservient) security acolyte. And it would certainly be in Australia's interests to carry itself with greater assuredness and imagination on the international stage.

The global economic outlook may be problematic. But there are major opportunities as the economies of South-East Asia expand and mature. This is where Australia and America can reinforce their cooperation as independent and mutually invested partners. And, given the extraordinary cultural alignment between the two, this is something that is quite within reach. We shall turn to that now.

# 6.
## Culture

Boomers rule, okay – except when Rupert Murdoch exerts control.

So, why this focus on the Boomers, this author's generation (well, almost)? The Baby Boomers have defined the contemporary mindsets and cultures of both America and Australia. Their mark is indelible. But are they really victims of their parents' choices? Have they really contributed nothing to the modern world? Are there no Boomers of note? Is the world of today nothing more than a tribute to their monumental ordinariness? Well, if the measure is Donald Trump, Bill Gates (Microsoft), Jeff Bezos (Amazon) – Boomers to a man – the answer is obvious. And note the absence of women. While, as in all populations, some have risen to the top by virtue of class, IQ, parental wealth, connections, ability or just plain luck, the confronting fact is that the legacy of the Boomer generation is little more than consumerism, escapism, passivism, racism, self-satisfaction and spectatorism. How could that be? With Joe Biden, a pre-Boomer, as American president and Donald Trump (a Boomer) breathing down his neck for re-election, it is fair to say that the Baby Boomers still enjoy massive influence over the modern world that they have done so much to mismanage.

Fintan O'Toole captures the problem with his characteristic precision:

> In the contemporary US, the gerontocracy seems even more exclusive and its membership even older than the one that was swept away in France by the July Revolution of 1830. The baby boomers who sang

along with Bob Dylan when he warned, 'Senators, congressmen/ Please heed the call/Don't stand in the doorway/Don't block up the hall,' now linger in the lobbies. Age has not withered their appetite for power. In 2014 the US elected the oldest Congress in its history. The record did not last long: It was broken in 2016. And then again in 2018. And yet again in 2020, when – remarkably – the majority of the incumbents who lost their seats were replaced by someone even older. In the 2022 midterms, the House did become slightly younger (the mean age of representatives dropped by a year, from fifty-nine to fifty-eight), but the mean age of senators continued to rise and is now over sixty-five.[1]

As a largely self-defining gerontocracy, the Boomers have constructed a political culture that both dominates the political life of America and Australia and defines the political standards of those nations that make up the emerging 'democracies' of Africa, Asia, Eastern Europe and South America. This is a worrying legacy that does little to remediate the frailty of those new democracies.

Australians and Americans born after 1945 continue to live in a world of their own, to channel the Seekers' saccharine and selfish refrain, first aired in 1965. No Australian generation was as readily Americanised as were the Baby Boomers. As they ride off ever so slowly into the sunset, it is just possible that their children will lament their passing – but, even then, only until their estates have been distributed and their ageing Gen-Xer offspring can afford to transport themselves to their parents' recently vacated aged-care facilities.

One of the most cynical, grasping and self-absorbed generations in history, the Boomers have left a legacy that will endure for generations. It will take that long for their children and grandchildren to recover from their excesses. As they cashed in the public investments of their parents' generation, they created their wealth by reducing taxes and increasing public debt. And then they paid for their additional excesses by reducing taxes even further and creating even more public debt, a legacy that is as mephitic as it is toxic. Passengers on the train of history, their hypocrisy is without parallel. While they imagine that they have created the world of the present, they have in reality bludged on the energies and imaginations of their parents – the people born into the horrors of World War I, who endured the Great Depression and then survived the genocidal brutality of World War II and the arrival of the Atomic Age. Born after 1945, they spent their adolescent years in a world shaped by those born mainly in the depressed interwar years. While the Baby Boomers like to claim the remarkable periods of change that were the 1960s and '70s, those changes were the gift of those who saw the possibilities of a new world.

It is far beyond the scope of this book to analyse and evaluate the myriad ways in which the cultural dynamics of Australia and America resonate within each nation and across the Pacific. Nor would an in-depth survey covering almost two and a half centuries – fascinating though that would be – offer much guidance about where the bilateral cultural relationship might go, as distinct from where it has been. So this chapter limits itself to drawing together the key features of the cultural milieu in which the Baby Boomers grew up. And since the Boomers' implicit prejudices and habits of mind continue to exert such a profound influence on contemporary Australia and America – the Boomers will not let go – an indicative approach to the topic will serve well enough.

To make a short examination of the cultural alignments between Australia and America manageable, the focus of this chapter is on the cultural influences that shaped the Boomers and made them the entitled, grasping solipsists they are. It is not intended to address the rich cultural phenomena of the twenty-first century, which may or may not be shaping the next generation of leaders. It is simply to identify some of the more indicative features of the cultural alignments that have brought Australia and America to where they are now. And, in most respects, it is a disappointing story.

# The Baby Boomers and their mindset

Perhaps the most significant agent of social change in America in the 1960s was Martin Luther King Jr, who led the civil rights movement from the mid-1950s until his assassination in 1968. A political philosopher of some note, he brought his oratorical and political skills to bear on the most fundamental issue that divides America (one that also resonates in Australia, and of which the failed constitutional referendum of October 2023 remains deeply emblematic).

For America, the 'steady-as-you-go' and exceptionalist administration of President Dwight D. Eisenhower (born 1890) gave way to the exceptionalist excitement of President John F. Kennedy (born 1917) and, as the only beneficiary of his assassination, the dead hand of President Lyndon B. Johnson (born 1908), who took his country and its Baby Boomers into the unmitigated disaster of the Vietnam War, despite what he did for America's Black population. And President Richard M. Nixon (born 1913) was the price that America paid for its exceptionalist folly.

In Australia, the staid – some might say stultifying – hand of Robert Menzies shaped the complacent politics of the 1960s, just as the imperious – some might say imperial – imagination of Gough Whitlam shaped the 1970s. Malcolm Fraser took a strong stand against apartheid but made little impression on much else. Menzies was born in 1894, Whitlam in 1916 and Fraser in 1930. Bob Hawke was born in 1929 and John Howard in 1939. Paul Keating pre-dated the Boomer generation by two years.

The Americans who shaped the cultural revolution of the 1960s, to which the Boomers lay claim, were all born before 1940. J.D. Salinger (whose novel *The Catcher in the Rye* became a Boomer icon) was born on New Year's Day 1919. James Baldwin, Norman Mailer and Andy Warhol were all children of the 1920s. Oral Roberts (born 1918) launched an abortive attempt to evangelise Australia in 1956, only to lose £40,000 for his trouble – possibly because his visit competed with the cricket.[2] Billy Graham (also born 1918) was much more successful. This smoothest of American evangelists drew 150,000 to his Melbourne Cricket Ground crusade to make their 'decision for Christ' in 1959. His (almost) namesake, the impresario and rock and roll promoter Bill Graham, was born in 1931, arriving in America as a Berlin-born Jewish orphan. (Is there a more American success story than that?) His mother died in Auschwitz. Bob Dylan, Joan Baez, Jimi Hendrix, Frank Zappa and Paul Simon were all pre-Boomers, as were Peter, Paul and Mary and the Seekers. The Seekers packed 200,000 people into the Sidney Myer Music Bowl in Melbourne in 1967, demonstrating that 'Come the Day' and 'A World of Our Own' were more attractive to Baby Boomers than Billy Graham's brand of eternal life. (If there is any hope to be had, it may be found in the fact that Taylor Swift's aggregate crowds during her 2024 Australian tour outnumbered those of both Billy Graham and the Seekers.)

It is perhaps a truism that all generations ride on the back of their pre-decessor: the generation that fought World War II shaped the world that followed, especially in Australia and America. They created the much adulated 'international rules-based order'. Their children inherited the boom times which the interwar generation created, enjoying improved diets, improved health systems, improved educational opportunities and eventually improved employment prospects. They made the most of the freedoms that arrived with Timothy Leary (born 1920), Gregory G. Pincus (born 1903, credited with the development of the oral contraceptive pill) and Elvis Presley (born 1935) – the patron saints of drugs, sex and rock and roll.

In America, the political environment shaped the minds of the young Baby Boomers: the ideological excesses of McCarthyism – fomented by the totalitarian tendencies of the FBI's J. Edgar Hoover – set in train the iconoclastic conservatism that has infected American politics for over seventy years now.[3] American state, municipal and school libraries are banning and burning books even today. A deeply anti-democratic form of political repression and fear campaigning saw the persecution of 'liberal' and so-called 'left-wing' people – academics, actors, artists, diplomats, human rights activists, politicians, scientists, unionists – which destroyed the lives and livelihoods of countless Americans, all in the name of 'anti-communism'.

While not so virulent, Australia's form of anti-communism took it down a similar path towards proscription. The federal parliament passed the *Communist Party Dissolution Act* in late 1950, thereby abolishing the Communist Party and permitting the seizure of its property without compensation, while authorising the governor-general to declare bodies 'affiliated' with the Communist Party, such as trade unions, to be unlawful. These were extraordinary powers, judged unconstitutional by the High Court in March 1951. Prime Minister Menzies then attempted to amend the Australian Constitution to confer on the government the power to abolish the Communist Party. The referendum, conducted in September 1951, failed, but only just. Ironically, while the people of Australia refused to destroy the Communist Party, international events would achieve this anyway over the next four decades.[4]

In the years immediately following World War II, the political left was under pressure, with membership of the Communist Party of Australia declining from 20,000 during World War II to fewer than a thousand by 1990. At the same time, the right in both Australia and America was growing steadily, with its deeply conservative values influencing political and social views on both sides of the Pacific. The National Civic Council, spearheaded by the formidable B.A. Santamaria, gave the Catholic right the policy and organisational capabilities to destroy the Labor movement from within, thereby splitting the Australian Labor Party and keeping it out of office for a generation.

The Moral Re-Armament (MRA) movement, which began in America in the late 1930s, expanded significantly in the immediate post–World War II years, establishing its international headquarters in a restored hotel in Caux, Switzerland. It attracted high-level political support in many countries, including America, France and Germany, and significant community support, especially among the conservative middle class. Founded by a Lutheran pastor, the MRA was evidently Protestant (the Catholic Church was as opposed to the MRA as it was to the Masonic Order) without being overtly denominational. By the late 1950s, the MRA was a significant promoter of conservative anti-communist values in North America, Australia, South-East Asia, Africa and Europe. It was particularly skilled in the use of film to distribute its message. The high production values of films like *Freedom* (1955) and *The Crowning Experience* (1961), supported by artists such as the American contralto Muriel Smith, lent authority and credibility to the MRA offering. The cloying wholesomeness of those films was reminiscent of *The Sound of Music*, but without the integrating skills of Julie Andrews. The adolescent Boomers were dragged away from their usual Saturday afternoon movie fare by their parents to attend a more sentimental form of cinematic indoctrination where the fundamental values propagated by the emanations of Hollywood and Caux scarcely differed.

In America, the Vietnam War was a catastrophic period for the Baby Boomers, exploiting their inherited social values (male chauvinism, misogyny and racism, for instance) while confirming them in the same values. If the MRA shaped the political conservatism of their teens and early twenties, the Moral Majority helped them on their journey beyond the Christian right towards a Republican Party transformed by a coalition of southern Baptists. The televangelist Jerry Falwell was a powerful and persuasive advocate for traditional family values, creationism, religious instruction in schools, the prohibition of abortion and same-sex marriage and opposition to equal rights and nuclear arms limitation. In many ways, Falwell took up where Oral Roberts and Billy Graham left off, consolidating broad political and social values that gave expression to a defining American mindset. The financial resources behind the Moral Majority were mind-boggling. Money enabled the fundamentalist, charismatic and pentecostalist traditions to compete with one another for influence while consolidating a conservative and traditionalist national mindset that afforded them a curious political unity: Republicanism.

This mindset resonated in Australia, albeit with some significant differences. While sectarianism remained strong in America, secularism was more prevalent in Australia, where general attitudes towards women's rights, gay and lesbian rights, the right to choose abortion, decriminalisation of drug use and religious observance became more liberal than was the case in America. Australians were more likely to favour gun controls and compulsory voting than Americans, reflecting perhaps a different balance between communalism and individualism. Moreover, Australian philanthropy was and remains notoriously parsimonious, failing to generate the enormous cash flows required for sustained media campaigns. Australia comes nowhere near America on that score.

## What is culture, anyway?

Ultimately, the institutional and structural arrangements that underpin any society – or any effective international relationship, for that matter – are artefacts of a shared culture. In that sense, culture is systemic. But the term 'culture' itself defies and evades definition. It is so diffuse in its applications and so diverse in its forms that it means a lot and a little, everything and nothing. That is the beauty of the word: it is not univocal, but reaches out to embrace a startling diversity of manifestations and shapes that combine to establish community, identity and society more broadly.

Culture is the glue that holds societies and nations together. It provides the background noise to national storytelling while at the same time providing content to the stories that give expression to the national imagination. And imagination is the matrix that affords culture both its meaning and its effect. In a transcendental sense, culture is as much the Dreaming of Australia's First Peoples and the creation stories of North America's First Nations as it is the many manifestations of *mythos* that substantiate the collective behaviours of the settler communities. The wonderful thing about culture is that it is at once popular and elite, highbrow and lowbrow, spiritual and secular, welcoming and intimidating, approachable and arcane, comforting and puzzling. Culture is multidimensional, aspects bumping into one another in chaotic ways that are as challenging as they are fascinating. It both defines difference and, by encouraging acceptance, drives inclusiveness. Yes, culture can be disruptive and even dystopian, but it auto-corrects in the interests of its own survival. Hence, culture is the ultimate determinant of the national mindset.

The class-based distinction between 'popular' and 'high' culture is ultimately meaningless as a tool for understanding how the broad, chaotic, dynamic and infinitely exhilarating swirl of cultural tropes both shape and reflect aspects of national identity and mindset. As the British philosopher and public intellectual Roger Scruton wrote, 'a high culture is the self-consciousness of a society' – for those, perhaps, who can afford to be self-conscious.[5] It is a precarious achievement, Scruton writes, enduring only if it is underpinned by a sense of tradition and a broad endorsement of the surrounding social norms. But it does concern itself with the life of the mind, which is in turn entrusted to academic and other institutions, because it is a social benefit that is the product of the knowledge it generates. As Scruton puts it, 'The life of the mind has its intrinsic methods and rewards. It is concerned with the true, the beautiful and the good, which between them define the scope of reasoning and the goals of serious inquiry.'[6]

For this reason, aesthetics, 'the arts', education, literature and philosophy play a critical, though not determining, role in shaping the cultural alignment between Australia and America. We shall return to these aspects of culture later in this chapter.

## Shaping the mindset

For both America and Australia, national culture both extends back into the distant past, when their respective First Peoples established their early links with the land, and leans forward to the myriad possibilities that inclusive multicultural societies represent – the wisdom of the past combining with the hopes of the future. Australian culture has its origins in the early migrations of peoples through the land bridges and seas of South-East Asia, the First Peoples arriving in Australia over 65,000 years ago. American culture has its origins in the similar migrations of peoples across the steppes of Eurasia and through the land bridges and seas between North Asia and North America some 30,000 years ago. The cultures of Australia and America can certainly claim antiquity. They can also claim continuity, the modern settler communities being simply the latest to have found their way to the Americas or the Antipodes and established their homes there.

The cultural alignments between Australia and America are astonishingly deep and extraordinarily extensive. They are also, on occasion, pervasive and pernicious, becoming the default influencers and normative expressions of Australian culture as they do that of America. Whereas these cultural alignments are very often American in origin, reflecting as they do American cultural evolution, to Australia they are seductive. They have been so for the best part of a century. The cultural vectors that permeate the Australia–America relationship are manifold, extending across the arts and sciences, literature, leisure, consumerism, education, sport and virtually every domain of human activity. Shared cultural inputs have shaped social mindsets on both sides of the Pacific, establishing a deep consonance in social assumptions, attitudes and expectations, not to mention biases and prejudices. While the emotional ballast of public discourse can differ substantially between Australians and Americans – Americans often appear to be more literal and invested than their Australian counterparts – urban Australians and Americans display many similarities, as do Australians and Americans who live in regional and rural areas. American ranchers and grain growers speak the same language as their Australian co-pastoralists, just as Australian retailers operate on the same wavelength (though perhaps not at the same scale) as their American commercial colleagues.

Precisely how the cultural convergence between Australia and America began is difficult to determine. For its first century or so, Australia was very British, defining itself by British cultural tropes – the slogan 'for King and Country' enticed young Australians to the Sudan as readily as to South Africa and the killing fields of Europe. But the advent and evolution of film offers as good a starting point as any – at least, since the American movie giants swamped Australia's innovative and thriving pre–World War I moving picture industry. *The Story of the*

*Kelly Gang*, the world's first full-length narrative feature film, made its debut in Melbourne in December 1906, and was quickly released in England, Ireland and New Zealand. The outbreak of World War I, however, put an end to Australia's flirtation with movie production, just as it provided the stimulus for American entrepreneurship to create and dominate the world's movie theatres. By the time Metro-Goldwyn-Mayer's *The Wizard of Oz* hit Australia's silver screens in 1940, Hollywood was shaping the imaginations of the English-speaking world, just as it was shaping the imaginations of Americans. And as the cultural tropes of America found their imaginative expression through film, they found their commercial home in neoliberalism. Hollywood and money became synonymous.

## What American and Australian kids read and heard

American and Australian children of the 1950s and '60s read much the same kind of stuff, to the extent that they read at all. With British publishers exercising almost total control over the Australian book market, few American publishers had access to Australian readers. The Dr Seuss books were the notable exception, as an introduction both to reading and to the implied values system that infused the stories.

It is fair to say that the literary values on both sides of the Pacific were pretty much aligned: male dominance, female subservience, racial subordination, 'family values', social conservatism and bourgeois privilege. Those fortunate enough to have been born into nurturing families, where reading was what everyone did in the evening after the materfamilias had prepared and served dinner, and then cleaned up, were exposed to good, wholesome literature that shaped their prejudices and then reinforced them. Engaged and enthusiastic teachers also encouraged their brighter students to read, and often inculcated good reading habits.

Australian and American girls shared *Little Women* and *National Velvet* (later a phenomenally successful film), and endless teen romances by

Beverly Cleary, Rosamond du Jardin, Janet Lambert, Aurelia Stowe and many others. Australian girls devoured Enid Blyton's Noddy and Big Ears stories, followed by countless *Famous Five* and *Secret Seven* stories as they approached their teens. Young American girls read the prolific and pseudonymous Carolyn Keene's Nancy Drew books which, like the Enid Blyton oeuvre, inculcated the passivism that, as the counterfoil to male chauvinism, became a key target of the feminist movement.

Australian and American boys enjoyed the novels of James Fenimore Cooper (*The Last of the Mohicans*, *The Deerslayer* and *The Pathfinder*, for example), the pseudonymous Mark Twain (*The Adventures of Huckleberry Finn*, *The Adventures of Tom Sawyer* and his collections of short stories) and Robert Louis Stevenson's *Treasure Island*, *Kidnapped* and *The Strange Case of Dr Jekyll and Mr Hyde*. Australian boys added Marcus Clarke's *For the Term of His Natural Life* and the pseudonymous Rolf Boldrewood's *Robbery Under Arms*, along with the novels of Walter Scott and John Buchan. There is always an exception, of course. In the South Australian bush, the literary diet was strictly British – Captain W.E. Johns' Biggles series, Paul Brickhill's *Reach for the Sky* and the totally wholesome *Eagle* comics – which explains a lot.

And if all that appears too highbrow, American and Australian men of all ages could not get enough 'dime Westerns' by prolific writers like Zane Grey, Ned Buntline, Max Brand, Edward Ellis, Ernest Haycox, Prentiss Ingraham and Edward Wheeler. Both cheap and inexpensive, the dime Westerns captured a hyper-masculinity that continues to distinguish those who modelled themselves on the Marlboro Man, drove a Ford F-100 or a foxtail decorated ute, and fancied themselves in moleskins or chaps. That was – and remains, the stereotype notwithstanding – a big, conservative and influential cohort.

Comics were a literary mainstay of the 1950s and '60s. They did not demand much word recognition, and the cartoon drawings conveyed all the conventional tropes – white supremacy, female subordination, non-white racial inferiority, the power of wealth, American exceptionalism in the form of the superheroes, and a generally Manichean view of right and wrong. *Mandrake the Magician* had his 'giant Nubian servant', Lothar, and the beautiful Princess Narda – all 'goodies', of course – while he battled the forces of evil in the person of The Cobra, his brother Derek and Aleena the Enchantress, the inevitable femme fatale. Another Lee Falk character was the Phantom – 'the ghost who walks, the man who cannot die' – another hypersexualised superhero, who enjoyed the enduring love of Diana Palmer and the pygmy Bandar tribe's devotion. They were Black, of course. And where would the Phantom have been without his white stallion, Hero, and his trained wolf, Devil?

In both America and Australia, *Mandrake* and *The Phantom* were enormously popular, as were other comics and any number of folk and western heroes – Batman, Flash Gordon (known as 'Speed Gordon' in Australia until the American GIs arrived in late 1941, because 'flash' meant 'trashy'), Dick Tracy, Hopalong Cassidy, Roy Rogers and Zorro, to name just a few, and not to omit Nancy and Sluggo and Joe Palooka. And as these comic-book characters found on-screen realisation, their role as cultural totems provided a secularised, though decidedly racist, common youth culture in the more sectarian world of the 1950s and '60s. Such was the reach of the Lone Ranger and his Indian sidekick, Tonto, that it was more common to hear children playing 'cowboys and Indians' in Australia's suburbs address each other as '*kemosabe*' (trusty scout) than 'pardner' or the more abusive epithets of the sectarian schoolyards.

## The armchair generation

According to the few who remain, the generation of the Great Depression made their own fun – trapping rabbits, catching yabbies and raiding the neighbours' fruit trees and raspberry canes. In the absence of reliable birth control measures, big families were the norm. Entertainment was largely confined to the 'Saturday night hop' at the local Mechanics' Institute or church hall, where any number of people could play a musical instrument and make up the band. It was a time of simple pleasures and modest expectations, where even access to a wireless receiver was restricted, especially in the bush. To the endless misery of the cats required to sacrifice their whiskers, children (usually boys, of course) who were able to construct coils, access primitive capacitors and headset amplifiers (occasionally the earpiece ripped from a public telephone box) would improvise crystal sets – a less than ideal solution to the creation of an informed and entertained public.

Newspapers filled that role, running both morning and evening editions, and providing the only mass media. Newspapers even published instructions on how to construct crystal sets.[7] And copies of the daily newspapers passed through multiple hands. As the country children who attended the ubiquitous city boarding schools could attest, along Australia's long-distance railways, fettlers and settlers alike would call, 'Paper!' as the trains chugged past – often to see a toilet roll flung out the window streaming in their general direction. Schoolboy humour has always had a certain quality.

It was a similar story in America. The war changed all that, with the AWA, Astor, Ferris, Healing and Kriesler valve wireless sets occupying pride of place in most suburban sitting rooms. While the evening news at six o'clock created a more informed adult population, the radio serials broadcast between four-thirty and six shaped the values and moulded the minds of their children. The daily fifteen-minute broadcasts of *The Air Adventures of Biggles*, *Superman*, *Tarzan*, *Hop Harrigan*, *The Sea Hound* and *The Lone Ranger* reinforced, or in some instances replaced, the attitudinal and behavioural tropes of the comics strips. The children of the comfortable and conservative middle class living in Hamilton Heights, Wahroonga and Glen Iris became 'Argonauts', members of the widely successful eponymous ABC club for children, while the children in the (then) fringe suburbs of Rocklea, Bankstown and Nunawading competed on Saturday-morning commercial radio for the Tarzan call of the week – doubtless wearing their Davy Crockett hats for effect.[8]

The early Baby Boomers enjoyed one further entertainment that, in some respects, defined the age, its passing unregretted: the Saturday afternoon movies. With nothing else to do, kids flocked to the Arcadia, the Odeon, the Regent or the Ritz for their weekly fare of the Cinesound Movietone News, a *Wile E. Coyote and the Road Runner* cartoon, a western serial and a B-grade 'feature', very often another western. As the 'usherette' wandered the aisles with her tray of ice-cream cups and choctops, Jaffas and Fantales (the dentists' favourite), the kids fired their pea-shooters and flicked rolled-up Fantales wrappers at each other, at least until the stage curtains parted, a hush fell and the real shooting started.

Whether in America or Australia, the serials (dominated by Columbia and Universal) were a critical part of the cultural diet. *The Cisco Kid* (with his sidekick, Pancho), *The Lone Ranger* (with his sidekick, Tonto), *Hopalong Cassidy*, *Roy Rogers* (with his ever-supportive female companion, Dale), *Zorro, Son of Geronimo*, and *Blazing the Overland Trail* (the last Columbia serial ever) were formative in their banality and subliminal messaging: heroic males, submissive women and the systemic oppression of non-white ethnic groups. Tom Mix, Audie Murphy, John Wayne, Gary Cooper, Alan Ladd, Burt Lancaster, Glenn Ford, Gene Autry and Roy Rogers (and the ever-smiling Dale) were the heroes of the Boomers' childhood. And Ronald Reagan movies – *The Last Outpost, Law and Order, Cattle Queen of Montana* and *Tennessee's Partner* – along with Walt Disney's *Davy Crockett: King of the Wild Frontier* – were evergreen hits, where too many showings were still not enough.

What the comic books, radio serials and Saturday afternoon movies all had in common was the constant repetition of the habits of complacency, entitlement, misogyny and racism – the drivers of a shared cultural matrix that largely determined their consumers' mindset and associated social preferences, whether in America or Australia. The advent of television only reinforced this.

Television was first broadcast in America just before the collapse of the financial markets that heralded the Great Depression. TV was technologically limited and broadcasts were restricted to small line-of-sight terrestrial broadcast areas of New York, Washington, Boston and Chicago. The viewing market was even smaller, given the expense and rarity of TV receivers, until a change in the regulatory environment and the commercialisation of wartime technologies brought entertainment to the American masses in the late 1940s.

Experimental TV broadcasting had begun in the late 1920s in Melbourne and Brisbane, but did not reach an eager public until late 1956, just in time for the Melbourne Olympics. While, with its rounded vowels and clipped pronunciation, the ABC (and Melbourne's GTV9, with its celebrity newsreader Sir Eric Pearce) remained a bastion of British propriety, the Americanisation of Australian TV proceeded apace. *Pick-a-Box*, which began as a radio variety show in the late 1940s, brought its hosts, Bob (an American) and Dolly Dyer, into primetime Saturday-evening viewing within six months of the launch of TV in Australia. Sunday mornings (after church, of course) was dedicated to another American compere, Jack Little, and his *Ringside with the Rasslers*, where iconic but completely rehearsed moves like the Step-over Toe-hold, the Brain Buster, the Flying Head Scissors, the Butcher's Axe and the Sleeper were the stuff of a week's factory-floor, office and playground conversation – for men, of course. Norlane, the Australian home of the Ford Motor Company, south of Melbourne, was not so very far from Detroit after all. Daytime TV was soon dominated by Tommy O'Hanlon Jr, a variety show comedian and magician whose background in American circuses endowed him with skills rarely seen in the Australian media.

In many respects, Australian television was indistinguishable from the American model, even down to the accent of the comperes. And it was not long before American TV serials began to dominate Australian broadcasts. It was less a question of American saturation of the Australian airwaves than one of providing Australian audiences what they wanted – essentially, US-sourced confirmation bias.

## Murdoch: The pre-Boomer whose legacy endures

In some respect, Rupert Murdoch personifies the Australia–America relationship. He also personifies the enduring control of the Boomer generation over significant elements of the national political and social infrastructure, particularly the fourth estate. His control of all forms of information and media – newspapers, radio, and terrestrial, cable and satellite television – affords him an unparalleled ability to frame the political agenda, advocate policy issues and shape how they are reported. Born in Melbourne in 1931, he now lives in New York and Los Angeles and is an American citizen. He is one of the wealthiest individuals in America, and has business interests across Australia, America, Asia and Europe.

Brilliant and ruthless, Murdoch rebuilt his father's struggling newspaper business, News Limited, which was structured around an Adelaide daily, *The News*. He also learned from his father the rare skill of owning and then disowning prime ministers. In the very early 1930s, Joseph Lyons had helped Keith Murdoch to start a radio station for his company in Adelaide. With Murdoch's backing, Lyons won the 1932 federal election. According to Jonathan Mahler and Jim Rutenberg: 'As Keith saw it, Australia's new leader served at his pleasure: "I put him there," he reportedly said when the two later squabbled. "And I'll put him out."'[9]

Through shrewd city and country acquisitions in Western Australia, Victoria, New South Wales, Queensland and the Northern Territory, by the early 1960s Rupert Murdoch had reformatted broadsheets into tabloids, and had given them considerably more popular appeal – sport, gossip, titillating photographs and provocative headlines. It was a formula he exported overseas as he began to expand his global media empire, News Limited, subsequently News Corp. He also translated it to his radio and television acquisitions, and to startups such as Fox News and SkyTV.

What makes Murdoch so interesting and so dominant is his ability to harness the aspirations and powers of political parties and the governments they form to deliver massive benefits to his corporate institutions – and, because those benefits can be monetised, to himself. In Australia, America and Britain, Murdoch has been an irresistible agent of political change, driven not by policy or political affiliation but by his need constantly to flex his political muscle and strengthen the ability of his corporate enterprises to generate political outcomes that favour their profitability. He campaigned for Gough Whitlam in 1972, as much because of his personal detestation of Menzies and McMahon as for McMahon's alignment with his archrival, Kerry Packer. Then, feeling that Whitlam had jilted him, he dumped Whitlam in favour of Malcolm Fraser in 1975. In retrospect, it is evident that Murdoch knew more about what was happening in Sir John Kerr's office at Government House than virtually anyone else in Australia or Britain.[10]

As the Fraser government began to flounder, Murdoch again switched allegiances – but not before he had secured a major change in television licensing laws to permit a non-resident rather than a non-citizen to hold a licence.[11] With the election of the Hawke government, Murdoch had to wait out the first term before changes to the cross-media ownership rules enabled him to grab the biggest prize of all – the takeover of the Melbourne Herald group his father once ran. This meant he could consolidate and dominate the Australian newspaper industry.

As in Australia, so too in Britain. Murdoch's support for Tony Blair secured government for Labour in the 1997 election with a thumping majority. Again, Murdoch's barracking was duly rewarded when British cross-media ownership rules were relaxed, enabling News Corporation to buy British free-to-air broadcasters.[12] Murdoch repeated the performance in 2007 when he backed Kevin Rudd, delivering government to Labor after a decade in opposition. And again, Murdoch fell out of love with Labor when the relationship had nothing more to give him.[13]

In America, Murdoch's ability to exploit the inconsistencies, vagaries and corporate complexity of American media ownership laws, particularly through his brilliant creation and constant transformation of Fox News, has secured him an almost unassailable position as a political kingmaker and media manipulator.

And so Murdoch has played a dominant role in the political culture of both America and Australia for half a century, and continues to do so, his 'retirement' notwithstanding. His political and social legacy is enormous. And it will outlive him. In Australia, his newspaper and radio outlets both influence voters and, more importantly, build compliance and convergence among the politicians they target.[14] The more serious effect of the Murdoch media empire, however, is less its influence on how politicians conduct themselves than on the deep mindset consequences – the idea that 'this is the way we do things around here'. In America and Australia, he has shaped both the medium and the message, to use Marshall McLuhan's phrase of sixty years ago.

Because Australians are a bit more laidback than Americans, Murdoch's impact on the national voting temper has perhaps been less disruptive than in America, where sectarianism and tribalism are more influential and pervasive. In America, he has both established and fomented a number of the fault lines that are reshaping the national mindset and, consequently, the nation. He has taken America on a dangerous path that exploits differences and legitimises intolerance. What is more, the runaway phenomenon that is Fox News has legitimised malice and malfeasance. Niall Stanage has captured this well:

> Trump has benefited greatly from the Fox News spotlight dating back to the middle of the last decade, when his regular appearances helped smooth his transition from the business world to his White House quest. Fox's coverage of him during his two impeachments is widely seen, by both supporters and detractors alike, as being of fundamental importance. The observation was made more than once that, had Fox been around when President Nixon was caught up in the Watergate scandal of the 1970s, Nixon would never have had to resign.[15]

It will require a new quality of leadership, and a new quality of media, to rectify this problem.

## 'The life of the mind': The bridge to the future

For most Australians born at the beginning of the twentieth century, the sign of academic and intellectual achievement, and the ultimate accolade, was the Oxbridge doctorate followed by employment at the Sir William Dunn School of Pathology or the Cavendish Laboratories. Similarly, acceptance by the Royal College of Music or a contract at Covent Garden advertised one's 'arrival' as a musician or opera singer. And while in some important ways international recognition was symptomatic of a national reluctance to self-affirm – the notorious 'cultural cringe' – it was also confirmation of the strong cultural alignment between Australia and the 'mother country', Britain.

In the immediate post–World War II years, the SS *Orontes* and SS *Oronsay* delivered their British immigrants to Australian ports, returning to London with escapees from Australia's sleepy suburbs – including Donald Horne and, later, Germaine Greer, Clive James, Robert Hughes and Barry Humphries. The arrival, however, of generous scholarships offered by American universities and well-endowed scholarship schemes such as the Fulbright Program attracted a growing number of outstanding Australian students to the leading American universities and colleges, especially in economics and the sciences.

The Fulbright Program may have been the first American exercise of 'soft power'. Emerging from a Congressional decision, sponsored by Senator William Fulbright, to apply repaid Lend-Lease credits to bilateral educational opportunities, the Fulbright Program has sponsored over 5,000 Australian and American students to cross the Pacific in pursuit of higher studies. It remains a powerful connection between the academic communities of both countries. This is amplified by almost 1,000 formal collaborative agreements between Australian and American universities to build deep relationships in innovation, science and education.[16] Australia is the seventh-most popular destination for American students, attracting a postgraduate population of some 12,000 at any one time, and a reciprocal postgraduate population of over 5,000 Australians. America is the leading research collaborator for Australia, as it is for most countries. Between 2011 and 2016, Australian and American researchers collaborated on almost 50,000 joint research papers.[17]

The links between Australian and American universities are replicated across virtually the entire gamut of the knowledge-creation institutions. Just as in the early days of television Americans crossed the Pacific to leaven Australia's entertainment diet, so Australians have long played a small but important part in the American creative arts world. Australians teach and study at some of the leading American music schools, such as the Curtis Institute in Philadelphia and the Juilliard School in New York. Errol Flynn and Peter Finch were mid-twentieth-century screen icons, and the late Heath Ledger's career was sadly cut short. Cate Blanchett is deservedly an international star of both screen and stage. So too are Nicole Kidman, Rachel Griffiths, Russell Crowe and the talented Sarah Snook, who dominated the HBO TV series *Succession*, purportedly modelled on the Murdoch dynasty. As a director, writer and producer, Baz Luhrmann is a phenomenon, winning Oscars, BAFTAs and Golden Globe awards. There are many other Australian screenwriters, Foley artists, and set and costume designers who work with their American colleagues to produce the spectacular shows for which Hollywood is famous.[18] It is unsurprising that American stage actors such as John Travolta, Johnny Depp and Amber Heard (along with Barnaby Joyce's favourite canines, Pistol and Boo), among many others, have found Australia an attractive location for their own films.

The world of contemporary music boasts innumerable genres and a vast range of artists and bands. They defy brief analysis. It is clear, however, that leading performers and groups appeal to the hearts and souls of entire generations. Bruce Springsteen has long drawn massive audiences on both sides of the Pacific. Keith Urban remains a country music legend. Singers such as Olivia Newton-John, Kylie Minogue, Helen Reddy, Delta Goodrem and Tina Arena have all enjoyed success in the highly competitive female artist market in America, while groups such as AC/DC, INXS, the Bee Gees, Men at Work, Crowded House, Midnight Oil and Savage Garden had successful American careers.[19]

The point is, of course, that the cultural and social mores that bring together Australian and American Millennials and their Gen Z successors are perhaps even more profound and probably more enduring than those that linked the Baby Boomers seventy years ago. The values that underpin contemporary cultural life differ significantly from those that formed the Boomers – young people on both sides of the Pacific are much less assuming, complacent and entitled than their forebears, and much more questioning and sceptical.

The deep cultural underpinnings of the national mindsets that determine the political life of America and Australia do not end there, however. They inform America's most favoured form of international interaction – war – and Australia's equally favoured form of signalling its relevance to its 'great and powerful friend' – unquestioning support. That merits reflection.

# 7.
# War

America has an itchy trigger finger: war is its default position. It has been involved in aggressive and punitive expeditions of all kinds for over 93 per cent of its national lifetime, across more than 225.[1] According to Tufts University's Military Intervention Project, 'the US has undertaken over 500 international military interventions since 1776, with nearly 60% undertaken between 1950 and 2017', and one-third of them occurring after 1999.[2] Indeed, armed aggression against Indigenous Americans dates back to 1609, with the war drums beating constantly until 1924 – a total of 315 years.[3]

The longest continuous engagement – the so-called American Indian Wars – was aggressive and expansionary, occupying and colonising Indigenous lands for eventual incorporation into the nation that is now the United States of America. The fact that so many American towns and cities begin with 'Fort' is testimony to the westward and southward settler expansion, as fortified encampments were established from which to mount territorial acquisition and suppressive military operations. In that peculiar sense, the American Indian Wars were 'internal', as was the original occupation of Indigenous lands after the settlement in Jamestown (VA) in 1607 and the arrival of the *Mayflower* in 1620.

Internal wars – the War of Independence and the Civil War – were also the most lethal in per-capita terms. Between 25,000 and 70,000 Americans died in the course of active military service during the War of Independence. Of these casualties, nearly 7,000 died in battle and at least 17,000 died from disease. Most died as prisoners of the British, generally in prison ships in New York harbour. At least 10,000 died in 1776 alone.[4] The War of Independence saw families split, as some supported the British colonial status quo and others sought self-rule. And in terms of deaths, injuries and the loss of property, it was also the costliest. Similarly, the Civil War was a catastrophe of unspeakable brutality. Recent population census analysis suggests that around 750,000 Americans died at one another's hands or from the wounds and diseases they inflicted on one other – over 400,000 Union casualties and over 300,000 Confederate casualties.[5]

Appalling though these numbers are, they are at least an order of magnitude less than the number of deaths inflicted on the Indigenous American population. In America, as in Australia, there is an enormous disparity between the 'official' casualty figures and the actual death rate due to pandemic disease, malnutrition resulting from land expropriation, and deaths in armed suppression operations. The popular imagination has been shaped by stories of individual encounters, such as the Battle of the Little Bighorn (Custer's Last Stand) and the Battle of Wounded Knee – bloody encounters with casualties in the hundreds. But the American Indian Wars, also known as the Frontier Wars (as in Australia), were characterised less by sharp military encounters than by a sustained war of attrition waged by frontiersmen, settlers and military forces employing the instruments of dispossession, alienation, the theft of lands and livelihoods, forced relocation, malnutrition and starvation, contagious diseases, armed attacks and the separation of children from their parents (as in Australia). Credible estimates suggest that at least 13 million Indigenous Americans perished between 1492 and the present. For the entire Western Hemisphere, that number blows out to an unfathomable 175 million people between 1492 and 1900.[6] By any measure, the depopulation of the Americas from Alaska to Patagonia was a genocide, 'an Indigenous Holocaust', to use David Michael Smith's term.[7]

During its march to independence, Americans fought against the forces of several European nations – Great Britain, France, the Netherlands and Spain – though most of these engagements were little more than opportunistic skirmishes as the settlers appropriated Indigenous lands and established borders or fired on the odd ship. America's foreign wars began in earnest with the North African Barbary Wars in 1801, memorialised in 'The Marines' Hymn' as 'the shores of Tripoli'. The US Navy undertook its first major foreign deployment in 1825, when it began piracy suppression operations in the Aegean, culminating in the sacking of Carabusa in early 1828. Four years later, the navy began its long tradition of punitive expeditions when it exacted reprisals against Acehnese privateers who had massacred the crew of an American merchant vessel named (ironically) *Friendship*. The bombardment of Kuala Batu – remembered in American naval history as the Battle of Quallah Battoo – bought a few years of calm before another merchant vessel, the *Eclipse*, was attacked and its complement massacred in 1838, thereby prompting the second Sumatran expedition.

**The Mexican–American War**

It was the war against Mexico that helped establish American ground forces as the formidable expression of American power that they have since become. Texas had gained its independence from Mexico on 2 March 1836 following a combination of guerrilla insurgency actions and pitched battles over the previous decade. Just a couple of days later, the Mexican president, General Santa Anna, laid siege to and destroyed the fortress at the Alamo, with Davy Crockett (whom we met briefly in the previous chapter) and his co-defenders dying in the process. Almost ten years later, Texas joined the Union as the twenty-eighth state, leaving some territorial tidying up to be done.

In some respects, the Mexican–American War was a conflict of con-venience ended by an American provocation, when a small US force was deployed across disputed territory to the Rio Grande to assert American territorial claims. Mexico understandably resisted, forcing the American troops to retreat in April 1846. This was enough for President James K. Polk to obtain US Congressional backing for his declaration of war on Mexico. American ground and naval forces moved quickly to establish military supremacy, and not just in the disputed territories to the south of Texas. By September, General Winfield Scott had taken Mexico City, paving the way for a peace treaty that saw the incorporation of Texas, California, Nevada and Utah, as well as disputed parts of Arizona, Colorado, New Mexico and Wyoming.

Mexico's resistance was doomed. Its independence from Spain two decades earlier had left the country with an inherently unstable political system and a barely functioning economy, and no credible military force. America's victory, on the other hand, was inevitable, as it acquired over half of Mexico's landmass: its economy was booming, with the demand for its agricultural exports, especially cotton, feeding the Industrial Revolution in Europe.

Commodity demand drove territorial expansion, and the energy behind America's southwards expansion revealed three additional facets of America's approach to war: spend whatever was necessary to achieve the aim; ignore casualties and losses, both military and civilian, American and enemy, incurred in achieving the military aim; and heavy-handedness brings its own rewards. As Stalin might have said (but in fact did not), 'Quantity has a quality all its own.'

While US losses were considerable, and certainly large enough to draw wide domestic criticism – America's first experience of 'war-weariness', perhaps – Mexico suffered enormous losses. Although 'to the victor the spoils' is true of all wars, the American predilection for heavy-handedness and brutality in its treatment of Mexican prisoners and civilians also drew criticism within the United States. The war with Mexico reinforced another aspect of the American approach to war: the link between winning and deterrence. A massive victory – with large numbers of enemy casualties and widespread destruction of infrastructure and property, the punishment of enemy leaders and tight controls imposed on the civilian population – exercises a powerful deterrent effect. A 'hearts and minds' approach to civilian control is fine, so long as the hearts and minds are not functioning too well.

## China and the Opium War

America's military involvement in the Second Opium War was a curiosity. As the world's dominant nation, Britain had used its military power to force a trade agreement upon the Chinese government that granted Britain most favoured nation status. This enabled Britain to address its trade imbalance with China, which ran heavily in China's favour, by exporting manufactures – and opium. Just as it had attempted to do in the First Opium War, China wanted to maintain a prohibition on the import of opium, but was unable to in the face of British military pressure and the narcotic susceptibility of its own population. The present-day export of fentanyl and other opioids by Chinese 'entrepreneurs' ('criminal gangs' is the preferred American description) is not entirely without precedent. France, Russia and the United States were quick to employ their diplomats to negotiate the same trading arrangements and a raft of other benefits – one in, all in, as it were.

As one of the principal treaty ports, where the foreign powers were able to conduct their business affairs unhindered by the Chinese customs authorities, Canton (Guangzhou) was the centre of American commercial interests in China. But as Britain continued to employ military force in the prosecution of its trading interests, there was always significant potential for ambiguity and unintended provocation. In his efforts to secure American commercial interests late in 1856, the US consul sought the assistance of the US naval squadron commander to protect the US compound against possible Chinese attack.[8]

The fog of war quickly descended, however, with both the American and Chinese leaders employing a combination of provocation and negotiation to secure their objectives. In return for a Chinese agreement to respect US commercial interests, the Americans agreed not to provide military support to the British and French forces. But as the American naval group was withdrawing up the Pearl River, the Chinese garrison manning one of the river forts fired on the Americans. Whether the attack on the American vessel was intentional or not, the American response was immediate and eventually overwhelming:

within two weeks, US marines and sailors captured and destroyed the four Chinese forts guarding Canton, leading to an apology from the Chinese authorities for attacking the American vessels and a neutrality declaration by both sides. The encounter had a perverse consequence: the Chinese forces learned important tactical lessons from their encounter with the Americans, subsequently defeating British and French naval forces at Taku, on the Hai River, three years later.

While this incident is little more than a footnote in the US Navy's remarkable history, it demonstrated – perhaps for the first time – three key features of the American approach to war: the idea that attack is preferable to defence; the importance of taking and keeping the initiative; and the fact that small forces with superior leadership and military technology defeat larger forces with inferior military technology. It also reinforced a principle established by Washington during the War of Independence: asserting and defending the power and rights of the state blurs the distinction between diplomacy and warfare. As America's military leaders have continued to demonstrate unapologetically, warfare is the continuation of diplomacy by other means (to channel Clausewitz). From Washington to Westmoreland, from Pershing to Paton, from Grant to MacArthur, from Perry to Nimitz, America is its military power.

After a couple of abortive overseas missions conducted by American forces – a defeat at the hands of the inhabitants of Taiwan in 1867, and an intervention in the Samoan Civil War in 1898–99 – America's war against Spain, which began in 1898, was the prelude to a militarily momentous century for America, when it morphed from being a significant Western Hemisphere power to global strategic dominance as the world's single and singular superpower.

The war with Spain began with a massive explosion in the forward magazines of USS *Maine*, an American second-class battleship at anchor in the port of Havana, Cuba, on 15 February 1898. In the already established tradition of American gunboat diplomacy, USS *Maine* had been dispatched to Havana to protect American interests as Cuba sought independence from Spain. American naval experts immediately concluded that the explosion on USS *Maine* was due to poor fire control practices in the coal storage compartments (the ship was fuelled by bituminous coal with a high methane content, producing volatile firedamp) leading to spontaneous ignition and the loss of the ship and most of its crew. This conclusion was subsequently supported by several investigations and inquiries, not least a review by Admiral Hyman Rickover in 1976.[9] But a combination of factors – including sensationalised tabloid journalism representing little more than 'fake news' – persuaded the US Navy to establish a board of inquiry, which identified an externally placed mine as the cause of the explosion. President McKinley was reluctant to cite the sinking of the *Maine* as an act of war, but in what was to become something of an American habit over the next hundred years, on 25 April 1898 America declared war on Spain anyway. This, as Rickover noted with considerable understatement, was 'a turning point in American history ... [leaving] us a legacy that still influences our nation'.[10]

And a turning point in American history it was, for the Spanish–American War quickly expanded into a war involving Mexico and the Philippines, setting the stage for a century of military adventurism, armed intervention and significant expenditure of American blood and treasure.

**An imperial adventure: The Philippines**

The war with Spain ended quickly. With the Treaty of Paris signed in December 1898, Spain lost what was left of its empire in Cuba, the Philippines and Guam, and other Pacific Island possessions that became the scene of bloody battles during World War II. Although America had made two very significant 'strategic investments' in the nineteenth century – Louisiana, purchased from Napoleon in 1803 for $15 million,[11] and Alaska, from Russia in 1867 for $7.2 million[12] – its purchase of the Philippines from Spain for $250 million was blind to the principle 'buyer beware'. Its transformation from a metropolitan power to a colonial power brought America nothing but trouble and a set of formative experiences that ill prepared it for its twentieth-century experiences in Japan and Vietnam. American naval and military units had taken control of Manila in July 1898, with the assistance of Filipino anti-Spanish guerrillas led by Emilio Aguinaldo, who was to become extremely problematic just six months later. America's gunboat encounters in China and Japan had not prepared it for a sustained and well-led insurgency – or 'insurrection', as Washington chose to describe it. Unsurprisingly, Aguinaldo did not wish to exchange the Spanish coloniser for an American one, and quickly turned on his one-time ally.

For its brutality and the deprivation experienced by the civilian population, the Philippine–American War was a disaster. Initially, Aguinaldo chose to fight a conventional war against forces superior in equipment, training and sustainment. Against overwhelming odds, Aguinaldo was forced to adopt guerrilla warfare techniques, with reduced losses but no appreciably greater success. This was due to the skills of the governor, William Howard Taft, whom President McKinley had appointed in 1900. Taft later became US president himself. The governor skilfully and successfully divided the Filipino community through his 'policy of attraction', winning the support of the landed, wealthy and better-educated upper classes, whom he gradually appointed to political positions in the legislature's upper house and to administrative positions in the bureaucracy. Taft entertained racially dismissive views of Filipinos as indolent and excitable, and encouraged Chinese immigration to build a more applied labour force, thereby further dividing the Philippines communities in ways that continue to reverberate over a century later. The assassination of President McKinley in 1901, however, brought Teddy Roosevelt to the presidency, and with him a considerably more muscular approach to the conduct of American strategic policy. Roosevelt appointed Taft as his Secretary for War, further entrenching their joint enthusiasm for America's new imperialist aspirations. In his annual address to the US Congress in 1904, Roosevelt announced his eponymous 'Roosevelt Corollary' to the Monroe Doctrine:

> If a nation shows that it knows how to act with reasonable efficiency and decency in social and political matters, if it keeps order and pays

its obligations, it need fear no interference from the United States. Chronic wrongdoing, or an impotence which results in a general loosening of the ties of civilized society, may in America, as elsewhere, ultimately require intervention by some civilized nation, and in the Western Hemisphere the adherence of the United States to the Monroe Doctrine may force the United States, however reluctantly, in flagrant cases of such wrongdoing or impotence, to the exercise of an international police power.[13]

The Monroe Doctrine of eighty years earlier was, in most respects, an American overreach, signalling America's exceptionalism and intent without the military power necessary to deliver or enforce its strategic preferences. It was much more than a statement of political bluster, however, for it demonstrated clear strategic ambition and enormous self-belief, which have remained characteristic of American approaches to war.

While the prospect of a debt default by Venezuela (do things ever change?) was the proximate trigger for Roosevelt's expansion of the Monroe Doctrine, it was in Asia that its implications were perhaps most profound, similar to President Nixon's Guam Doctrine sixty-five years later. As president, Roosevelt certainly toughened Taft's approach to the colonisation of the Philippines and paved the way for almost forty years of American strategic control of that country. Taft, who had initially favoured a managed progression to Filipino independence and statehood, was converted to Roosevelt's more imperial approach to the realisation of America's global strategic interests, an approach he worked to implement when he in turn was elected president in 1908. David Vine points out that 'Roosevelt's Corollary' also legitimised the policy of 'forward presence' – perhaps more accurately termed 'basing' – as an essential vehicle for American power projection.[14] This practice had already been adopted by the US Cavalry as it seized and claimed ownership over the Indigenous and Mexican lands that were eventually incorporated into the continental United States. The seizure and occupation of the Hawaiian island, and the eventual admission of Hawaii as the fiftieth state in 1959, followed a similar pattern.

It is never useful to regret what might have been. A textbook transfer of governmental authority from a colonial power to local inhabitants would have saved both money (the $250-million Philippines purchase price and the cost of three years of military operations) and lives (over 4,000 American troops and 20,000 Filipino combatants, not to mention some 200,000 Filipino civilians who died from violence, disease or malnutrition). The rejection of an imperial future and a peaceful transfer of power enjoyed wide support among American citizens. But with respect to the Philippines, another feature of America's instinctive approach to war emerged: the administration and the Congress pursued 'strategic objectives' – in this case, the strategic denial of the Philippines to Germany or Japan – over a preference for 'statecraft' that might have established a critical postcolonial precedent. To paraphrase Clausewitz, war is always the continuation of diplomacy by other means – more prickles and less politesse. At this point, America's instinctive preference for confrontation over statecraft had identified itself as a core feature of its approach to war.

## World War I

As the US government settled into its newfound imperial dream in archipelagic South-East Asia, the American people settled into a more neutral and less globally engaged frame of mind. The American governmental and bureaucratic elite, most of whom lived on the eastern seaboard, generally sympathised with Britain when World War I commenced in August 1914. But decades of high-flow immigration from Ireland, Scandinavia and Germany, and the strong linkages between the immigrant communities and the major Catholic and Protestant denominations, meant that the expanding communities in America's industrial cities were significantly less pro-British, particularly following the Easter Uprising in 1916, and equally disinclined to support a war against Germany. Early pro-German sentiment – numbers of German Americans tried to enlist in the German Imperial Army – declined sharply with the sinking of the RMS *Lusitania* and the loss of almost 1,200 people (just over 10 per cent were Americans) in May 1915.

But it was one thing to support an outcome in Europe favouring the British and the French; it was altogether another for Americans to commit to that outcome. America's bankers and industrialists saw economic opportunity and massive profits resulting from American military engagement in Europe, sowing the seeds of the industrial–military complex that has come to dominate contemporary American war planning. And the economic elites were pretty well aligned with the intellectual and policy elites of Washington, Philadelphia, New York and Boston.

These 'dogs of war', however, were effectively corralled by the kittens of peace – mostly the ethnic-based industrial working class and the deeply isolationist American farming and rural communities. Democratic president Woodrow Wilson, who had been slowly building a pro-intervention constituency in the Congress, found himself snookered by the Congressional Democrats. Plans to strengthen America's military and naval forces were voted down, generating renewed confidence in Berlin that American participation in the European war could be discounted, improving the chances of a German victory. Thus emboldened, imperial Germany determined upon a policy of unrestricted submarine warfare and commenced secret negotiations with Mexico – revealed in the infamous 'Zimmerman Telegram' – to combine in a war against a weak America. So, in a perverse reversal, Congress's decision to reduce military spending and keep America out of the war provoked exactly the opposite outcome.

As the Imperial German Navy's U-boats sank American cargo vessels and the American people digested the implications of the Zimmermann Telegram, Congress acceded to President Wilson's request for a declaration of war – a *volte face* that released the enormous power of American industry to build a military behemoth, significantly increased the chances of a British and French victory in Europe and, even more importantly, introduced the American way of war to Europe. America's late entry into the European war changed the way America did things domestically and internationally.

Congress's decision to go onto a war footing generated a newfound sense of national purpose in the way America organised its supply chains in virtually every sector – agriculture, communications, energy production, industry, mining and transport – and, more significantly, the way it funded itself. It introduced a progressive taxation system and democratised the war bonds system introduced by Britain at the outbreak of World War I to extend capital-raising to individuals and families through innovative advertising campaigns. It then internationalised its capital-raising by issuing bonds to foreign countries, in a precursor to the Lend-Lease system of World War II. It initiated the employment of women in roles that had traditionally been filled by men – assembly lines, machine operators, industrial processing – along with a substantial increase in the numbers of women attending university and joining the professions. Although most women subsequently returned to domestic and household roles after the doughboys returned from Europe, it established a precedent that ultimately rendered deep social change irreversible. Perhaps more significantly, in terms of how the rest of the twentieth century unfolded, it was by becoming a belligerent that America guaranteed a place for itself at the post-war negotiating table and in the construction of a post-war order – which was central to Wilson's strategic calculations.

So it was that, at the end of 1917, the American Expeditionary Force (AEF), a hastily trained army under the command of General John 'Black Jack' Pershing, was dispatched to the killing fields of Europe. Their participation was decisive. They fought under their own flag rather than in combined Allied units, a practice Pershing insisted upon (to the irritation of Allied commanders) and which has remained American combat doctrine ever since. A rare exception was Lieutenant Colonel George Patton's tank regiment, which fought under General John Monash's command at the Battle of Le Hamel in July 1918, a 93-minute encounter that some claim was the turning point of World War I.[15] Patton would achieve both fame and notoriety in World War II. The AEF sustained considerable losses: over 53,000 killed, over 200,000 wounded and over 63,000 non-combat-related deaths, due mainly to the outbreak of influenza at the end of 1918.[16]

In little more than a year, America had demonstrated that it could mobilise its entire economy and population to generate and deploy massive military forces, virtually from a standing start. It also redefined defeat to include economic destruction of the adversary, not just in the allocation of guilt and responsibility, but also in the imposition of costs and penalties. It did this with the full cooperation of its allies, who, as Christopher Clark has detailed in his brilliant study *The Sleepwalkers*, were complicit in the decisions to declare war in 1914.[17] For America, victory in war is not enough: domination in peace is a necessary corollary.

Its late entry notwithstanding, America emerged from World War I as the major Allied power and the undisputed leader of the 'Allied and Associated Powers' signatory to the Treaty of Versailles. This was not quite what Britain or France had in mind as they welcomed the arrival of the American forces at the beginning of 1918. Nor was it what Australian prime minister Billy Hughes had in mind as he sought to maximise Australian advantage in the distribution of the spoils of Germany's erstwhile colonies in the Pacific. Nor was it what Japan had in mind as it negotiated for (and nearly won) recognition for racial equality – Billy Hughes put paid to that. But the 'war to end all wars' established America's economic, political and strategic pre-eminence in a world that was almost bankrupted by the war, and was then effectively mortgaged to the United States as its belligerents repaid their loans and met their huge debts for materials and armaments. President Woodrow Wilson's 'Fourteen Points' set the terms and the tone of the ensuing peace, aspects of which we shall examine in the next chapter.

They also set the premises on which the US Congress refused to ratify America's membership of the League of Nations – thereby depriving it of authoritative leadership – segueing to the disaster that was to unfold a mere twenty years later.

## World War II

By virtue of Congress's decision to reject membership of the League of Nations, America became aloof from Europe. Nonetheless, America had watched the rise of Nazism and Hitler's adventurism and aggression with increasing concern. But that interwar aloofness, the fact that America's strategic interests were not directly engaged in the annexation of Austria, the occupation of the Sudetenland (and the fall of Czechoslovakian government) and the invasion of Poland all failed to persuade President Franklin D. Roosevelt's administration to seek Congress's agreement to a declaration of war on the side of Britain and France. American public opinion was decidedly pro-Allies and anti-Axis, but this did not encourage America to move towards any kind of war economy. It took the attack on Pearl Harbor to jolt America onto a war footing. From 7 December 1941 onward, the American engines of war have not stopped.

World War II is perhaps the most studied of all America's wars. For the purposes of this book, however, the topography of the war is not so relevant. What emerges from America's experience of a massive strategic shock – and Japan's attack on the fleet at Pearl Harbor was certainly that – has become part of the blueprint for America's approach to warfare. The Treaty of Versailles was a humiliation for Japan. Not only had it been excluded from the leadership group of nations – essentially a 'white man's club – on what were essentially racist grounds (fomented largely by Australia's Billy Hughes), but it had been treated with disdain as it was awarded a few of Germany's colonial trinkets in the Pacific. No country, least of all Australia or America, could have foreseen the use to which these island relics would be put by Japan two decades later.

In the immediate post-World War I years, Japan moved to secure its political and strategic interests in Asia through an assertive foreign and economic access policy and an aggressive military build-up. Due to restrictive trade policies on the part of America and Britain, Japan was ready within a decade to invade Manchuria, to capitalise on the political unrest in northern China by attacking China, and to begin positioning for the realisation of its Greater East Asia Co-Prosperity Sphere.[18] The combination of the Great Depression and its insistent disengagement engendered a flat-footed diplomacy during the 1930s and a refusal to sanction Japan's expansionist tendencies by employing direct political pressure backed by military posturing. In effect, the more Japan pushed in Asia, the less America responded – until Japan surprised America.

This was a fatal strategic error on Japan's part. The assumption that an attack on the American fleet at Pearl Harbor would persuade America to retreat into its isolationism misread America's sense of its own 'manifest destiny' and 'exceptionalism'. It also misread the American character and America's capacity for massive retaliation. Whatever else it might have been, Japan's attack on Pearl Harbor was not the prelude to an invasion of continental America. Rather, it was a form of coercive diplomacy – a pre-emptive attack intended to deter American involvement in affairs in Asia that, in Japan's view, were none of America's business. Just as Japan had, in 1905, humiliated Russia in its bid to carve out and maintain a role in North Asia, so it thought it could land a paralysing blow that would reconfirm America's isolationism. As a deterrent, however, it failed catastrophically because it forced America's hand.

President Roosevelt's response was immediate. Speaking to Congress on 8 December 1941, he announced America's declaration of war. In one of the most quoted speeches of the twentieth century, and deservedly so, Roosevelt said:

> No matter how long it may take us to overcome this premeditated invasion, the American people in their righteous might will win through to absolute victory. I believe that I interpret the will of the Congress and of the people when I assert that we will not only defend ourselves to the uttermost but will make it very certain that this form of treachery shall never again endanger us.[19]

Roosevelt's speech is worth close exegesis for its construction and its ineluctable rhetorical force, but also for its lapidary articulation of an

American philosophy of war. It is determined, grim and menacing. It is also absolute.[20] The speech is five hundred words of 'exceptionalism' and 'manifest destiny', though it does not employ those terms. It does not need to. In his declaration that '[n]o matter how long it may take us to overcome this premeditated invasion, the American people in their righteous might will win through to absolute victory', Roosevelt gives vent to an implacable certainty that America is invincible. America will do 'what it takes' to protect and promote its interests. And there is no clash with values here, no binary: the values that inform American interests are implicit in its unswerving manifest destiny.

*Le hachoir à viande*, 'the meatgrinder', was the macabre term the French used to describe one of the most pointless battles of World War I, the attack on Verdun, an entirely French and German affair that cost over a quarter of a million killed in action and half a million wounded. It was attrition gone mad. Yet the attrition model is deep in America's warfare DNA. In World War I, of the almost 5 million persons enlisted in the US military, there were just over 320,000 American casualties, 53,000 killed in action in less than a year, with just over 63,000 non-combat related deaths. In World War II, of the more than 16 million who enlisted in the American services, there were more than a million American casualties, with just over 290,000 killed in action.

No nation welcomes the death of its youth in war. But as the command tensions between General John Monash and the Allied commanders in World War I (principally the British, but Pershing included) bore testimony, Australia has a significantly more parsimonious approach to the loss of blood in warfare than do its allies. At its simplest, America's tolerance of battle casualties reflects its 'victory at any price' ethos, which was forged in its experience of war in the first half of the twentieth century and echoed its military adventures of the nineteenth century.

America ended the bloodshed of the Pacific War with two nuclear detonations. The destruction of Hiroshima and Nagasaki and the hundreds of thousands of Japanese civilian deaths and casualties precipitated Japan's capitulation. It was not a glorious end for Japan. Nor was it for America. The first use of a weapon of massive destruction was a strategic decision the moral foundations of which continue to be contested. So they should be. The moral dimension of America's ascension to global leadership – global domination, in the view of some – remains equally contested. In consequence, America's moral authority is clothed in ambiguity. As commander-in-chief, President Harry S. Truman took a decision he was authorised to take. America, however, was left carrying the moral responsibility for the emergence of the nuclear age. As General Douglas MacArthur accepted Japan's surrender aboard USS *Missouri* on 2 September 1945, he represented both his president and his country's responsibility for the unanswered and unanswerable questions that are forever associated with an overwhelming end to a war that had already been lost. That, perhaps, is part of America's manifest destiny.

## War in Korea

General MacArthur was the central character at the conclusion of one drama and at the beginning of another. At the end of World War II, MacArthur returned to the Philippines as a conquering hero, and then ruled Japan as America's pro-consul and the real power behind the imperial throne. No American commander since George Washington had enjoyed the adulation, authority and respect that the people of America, the Philippines, Japan, Korea and Australia accorded to Douglas MacArthur. MacArthur forged a close relationship with Prime Minister John Curtin, to the enduring irritation of General (later Field Marshal) Sir Thomas Blamey. That relationship both initiated and cemented Australia's deferential subordination to America's military leadership, and remains emblematic of Australia's strategic cringe towards America today.

Much has been written about MacArthur's abilities, command style and personality, and there is no need to add to that here, except to note that he was a gifted and thoughtful leader, and an exceptional strategist with a finely honed sensitivity to the role of the military leader in a democracy. He was certainly adept at managing and manipulating Prime Minister Curtin. He brought an entirely new character to the post-war rule of a defeated nation by the victorious power. Though much oversimplified, it is fair to say that post–World War II Japan owes much to MacArthur's sensitivity to Asian mores and values, and to his respect for the enduring features of Japanese identity, especially respect for the imperial institution. Yes, he was arrogant, brash and supremely self-confident, with a tendency to hubris. But, as Clausewitz does not say in his enigmatic chapter on military genius in *On War*, those qualities are probably indicative of all great military leaders.[21] Some would say that they also distinguish military fools. The difference, of course, is that great military leaders have much to be arrogant, brash and self-confident about.

America ended World War II on a high. It was globally victorious and the undisputed leader of the free world, as well as the dominant global power. Its victory, however, had come at enormous cost, and it entered into the creation of the post–World War II 'rules-based order' with three main objectives: to prevent future wars by establishing a new world order – the United Nations – that imposed effective constraints on any nation that sought to employ armed force; to avoid the need for America to resort to war itself; and to contain the spread of communism. As became clear far too quickly, these objectives were not mutually achievable.

Berlin was barely occupied before America and the Soviet Union became implacable foes locked in an intense battle for global influence with deep strategic consequences. America and China quickly found themselves opposed due to serious missteps on both sides, critically influenced by the fact that Japanese forces in China had remained undefeated. And, American efforts notwithstanding, the victorious colonial powers failed to appreciate that the world had changed in fundamental ways. The immediate post-war environment was one of political jostling, countervailing objectives, hidden agendas, duplicity (by everyone) and diplomatic skulduggery, not to mention espionage, subversion, terrorism (in some instances supported by state third parties) and the odd bit of proxy warfare as states tested the resolve of the colonial powers.

This might perhaps be described as 'the real world', where optimism and any hope for a better existence are seen as naive, romantic or sentimental – or all three. Yet the catastrophe of World War II – at least 40 million civilian deaths, 15 million military deaths, countless civilians injured and over 25 million wounded, and perhaps 10 million people in the various Asian theatres – and America's resolve not to repeat the folly of its rejection of the League of Nations engendered a global sentiment that the world community could do better. The UN Charter is testament to that. The world of realpolitik and MacArthur's world of East Asian reconstruction, however, were not in sync. It was in this strategic chasm that the North Korean People's Army crossed the 38th parallel into South Korea on 25 June 1950. And MacArthur was not prepared for it.

President Truman called upon General MacArthur to fix the problem, and the general was confident that he could – by Christmas (famous last words for those who recall August 1914). Like Westmoreland in Vietnam, MacArthur in Korea misunderstood and underestimated the cultural and social forces that supported 'communist' ideologies. Truman wanted to stop the spread of communism. MacArthur wanted to roll it back, even if that meant war with China.[22] And in that disagreement lay the seeds of failure. Over 36,000 Americans died and over 100,000 were wounded. Overall, more than 4 million Korean and Chinese people died in a war that has not yet ended.

The multidimensional tension between politics and strategy, cultural traditions and emerging social forces, colonialism and national independence movements that has undermined American policy for the last seventy years had its origins in Korea. And central to that has been the continuing inability to come to terms with China. The testimony given by generals Omar Bradley, Hoyt Vandenberg and Joe Collins to Congress at the time of MacArthur's dismissal reveals a profound misunderstanding of China, its culture, its politics and its historical strategic interests and ambitions – a misunderstanding that

MacArthur shared.[23] The difference between them centred on how that misunderstanding should be actioned.

With the benefit of hindsight, they were all wrong. Regardless, the Korean War confirmed habits of military thinking that continue to distinguish America's conception and prosecution of war today.

## The Vietnam debacle

Were it not for the principled stand and astonishing moral courage of Daniel Ellsberg, and the flawed retrospective of Robert McNamara, America and Australia may still not know just how truly momentous a strategic and political catastrophe the war in Vietnam was.[24] Nearly 9 million Americans were drafted for service in Vietnam. Over 58,000 died, 47,500 in battle. Over 300,000 were injured or wounded. With the benefit of conscription, over 60,000 Australians went to Vietnam between 1962 and 1973, of whom 523 died and 2,400 were wounded.[25] Nothing was gained in return for the massive loss of blood, treasure and national dignity.

In defiance of public sentiment, and blind to Australia's national and strategic interests, the Australian government played the little lamb to America's Mary. When Prime Minister Harold Holt proclaimed 'all the way with LBJ', he set the tone for subsequent Australian prime ministers to go all the way with the USA.

In the minds of many Americans at the time, the Oval Office and the Situation Room brought together those whom David Halberstam termed 'the best and the brightest' – many self-identified and self-anointed as such, deaf to the irony of the phrase.[26] Like Henry Kissinger, who quickly became their doyen, they were arrogant, self-assured and careless of the national polity whose children provided the cannon-fodder of war. They were men (predominantly) whose total unfamiliarity with the horrors of combat brought no constraint to their assumption that military power best achieves policy objectives. Their confidence in America's military and moral supremacy – and their inability to understand the dynamics of geo-strategic relationships except through the lens of their exposure to European political and military history – blinded them to the political realities of postcolonialism.

McNamara, in many respects, personified America's 'exceptional-ism' and high-handedness, allowing image and national prestige to triumph over national interests in the expenditure of blood and treasure.[27] He also personified, as did Kissinger, an egregious error in understanding and applying the principle of military subordi-nation to civilian control. Responsibility and accountability for the control of the military rests with the president and Congress: the president as commander-in-chief and Congress as the authority for the expenditure of funds. It does not rest with the civilian advisers to the president, as those surrounding presidents Kennedy and Johnson seemed to think. In Australia's case, civilian control rests with the executive and the Parliament – though some would argue that the latter should exercise more control than it currently does.

The Vietnam War continues to attract enormous scholarly interest. It was a multifaceted war that replicated every problem the American military machine had encountered in its previous two centuries, and then some. But there are three aspects that perhaps contributed to the war's catastrophic conclusion more than any other, and which continue to colour America's approach to war.

First, there was almost no deep on-the-ground knowledge of the cultures and societies with which America was engaging, nor any interest in acquiring that knowledge. Cultural sensitivity was dis-missed as an unnecessary distraction when all one needed to focus on was America's power and the mechanisms for employing that power. Second, the uncontested mutual validation that is often a hallmark of academic elitism created an echo chamber that precluded argu-ment and contest of views. The area and subject-matter expertise of America's diplomats was ignored in favour of the elegant constructs of political-science theorists. In fact, theoretical confirmation bias mar-ginalised practical diplomatic experience. The State Department has never recovered. And third, conventional warfare between heavily armed and well-trained armies relying on established military doctrine is largely irrelevant in meeting the demands of irregular warfare, insurgency and guerrilla operations.

General Westmoreland attempted to take the attrition model of warfare to its limits – only to discover that it alienated the population of Vietnam, rendered the situation on the ground increasingly less secure and inflicted little damage on a highly mobile and agile force, which could appear and disappear more or less at will. In his excoriating biography of Westmoreland, Lewis Sorley provides ten core reasons for the strategic failure that was Vietnam. Because they are relevant to America's subsequent wars, they are worth listing: Westmoreland, an artillery officer, was untrained in command and narrow in his experience; his senior staff lacked diversity; he rejected contestability; he prevented the South Vietnamese from exercising any meaningful role in their own defence; he denied them up-to-date weapons; he denied access to accurate intelligence assessments to the senior civilian advisers ('the best and brightest'); his war of attrition left the enemy insurgency infrastructure intact; he underestimated the enemy's endurance and resilience; he overestimated America's acceptance of the casualty rate; and, most critically, he squandered four years of support by the people, Congress and the media.[28]

When the years of deception and lies that surrounded the entire Vietnam adventure are taken into account, the destruction of popular trust in the accountability of government to the people is perhaps the most significant legacy of the Vietnam War. It is surely one of the fundamental causes of America's current malaise.

From a policy perspective, America's failure in Vietnam suggests once again that strategists must apply imagination to the task of planning. The unimaginable cannot be unthinkable. Yet a classified Central Intelligence Agency (CIA) report prepared in 1967 illustrates exactly what happens when disaster cannot be imagined:

What we mean by an 'unfavorable outcome' needs to be defined with some realism. We are not discussing the entirely implausible hypothesis of a political-military collapse, say, the precipitate withdrawal of American forces or sweeping political concessions tantamount to granting Hanoi outright achievement of its aims in the South.[29]

The extraordinary scenes of helicopters evacuating staff from the US embassy in Saigon at the end of April 1975 – over 7,000 people were evacuated in a single day – and the subsequent dumping overboard of perfectly serviceable aircraft from the flight decks of USS *Midway* and USS *Okinawa* began with a failure of imagination thirteen years earlier. The Vietnam War ended with the same failure.


## On to Afghanistan and Iraq

The Gulf War was a tidy and contained short war that defended and freed Kuwait against an attack by Saddam Hussein's Iraq. Supported by UN Security Council resolutions, thereby making the subsequent war lawful, America formed a coalition of some forty-two nations that mounted a campaign in two phases: a five-month build-up phase beginning in late August 1990, and then a six-week operational phase that restored the Kuwaiti government to power at the end of February 1991. It was a classical military operation with a clear strategic objective and a defined 'end-state'. It both recognised and validated American authority, power and prestige. Iraq's aggression was sanctioned and responded to, and Kuwait was liberated. Iraq was forced to withdraw behind its established borders, with a chastened Saddam Hussein continuing to govern in Baghdad.

It was in every respect a lopsided war, as Iraq's forces proved no match for the dominant American military. America resisted the temptation to invade Iraq, choosing instead to destroy key strategic targets and significant associated infrastructure. President George H. Bush resisted suggestions that he destroy Iraq and remove Saddam Hussein – a correct decision that was in total conformity with the principles of warfare and the law of armed conflict.[30] But the Gulf War was, with the benefit of hindsight, a prelude to the Iraq War a decade later. The strategic discipline of the Gulf War would not extend to the Iraq War, however.

The terrorist attacks on the Twin Towers of the World Trade Center, New York, on 11 September 2001 were as much an attack on America as was the bombing of the battleships at Pearl Harbor on 7 December 1941. America was shocked. America was angry. And America wanted revenge. These are among the worst of reasons for going to war, because they foment the domestic political pressures that encourage political leaders to take decisions unconnected with protecting or promoting the national interest (the power of the nation) or realising the national interests (the strategic aims of the nation). Someone had to pay – and who better than the Taliban government in Afghanistan, which had provided the training and the facilities to the al-Qaeda operatives who had planned and executed the Twin Towers bombings? In its exhaustive investigation, the 9/11 Commission identified an enemy 'who is sophisticated, patient, disciplined, and lethal.'

> The enemy rallies broad support in the Arab and Muslim world by demanding redress of political grievances, but its hostility toward us and our values is limitless. Its purpose is to rid the world of religious and political pluralism, the plebiscite, and equal rights for women. It makes no distinction between military and civilian targets. *Collateral damage* is not in its lexicon.[31]

An enemy such as this is less a threat to the nation than to the global system, and as such demands extreme care in how military force is to be employed, lest the strategic task exceeds the military resources available. It is precisely here that the seeds of the failure in Afghanistan were planted. America's two-decade involvement in Afghanistan – its longest foreign war – replicated the manifold faults of Washington's strategic decision-masking processes since World War II. An uncalibrated, open-ended commitment without a sharply defined strategic purpose, a clear idea of the desired strategic outcome (the 'end-state') and a clearly delineated pathway to withdrawal (the 'exit strategy') is a prelude to strategic disaster. And that, like the Vietnam and Iraq wars, is what the war in Afghanistan became.

Following the 9/11 attacks, President George W. Bush, in consultation with his principal advisers, demanded Osama bin Laden's extradition from Afghanistan to the United States. The Taliban, a fundamentalist organisation that overthrew the Afghan government in 1996, refused. And so the war began. It was hastily conceived and the supporting coalition, including Australia, was hastily assembled. As with most of the coalitions formed in support of the US, the partners each had somewhat different strategic and political objectives, and each operated under different rules of military engagement. While the coalition enjoyed the support of a UN mandate, it extended initially only to the region immediately surrounding Kabul, which meant that the Taliban were able to find sanctuary in Pakistan and in the remote valleys of Afghanistan.

As the British had discovered in the nineteenth century and the Soviet Union a century later, Afghanistan presents insoluble operational problems to any invader. Afghanistan's tribal structures are resilient and resourceful, and its fighters, like the Viet Cong, were indistinguishable from the civilian population. The coalition enjoyed early tactical success at both the political and military levels, installing a favourable government in Kabul and creating a tolerable security environment for the population, at least in the major urban centres. But this early success was blown out of the water by the Bush administration's refusal to support any negotiation between the Karzai government and the Taliban. Multi-party negotiations may have led to some form of Taliban representation, or even some measure of power sharing.

America's intransigence on this matter reflected three connected but totally misunderstood factors: that the strategic purpose of the war was unclear; that America did not comprehend the politically and socially embedded character of the Taliban; and that it failed to understand the consequences of negotiating with the Taliban, which would legitimise them in the eyes of the Afghan population. From the corruption of Afghan civil administration officials to the occurrences of 'green on blue' attacks (Afghan National Army soldiers murdering coalition forces), the preconditions for strategic failure were established in 2002. From then on, the insurgency intensified, the Afghan government became increasingly unstable, and the coalition was barely able to maintain a tactical status quo.

Peace overtures and side deals notwithstanding, America was unable to generate trust in Afghanistan. From 2018 onwards, Afghanistan became increasingly chaotic until President Biden, confronted by a war-weary America, had no option but to withdraw the remainder of America's forces and its diplomatic staff. It was a total strategic humiliation, for America as for its allies. For Australia, forty-one soldiers died and more than 260 were wounded. Australia's image, and that of the Australian Defence Force, was significantly damaged by allegations of war crimes committed against Afghan civilians, alleged crimes that themselves bear witness to the lack of moral purpose in a war that lacked strategic purpose from its inception. There are many lessons to be learned.

In most respects, the Iraq War was a self-imposed sideshow. It undermined America's ability to address the strategic issues created by its engagement in Afghanistan by forcing it to fight on two quite different fronts simultaneously, at least for the duration of the main campaign in Iraq. The Iraq War was the product of mischief, misinformation, mistakes and misunderstanding. It was also the product of deception and lies directed at the American, Australian and British publics, as well as the UN and the international community more broadly.

As the American philosopher Susan Neiman has argued, the language swirling around the attack on Iraq by America, Australia and their allies is indicative of muddiness and obfuscation in both moral and strategic purpose. Neiman suggests that terms like 'moral authority', 'democracy' and 'freedom' were thrown about to disguise the manifest inadequacies of the Bush administration, considered at the time 'the worst presidency in American history'.[32] (The Trump presidency was yet to come.) President George W. Bush took America on a journey that sapped its energy, wasted its money and eroded its authority, credibility and legitimacy as the world's leading power. Its actions in Iraq were ill-judged, wilful and petty.

Those surrounding the president – Vice President Dick Cheney, Secretary of Defense Donald Rumsfeld, his deputy Paul Wolfowitz, Secretary of State Colin Powell and National Security Advisor Condoleezza Rice (later to replace Powell) – could not see beyond the 'shock and awe' use of American military power to resolve the complex political and social forces that lay behind the destruction of the Twin Towers. Rumsfeld, cocky, confident and convincing, dominated the Bush team, spurring the president to a decision against the better judgement of America's military leaders. Powell gave bogus testimony to the United Nations in February 2003, a sad betrayal of his personal authority and his long experience as a senior military commander. Rice, a talented classical pianist, understood well the analysis and study that one must devote to the mastery of even a single serious adventure into music, yet she appeared dazzled by the mansplainers around her as they dragged America into the quagmire of Iraq.

Without analysis, comprehension and preparation, war is to be avoided at all costs. Yet America rushed headlong into disaster. And the lessons that might have been learned from General MacArthur's political leadership in Japan almost sixty years earlier were forgotten or ignored when Ambassador Paul Bremer was appointed head of the Coalition Provisional Authority to administer Iraq after the fall of Baghdad. Bremer, who had never been to Iraq and spoke no Arabic, destroyed Iraq's Ba'athist civil administration, thereby establishing the preconditions for a destructive and murderous civil war. Incitatus, Caligula's favourite nag, would have done better. One hopes that Bremer had more skill as a ski instructor than he displayed as a civil administrator.[33]

As with the Vietnam War, the adventurism that distinguished the Iraq War was founded on profound misconceptions – it was not simply the product of lies. The weapons of mass destruction, chemical and nuclear, were a chimera: they did not exist, and there was no evidence that they did. Secretary Rice's casual reference to a mushroom cloud as the smoking gun was not simply an exercise in scare-mongering. It was a pre-emptive distortion of the facts. Yet the complete absence of evidence, aligned with the informed commentary of experts, failed to convince otherwise intelligent people that the preconditions that confer legitimacy on the decision to embark on war existed. For that reason, among others, as Britain's Chilcott Inquiry found, the Iraq War was as illegal as it was unnecessary.

In joining America's illegal war, Australia, together with Britain, acted illegally. Just as America's rationale for attacking Iraq was to alleviate domestic political pressures, so it was for Australia and Britain. Alliance with America, and the domestic political benefit derived from 'all the way with the USA', may have strengthened the domestic image of prime ministers John Howard and Tony Blair as determined and muscular leaders. In Blair's case, there was the attraction of snatching Prime Minister Thatcher's Falkland Islands mantle. And for Howard there was the attraction of burnishing his 'man of steel' credentials.

Yet none of this amounted to any kind of strategic justification for a war in which nearly 4,500 American soldiers and nearly 200 British soldiers died. No Australian service personnel died in combat in Iraq: Australia prefers to provide its flag and avoid casualties. According to research conducted by four American universities, however, nearly half a million Iraqis were killed.[34] The historical enmities between the Sunni and Shia communities in Iraq were allowed to explode by American civilian and military administrators who had no idea of the underlying grievances or the traditional compromises needed to contain them. As in Vietnam, the lack of cultural sensitivity probably doomed the mission from the outset. Complicated lessons are hard to learn.

### America's anatomy of war

There are all sorts of wars, and America has a taste for all of them. By and large, America is good at fighting wars – except when it is not. They range from conventional and unconventional warfare to include small wars, low-intensity conflict, guerrilla war, proxy war, civil war, interstate war, limited war, cyberwar, ground-sea-air-space war, urban war, grey-zone war, declared war, undeclared war, global war, theatre war, colonial war, revolutionary war, culture war, economic war, trade war and an endless list of categories that intersect more or less randomly.[35] This might be called the taxonomy of war.

But no matter what category of war America might like to engage in at any particular time, it follows a clear set of decision principles that together constitute an anatomy of war. While the following list is neither exhaustive nor normative, it may assist in the appreciation of what informs American decisions to employ armed force. This quick and necessarily compressed account of three centuries of America's wars – wars that also engaged its allies, such as Australia, during the past century at least – suggests a set of decision elements that illustrate the American way of war.

- America takes and keeps the initiative.
- Big forces defeat small forces.
- America spends what is needed to win.
- Attack is preferable to defence.
- War *is* diplomacy (kinetic diplomacy).
- America wages war because it can.
- Massive victory creates deterrence.
- America fights when it chooses.
- Forward basing creates options.
- War becomes its own end.
- Prevention needs minimal diplomacy.
- Strong leaders defeat weak leaders.
- Technology wins.
- America ignores casualty numbers.
- Force (heavy-handedness) wins.
- War trumps diplomacy.
- Domination, not just victory, is peace.
- America fights on its own terms.
- Retaliation justifies massive response.
- War is an end in itself.
- War demands massive military strength.
- America *is* its military power.

- It is America's anointed task to lead.
- Policy is the continuation of war.
- Power is preferred to persuasion.
- Presidents do not lose wars.
- American strategy is franchised.
- Moral questions are an indulgence.
- Policy elites construct echo chambers.
- Politicians determine America's wars.
- The military-industrial complex rules.
- Allies follow America's lead.
- Diplomacy is the servant of war.
- Generals win wars (personality reigns).
- Bomb or be damned.
- The CIA 'holds the ring'.
- Disaster is unimaginable.
- The civil–military divide is critical.
- Soldiers execute America's wars.
- Loss of popular support matters.

These elements may generate military success. They also harbour the possibility of strategic failure. To maximise the possibility of success in war, its conduct must be considered, deliberate and patient. Yet unsuccessful long wars have driven American planners – especially the academic civilian planners – to an impatience that persuades them that short wars are best. That impatience almost guarantees long wars as the operational norm. This creates a dangerous risk for America and its allies. As RAND Corporation commentary has put it:

> U.S. adversaries – be it the Taliban yesterday, Russia today, or potentially China tomorrow – bank on Washington's strategic impatience. They presume that if they hold on for long enough, Americans' desire for short wars will sabotage their efforts in time. If the U.S. objective is to win, the only thing worse than fighting a long war may be thinking it's possible to avoid one.[36]

For America and Australia, war and peace do not constitute a binary relationship, one depending on the absence of the other. America has been in a constant state of war. Yet Americans see themselves as peace-loving people, just as they see America as a peaceful country.

There is a contradiction here. The reasons for America's frequent resort to armed force are elusive. Americans are friendly, generous, gregarious and capable of extraordinary kindness. Perhaps, like Australia, America is beset by the kinds of insecurities that stem from being strangers in their own land, a beautiful but often forbidding and unforgiving land of extremes. Its early-seventeenth-century settlers were unable to tame it, and died, while its First Peoples looked on, simultaneously amazed and threatened. Perhaps, like Australia, America is beset by its inability to come to terms with its racial diversity and the deep misogyny that affects so many aspects of its way of life. Perhaps, like Australia, it projects its insecurities as threats, instinctively resorting to armed force to deal with them.

Yet, like Australia, America values peace, not as the absence of war but as the necessary precondition for happiness and wellbeing, which is where security really lies. So how do America and Australia go about building the peace that is coterminous with prosperity? It is to that question we now turn.

# 8.
## Peace

War and peace are often represented as the poles of an existential binary intrinsic to human experience, and possibly to 'the human condition'. The traditional cultural and popular image of war and peace was shaped by the Western preference for the kind of dialectic employed, for example, by Suetonius in his *Lives of the Twelve Caesars*, in which he described Titus (39–81 CE), who was more famous for building the Colosseum, as having 'facility in nearly everything concerning the arts of war and peace and ... capable of the greatest duplicity'.[1] Titus sounds quite contemporary. The same binary underpins the well-worn aphorism *Si vis pacem, para bellum* – 'If you want peace, prepare for war' – though a more ethical approach might be 'If you want peace, prepare for peace'. George Washington riffed on the war–peace idea in his first 'state of the Union' (as it later became known) address to Congress, in January 1790, when he said, 'To be prepared for war is one of the most effectual means of preserving peace.'[2] Clearly, the Revolutionary War continued to weigh heavily on the President's mind. But, as we saw in the previous chapter, peace as the consequence of capacity for and success in war was cemented into the American mindset even before the first meeting of Congress.

Tolstoy sharpened the modern conception of war and peace. In his magisterial novel – part fiction, part history and part philosophy – Tolstoy delivers an extended contemplation of the human proclivity for creating happiness, or at least contentment, out of suffering. *War and Peace* resolves the tension between the mechanics of destruction and the societal transformation that war is supposed to create by celebrating the triumph of the human spirit over adversity – for the winners, perhaps. The novel is at once teleological and theological.

But for America, war and peace do not constitute an existential binary. Rather, peace is simply the continuation of war by other means and *vice versa*, which partly explains why America has been prosecuting war for most of its 300-year history. Peace, like war, is a dimension of power. The Orwellian 'international rules-based order' is code for 'Pax Americana', just as 'Pax Americana' could be code for a more neronic phrase like 'Dominatio Americana' – it is all a matter of degree. For the fact is that just as America does not do war very well, its success at building and maintaining the infrastructure of peace is patchy. Like Longfellow's 'Girl with the Curl', when America is bad, she can be horrid. Quite simply, its default to armed force makes it hard for America to stay the course.

And that is the problem: notwithstanding the triumphs that have made the world a better place, America has trouble maintaining the energy, investment, momentum and perseverance necessary for a sustained diplomacy. So too does Australia: hundreds of billions of dollars on nuclear-powered AUKUS submarines is far preferable to tens of millions of dollars on a reinvigorated diplomacy!

Australia's AUKUS decision, endorsed by both sides of the political spectrum, is emblematic of the policy and planning conundrum faced by each of the three participating governments – America, Australia and Britain.[3] As President Eisenhower warned, the military-industrial complex has a vested interest in barracking for as ambitious and enormous a defence budget as possible. Profits are maximised on the back of technical and manufacturing risk, with 'project varia- tion' providing unbounded opportunity for contract rorting, massive overcharging and fraud. AUKUS is a tribute to the cynicism of the leaders of each of the three governments – especially Australia's – and the opportunism of their naval advisers. The ABC series *Nemesis* (episode three in particular) was gobsmacking for its revelation – in the live-to-camera words of responsible ministers – of the cavalier decision-making by enthusiastic amateurs whose knowledge of submarines seemed limited to repeat viewings of *Run Silent, Run Deep* (Clark Gable), *The Hunt for Red October* (Sean Connery and Sam Neill) and *Das Boot*.[4] To commit $368 billion (certainly a significant underestimate) over a forty-year timeframe (another underestimate) on the basis of a fear of China, guesswork and a hunch or two. As Hugh White has argued, the AUKUS proposal must 'surely count as the most disastrous defence-policy mistake in our history and one of the worst on record anywhere'.[5]

If war is a policy choice made by a nation-state to contain, control and defeat an enemy (which may or may not be a nation-state), peace is both a state of being and a policy outcome underpinned by law. In his vast and rather gloomy *The Shield of Achilles*, Philip Bobbitt surveys Europe's history of international constitutional development and reform, often (indeed usually) expressed in treaties.[6] His very bleak observation is that war is the crucible in which constitutionality is formed and in which constitutional change becomes possible. So peace, as a political and social phenomenon, is dependent on international constitutional agreement that establishes law – often expressed as the rule of law – as the glue that holds the edifice of peace together. And the rule of law itself depends on a fundamental acceptance that human beings have dignity and value by virtue of their shared humanity. Hence, peace is much more than the mere absence of war, just as health is much more than the mere absence of illness.

Like health, peace is a state of being where the preconditions – the causation factors – coalesce to produce the outcome we call peace. So conditioning factors like stability, confidence, harmony, wellbeing, contentment, security (in the Ciceronian sense of having no worries), equanimity, prosperity, environmental and social amenity, benevolence and graciousness together constitute the state of being that, when codified in law, the global community calls peace. For peace to be sustained, it cannot be the consequence of an armistice or a cessation of hostilities. Peace must always be the cause of policy, not just its consequence. Unfortunately, many nations, evidently including America and Australia, have a problem with this idea.

America has the extraordinary habit of authorising its diplomats to negotiate the legal frameworks that give formal expression to peace and the conditions and benefits of peace, and then walking away from them on the grounds of its own exceptionalism – its actions do not need to be governed by the agreements that constrain other nation-states because it is above all that. So America negotiated the League of Nations, then failed to join it. It negotiated the UN Charter, but gave itself and the other permanent members of the Security Council the power of veto. In a 2023 study to establish an index of UN-based multilateralism, the United States ranked last, below Israel, Ethiopia, Pakistan, Russia, India and Saudi Arabia.[7] It negotiated the Law of the Sea Convention, then refused to ratify it. It helped to create the World Trade Organization, then (under the Trump administration) stymied its disputes resolution system by refusing to confirm judicial appointments to its Appellate Body.[8] It also helped to negotiate the Rome Statute that established International Criminal Court, but subsequently withdrew its signature, informing the secretary-general that it would neither ratify the statute nor entertain any obligation towards it. It has maintained a testy relationship with the International Court of Justice. If peace, in part at least, is a product of a functioning international rules-based order, America is clearly not a major investor. It would appear that America does not have a clear contemporary idea of what peace is.

There are two principal reasons for this. First, it is easy to confuse cause and consequence, as Washington did in his first address to Congress. This failure in the logic of public policy is a common feature of political discourse. Politicians are frequent offenders when they allow the immediate to swamp the important, thereby perpetuating the missteps that result from unforced errors. Among military planners and commanders, this phenomenon is amplified when means become ends. That was a constant feature of decision-making in Vietnam and Iraq, which ultimately enabled President Nixon to declare the 1973 Paris Peace Accords as 'peace with honour', while in reality the United States (and Australia, along with the other allies) ended its war in defeat and dishonour. The strategic truth is that a pointless and dishonourable war usually leads to a pointless and dishonourable peace.

Second, within binary frameworks where there is no middle ground, it is easy to consider things only in the terms of their supposed opposites. False dichotomies are commonplace, particularly in the world of politics and political rhetoric. The 'either/or' proposition is advanced at the expense of the 'both/and' outcome: the patent nonsense that 'voters may own a house or pay compulsory contributions to a superannuation fund' was an argument against legislated superannuation in Australia, for example. So war and peace are represented in terms of victory and defeat rather than entirely separate non-polar states of being that are causally and consequentially different.

This has not always been the case, because peace has never been the primary objective of American foreign policy. The objective of American foreign policy has always been the acquisition and assertion of power. But, equally, America has not always acted in a manner that appears to undermine global peace rather than build and sustain it. And where it has acted in the interests of world peace, like-minded countries have been quick to join it, just as America is good at accommodating and implementing the ideas of others. Australia worked closely with America in its response to the calamities and horrors of both World War I and World War II. And if America hopes once again to back its military authority with the moral authority necessary to support its claims to global leadership, it will need to rediscover the distinctive world of peace and its preconditions, recognising that power must always respect its intrinsic moral dimension, and that, in consequence, diplomacy becomes the principal instrument for a sustained statecraft.

## The League of Nations and the United Nations

Though intellectually brilliant, President Woodrow Wilson may not have been the most worldly of statesmen, just as Billy Hughes was not the most diplomatic of Australian prime ministers. Like a blowfly at a picnic, Hughes buzzed around the Paris Peace Conference, irritating everyone but having little substantial impact on the outcome of the conference. It happened to suit the great powers, and President

Wilson, to exclude Japan from the 'high table' of global management on race grounds: race-based policies were in force in America and Australia, and in most European countries. It also happened to suit the European powers, and America, to cede former German possessions in China and the Pacific to Japan (a sop for its exclusion from the 'high table'), just as it suited the European powers and America to back the continuing colonial aspirations of World War I's victors. And it happened to suit the European powers that Australia took responsibility for the former German-administered territories of New Guinea. So Hughes got what he wanted, not a bit of which mattered to the key European powers, or to America. President Wilson, on the other hand, did not get what he wanted. Frustrated and outmanoeuvred by France's President Clemenceau and Britain's Prime Minister Lloyd George, he was ultimately defeated by his own Congress.

Wilson's post-war policy rested on two core principles: that the maintenance of peace was a responsibility shared between all governments; and that the legitimacy of those governments depended on the consent of the governed. In his address to the US Senate in January 1917, he said:

> [I]t is taken for granted that that peace must be followed by some definite concert of power which will make it virtually impossible that any such catastrophe should ever overwhelm us again … It is inconceivable that the people of the United States should play no part in that great enterprise … Only a tranquil Europe can be a stable Europe. There must be, not a balance of power, but a community of power; not organized rivalries, but an organized common peace … It must be a peace without victory … Victory would mean peace forced upon the loser, a victor's terms imposed upon the vanquished. It would be accepted in humiliation, under duress, at an intolerable sacrifice, and would leave a sting, a resentment, a bitter memory upon which terms of peace would rest, not permanently, but only as upon quicksand. Only a peace between equals can last. Only a peace the very principle of which is equality and a common participation in a common benefit … I am proposing that all nations henceforth avoid entangling alliances which would draw them into

competitions of power, catch them in a net of intrigue and selfish rivalry, and disturb their own affairs with influences intruded from without.[9]

Wilson translated the idealism underpinning his recipe for liberal internationalism into the more specific Fourteen Points enunciated a year later in an address to the US Congress. At its conclusion, Wilson noted:

> An evident principle runs through the whole program I have outlined. It is the principle of justice to all peoples and nationalities, and their right to live on equal terms of liberty and safety with one another, whether they be strong or weak. Unless this principle be made its foundation no part of the structure of international justice can stand. The people of the United States could act upon no other principle; and to the vindication of this principle they are ready to devote their lives, their honor, and everything that they possess. The moral climax of this the culminating and final war for human liberty has come, and they are ready to put their own strength, their own highest purpose, their own integrity and devotion to the test.[10]

'Wilsonianism', as it came to be known, was deemed a failure because the European hard-heads, the 'pragmatists' and 'realists', appreciated better than an American intellectual ever could that victory demanded punishment and reparations. The skulduggery and narrow self-interest that began the war was still in play at its awful end. The failure in fact lay with the hard-heads, who could not contemplate a world in which the rule of law could sustain an enduring peace or the idea that magnanimity could coexist with economic reconstruction. The collapse of Europe into World War II less than twenty years later demonstrated just how great the hard-heads' failure was. They considered war, not law, to be the force that shapes the international system and the nations that populate it – a view shared by Philip Bobbitt when he wrote that 'we must see clearly what role violence and war have played, and will continue to play, in shaping that system'.[11] It is easy, however, for bleak and destructive 'realities' to engender fatalism and pessimism, and even easier to give in to the anarchic forces that dismiss idealism as an adolescent affliction and humanism as naive. The pursed lips of the cynic always signal bitterness. But the cynicism of Kissinger and his coterie notwithstanding, the fact is that most American presidents have espoused optimism and values as the basis for American exceptionalism and its manifest destiny. Even an analyst as hard-bitten and provoking as Walter Russell Mead can recognise that 'the Wilsonian vision is too deeply implanted in American political culture, and the values to which it speaks have too much global appeal, to write its obituary just yet'.[12]

It is widely held that Wilson's, and hence America's, inability to deliver a liberal rules-based international order at Versailles was the product of his inexperience and ineptitude, the dominating influence of his policy amanuensis, 'Colonel' Edward House, and the bitter domestic politics of 1920 that saw Congress vote down America's membership of the League of Nations. House did play a significant role as the President's intermediary in Washington and in Europe, though his authority came from the President and nowhere else. He was a wheeler-dealer whose diplomatic agility during the peace negotiations of 1919 was to America's advantage. But House did not keep Wilson fully informed, and hence lost the President's confidence, which was not to the advantage of House or his President.[13] So George Kennan and Henry Kissinger, both incendiary 'realists', are deeply dismissive of Wilson's 'naïveté', advocating a policy based on balance of power in preference to legal and moral principle. If the Vietnam War, the war in Iraq and the lengthy war in Afghanistan are any guide, balance of power appears to eschew peace in favour of disgrace. Bobbitt wryly comments: '[B]ut I wonder who is really the *naïf* here?'

> A politician twice elected president from a minority party, who skillfully took his country from a stubborn isolationism to world leadership, is unlikely to have based his decisions on a childlike view of human nature ... [Kennan and Kissinger] exaggerate the role of litigation and then substitute that rather limited role of law ... for the more pervasive and profound pull of legal grammar in a constitutional society like the United States.[14]

Wilson's 'failure' was less in the conception of the idea than in its delivery. As the League of Nations struggled, largely due to America's non-membership and non-leadership, and Europe descended into political chaos and strategic catastrophe, Wilson's imagination and idealism were increasingly seen as an opportunity lost, a failure to remember and reflect upon history. Not by President Roosevelt, however. He understood instinctively that a law-based domestic policy that delivered improved economic equity, inclusion, participation and prosperity was the wellspring of a durable foreign policy, and that a durable foreign policy was the necessary precondition for world peace. As Daniel Deudney and John Ikenberry have noted, 'the America that brought unprecedented peace, prosperity and security into the international system was the America brought into existence by Roosevelt's New Deal'. The link between the New Deal and global peace after World War II was not accidental. The 'international rules-based order' formed out of the crucible of the Great Depression and World War II was an artefact of Roosevelt's New Deal, which provided the foundations of American foreign policy (where America had one) for the rest of the twentieth century.

With Roosevelt's death in 1945, the liberal internationalist mantle passed to Vice President Harry S. Truman. Truman was essentially unlettered, but a wily politician: a protégé of powerful Texans, he exploited their networks as he created his own. He was without compunction, unaffected by any moral scruple in authorising the use of the *Little Boy* and *Fat Man* nuclear bombs on Hiroshima and Nagasaki. A Wilsonian internationalist by predisposition, he was also aligned with Roosevelt's approach to a post–World War II dispensation, where global peace was not predicated upon the cessation of hostilities but upon the creation of an internationalist world order built on prosperity as a precondition for a sustained peace upheld by strong institutional structures. The Marshall Plan was the principal agent of economic reconstruction, and the United Nations was the platform on which international institutional arrangements could be established.

As it went to war after the bombing of Pearl Harbor, America was already investing considerable intellectual capital into the development of the UN Charter to secure global peace. As early as 1943, Roosevelt had commissioned initial planning for the post–World War II world, in which the global community would organise itself around constitutional arrangements founded upon the rule of law – the key elements of which ultimately found expression in the preamble to the UN Charter. This work was given greater authority when the major powers – America, Britain, China and the Soviet Union – met at Dumbarton Oaks, in Washington DC, from August to October 1944 to hammer out the basic structure of the post–World War II political dispensation. As the tide of war turned and the Allies sensed victory, the stage was set for America to lead the global community into what it hoped would be an enduring peace. President Truman opened the first preparatory meeting of the United Nations in San Francisco on 25 April 1945, which happened to be Anzac Day in Australia.

Speaking by radio from the White House, Truman said:

> Each of you can remember ... courageous champions, who also made the supreme sacrifice, serving under your flag. They gave their lives, so that others might live in security. They died to insure justice. We must work and live to guarantee justice – for all ... Let us labor to achieve a peace which is really worthy of their great sacrifice. We must make certain, by your work here, that another war will be impossible. We, who have lived through the torture and the tragedy of two world conflicts, must realize the magnitude of the problem before us.[15]

Deputy Prime Minister Frank Forde led the Australian delegation to the San Francisco conference. But Dr H.V. Evatt, the Minister for External Affairs and Attorney-General, did the heavy lifting. In equal measure acerbic and pugnacious, Evatt was not a popular negotiator, rather like Billy Hughes in Paris two decades earlier. But what Evatt lacked in style was made up for in his cut-through intelligence and relentless work ethic. Evatt laboured tirelessly to ensure that the middle and smaller powers could project their voices as effectively as the permanent members of the Security Council. In that, he won the grudging respect of America's lead negotiator, Edward Stettinius.[16]

In creating the United Nations, America did the heavy lifting. Consent, however, works when it is freely given, not extorted or imposed. So it was that in San Francisco, America worked hand in hand with allies like Australia and partners from every continent to secure world peace on a solid platform of rules supported by the UN Charter. That was America at its best, employing its power both to its own benefit and to the benefit of the global community.

## Franchised foreign policy and cleaning up the mess

Foreign policy is evolutionary. The American foreign policy institutions entertain themselves with an ongoing discussion that resembles the endless disputations between the scholastic theologians of the Middle Ages. The debate on whether Wilsonianism failed the twin test of pragmatism and realism, and whether Rooseveltism (of the FDR variety) succeeded because it passed the twin test of pragmatism and realism misses the point. Times change. The global situation changes. The actors on the international stage change. And the problems confronting them change. While theoreticians may see significant comparative differences between the foreign policy approaches of Wilson and Roosevelt (and Truman), the more important fact is that liberal internationalism remained a constant in America's twentieth-century diplomacy. The previous chapter dealt with some of the massive U-turns in America's practice of liberal internationalism as it franchised its diplomacy to the CIA and the Pentagon.

The CIA is in the business of intrigue and subversion, just as the Pentagon is in the business of demonstrating America's military supremacy, which means winning wars. The CIA-managed 1953 overthrow of the elected prime minister of Iran, Mohammad Mosaddegh, and the ensuing consolidation of the Pahlavi 'dynasty', went well. The next seventy years not so much. The Shah became increasingly despotic until he was deposed by the Ayatollahs in 1979, and Iranians have lived under a theocracy without any meaningful civil or political rights ever since. And America has no effective relationship with one of the principal players in the Middle East. Again, the CIA's role in the removal of Indonesia's President Sukarno in 1965 and his replacement by General Suharto may have saved Indonesia from communism, but annihilated the estimated 500,000 Communist Party (PKI) members and ethnic Chinese who were slaughtered in a frenzy of ethnic cleansing tantamount to genocide.[17] The CIA's meddling in so many of the countries of South America, including Chile (where Australia had a bit role), has done nothing for the continent's stability or prosperity, or for the security of its peoples. And the Pentagon's bombs have done nothing for the peoples of Vietnam, Cambodia, Iraq or Afghanistan.

But when, after calamities such as these, America reverts to its better nature, it demonstrates repeatedly just how effective its diplomacy can be. American diplomats are among the most applied and assiduous in the world. In the management of ongoing bilateral relationships, they practise a well-calibrated and constant attention to diplomatic detail. Their analysis and reporting are second to none. And when America puts its mind to a major international diplomatic task, it brings tremendous intellectual and financial resources, and its boundless energy, to bear. The creation of the United Nations and the design and implementation of the Marshall Plan underpinned the relationship that America enjoyed with post-war Europe until President Trump walked away from America's leadership role and insulted its allies as he did. President Biden and the State Department have worked successfully to restore trust in the United States by members of the European Union and NATO alike. President Eisenhower's 'Atoms for Peace' proposals in 1953 kick-started a period of oftentimes difficult and tense diplomacy, which endured until President Trump decided to terminate critical agreements unilaterally. Speaking at the United Nations, Eisenhower said:

> I would be prepared to submit to the Congress of the United States, and with every expectation of approval, any such plan that would, first, encourage world-wide investigation into the most effective peacetime uses of fissionable material, and with the certainty that

the investigators had all the material needed for the conducting of all experiments that were appropriate; second, begin to diminish the potential destructive power of the world's atomic stockpiles; third, allow all peoples of all nations to see that, in this enlightened age, the great Powers of the earth, both of the East and of the West, are interested in human aspirations first rather than in building up the armaments of war; fourth, open up a new channel for peaceful discussion and initiative at least a new approach to the many difficult problems that must be solved in both private and public conversations if the world is to shake off the inertia imposed by fear and is to make positive progress towards peace.[18]

This speech authorised America to begin the processes that led to the creation of the International Atomic Energy Agency in 1957. It also delivered the Treaty on the Non-Proliferation of Nuclear Weapons in 1968, after three years of difficult international negotiation and initiated the bilateral consultations with the former Soviet Union that produced the Strategic Arms Limitation Talks (SALT) agreements in 1972 and 1979. These agreements in turn set the stage for the Intermediate-Range Nuclear Forces Treaty (INF), signed by President Ronald Reagan and General Secretary Mikhail Gorbachev in 1987, and the Strategic Arms Reduction Treaty (START), signed in 1991 by presidents George H.W. Bush and Mikhail Gorbachev. In the world of containment and distrust, underpinned by the 'mutually assured destruction' doctrine of the nuclear strategists, these were signal achievements. President Nixon, justifiably regarded as the villain of Vietnam, took the momentous decision to initiate overtures to Beijing, which led to his visit to China in 1972 and the normalisation of diplomatic relations on 1 January 1979. The Camp David Agreements of 1978 and 1979, negotiated between Egypt's President Anwar Sadat and Israel's Prime Minister Menachem Begin, were a triumph for President Jimmy Carter.

America also played a crucial role in the reunification of Germany and Germany's ascension to its role as the economic powerhouse of Europe. President Reagan's 1987 speech, delivered at the Brandenburg Gate in Berlin, was a clear product of America's liberal internationalist tradition. Reagan said: 'We in the West stand ready to cooperate with the East to promote true openness, to break down barriers that separate people, to create a safe, freer world. And surely there is no better place than Berlin, the meeting place of East and West, to make a start.'[19]

America's authority as a global leader and its credibility as a resourceful broker and negotiator afford it a continuing role in European affairs similar to its role in global affairs. These were put to the test in a number of European crises following the collapse of the former Soviet Union.

The prolonged warfare and crimes against humanity that followed the dissolution of the former Socialist Federal Republic of Yugoslavia inflicted massive suffering on the peoples of the Balkans. The brutality inflicted by the military forces of several of the new republics against the civilian populations of traditional rivals shocked the global community for its barbarism and breadth. 'Ethnic cleansing' – a grotesque euphemism for genocide – was widespread. The NATO members were assiduous in their efforts to bring the warring factions to the negotiating table, but the Balkan preference for 'negotiation by media', and for serial grandstanding, rendered progress glacial. America mobilised its strategic authority and diplomatic power to convene the warring factions at a remote air base in Dayton, Ohio, to hammer out the Dayton Accords. Warren Christopher, the Secretary of State, and the ebullient and totally non-self-effacing Richard Holbrooke brokered a deal that only America could facilitate.

The Dayton Accords did not solve the problems of the Balkans. But they did bring down the levels of violence and provided a shaky start to further political resolution of the underlying cultural, economic, religious and social issues that have made the maintenance of any durable peace in the Balkans so difficult. The Dayton Accords also authorised NATO to deploy a peacekeeping force to the Balkans. This was particularly significant, in that 'out of area' deployment by NATO forces both signified a new role for NATO in the post–Cold War world and encouraged an expansion in its membership.[20]

## Working with 'mates'

America is good at taking the initiative. But for a nation so self-evidently exceptional and endowed with 'manifest destiny', America is also good at working with its partners. There are many opportunities for creative problem solving in a chronically disrupted world. Examples of America's cooperation with its European partners abound. President Trump's disdain for NATO and President Emmanuel Macron's gallic mordancy in diagnosing NATO's brain death are well known.[21] Yet America has supported and led what is tantamount to a reformation of NATO since the end of the Cold War. NATO's newfound confidence in operating 'out of area', together with its expansion (though the latter has not been without serious consequences), are not simply a reaction to changed security circumstances in Europe. They are completely consistent with America's historical ability to create an opportunity out of a problem. And while America and its NATO partners could have been more nuanced and skilful in the way they managed Russia's strategic sensitivities – now, there's a country with anxieties and insecurities! – it was always prepared to seize the initiative.

Australia's experience working with America has too often been that of a highly dependent subordinate, a willing acolyte ready to replace the national colours of green and gold with fawn and yellow. Australia likes to tug the forelock and display deference, yet is always reluctant to sustain casualties in support of America's foreign adventures. The more acerbic US military commanders comment that Australia's willingness to step up to the plate is code for its unwillingness to take the hits. Given Australia's enormous casualty lists in World War I and World War II, the resistance by successive governments to body bags is laudable. But if support for American adventurism is expected to be at 'no cost', perhaps the support itself has little merit or wisdom.

To many senior Americans, Australian participation is invisible. Speaking about Vietnam in the prize-winning documentary *Fog of War*, Robert McNamara observed: 'None of our allies supported us. Not Japan, not Germany, not Britain or France. If we can't persuade nations with comparable values of the merit of our cause, we'd better re-examine our reasoning.'[22]

Just when did the ANZUS partners Australia and New Zealand cease being allies? Sycophancy comes at a price when even Robert McNamara forgets us. When Australia has decided to act in the interests of its neighbours and itself, as it has in recent decades in Bougainville, Solomon Islands and Timor-Leste, it has been able to do so without casualties and without American forces. In those instances, America's support was both subtle and effective. America's contribution to Australia's national defence and strategic intelligence efforts is overwhelming, playing a cardinal role in ensuring that the Australian Defence Force can operate effectively and efficiently. And when America puts its shoulder to that wheel, it provides commensurate diplomatic support. In such situations, Australia does not act under the authority or with the blessing of America, but in partnership. That is well understood in the region.

Perhaps the clearest examples of America and Australia working collaboratively to respond to crises, establish sustained prosperity and secure the prospects for long-term peace have been in the field of economic management. During a visit to Seoul in 1989, Prime Minister Bob Hawke had set in train a trade liberalisation idea that had been around for a few years – a peak forum of regional leaders to give the idea the top-level authority it needed. With a positive response from South Korea's President Roh Tae-woo at a meeting in January 1989, Hawke outlined his thinking in a speech delivered the next day. Wishing not to frighten the ASEAN leaders (Malaysia's Prime Minister Mahathir Mohamad was opposed to the idea), Hawke omitted any reference to America, which generated some irritation in Washington. But eventually Washington got on board, and the first Asia-Pacific Economic Cooperation (APEC) meeting was held in Canberra in November 1989, at the ministerial level. Energetic diplomacy both preceded and followed that meeting. America and Australia conducted a busy diplomacy around the Pacific rim, but found it difficult to secure broad agreement for APEC to meet at the heads of government level.

Prime Minister Paul Keating and President George H.W. Bush were an unlikely combo. When they met in Sydney on New Year's Day 1992, Keating was his usual eloquent self in advocating the need for a regular heads of government forum in Asia, which, alone among the world's regions, lacked high-level collaborative leadership. For his part, Bush was positive but noncommittal. So Keating set to work to build both commitment and enthusiasm, knowing that, without American participation and support, the project was doomed. He met heads of government like Indonesia's President Suharto and Japan's Prime Minister Miyazawa, wrote more letters in a year than most prime ministers write during their time in office, and kept on Bush's case. With Bush's defeat at the end of 1992, Keating saw in President Clinton the opportunity he was waiting for. But Keating understood better than most that the opportunity of a lifetime lasts only as long as the lifetime of the opportunity. He pounced, playing to Clinton's sensitivity to the need for the US to restore its leadership role in the Asia-Pacific region. And Clinton responded. At Clinton's invitation (itself demonstrating clear US support and leadership), APEC heads of government met in Seattle in November 1993. APEC is now an established part of Asia's economic architecture.

In September 2008, the massive Lehman Brothers bank collapsed. When the world's largest insurance company, AIG, also found itself on the edge of collapse, the US government moved quickly to underwrite it. The global financial crisis had arrived: the world's major economies were facing a recession on a scale not experienced since the Great Depression of 1929. In his wonderfully panoptic *Fear of Abandonment*, Allan Gyngell comments with his trademark understatement that 'the domestic economic policy challenges facing the government from the Global Financial Crisis were immediate and practical, but its foreign policy implications were longer-term and institutional'.[23]

To his enormous credit, Prime Minister Kevin Rudd could see the danger and the opportunity of the GFC, and with characteristic energy set about instituting a fundamental change in the way that the leading economies dealt with global economic threats.[24] And he knew instinctively the role that America would have to play. The question was: how to turn a global crisis into an institutional solution? Speaking at the UN General Assembly in the days following the Lehman Brothers collapse, Rudd laid out the case for the G20 to serve as the peak economic coordinating body, rather than the IMF or the Financial Stability Forum, both of which lacked the political authority to instigate or deliver reform. Rudd then began a major diplomatic campaign to persuade President George W. Bush to back the G20 as the peak body and to see off the growing number of opportunistic counterproposals. In his last month in office, and in a display of indifference and indolence, Bush agreed and convened the first G20 leaders' meeting, in Washington DC on 14–15 November 2008.

Like Keating with APEC, Rudd appreciated implicitly that the G20 had to be institutionalised if it were to effect its new role, so he set off in pursuit of this new goal just as tirelessly. Rudd and Australia's diplomats, in an extraordinary display of traditional and shuttle diplomacy, garnered members' support for the idea, enabling Rudd to visit the new president, Barack Obama, in April 2009 to close a deal. Obama invited the G20 leaders to a third meeting, in Pittsburgh in September 2009, with a number of key European leaders still resisting. At Obama's invitation, Rudd opened the discussion of the G20's future. With the American president and the Australian prime minister working hand in glove, the G20 was transformed into the world's premier economic and financial institution. It was a singular diplomatic achievement.

### Escaping the doldrums: Rediscovering diplomacy

The reshaping of America's domestic politics over the past few decades, sketched out in Chapter 3, has impacted negatively on America's sense of identity and has exacerbated the insecurity that lies deep within America's national psyche. The confidence with which America set about delivering significant results that bolstered world peace and stability has eroded as it tackles its deep internal fault lines and the disrupted external environment. This has manifested itself most clearly in the tentative manner with which the US has dealt with

Russia, a protagonist it knows well, and the clumsy way it has dealt with China, a protagonist it knows hardly at all.

America's preoccupation with the dynamics of 'great-power rivalry' – a lazily reductionist concept if ever there was one – has blinded it to the nature and vitality of its own power, and to the fact that American power is qualitatively and quantitatively different from anything that has preceded it. Power is not a univocal concept, particularly when it represents a correlation of elements that are historically and socially unique. That is America. It is what Americans have traditionally meant by 'exceptional', and why they refer to their 'manifest destiny'. The fact is that America has no peers: it has nuclear competitors, of course, but no state has ever enjoyed the wealth, resources (of all kinds) and competitive energy that defines America. Unlike its would-be competitors, it is self-sufficient.

As noted earlier, America, like Australia, does suffer a deep-seated sense of insecurity that goes back to the beginning of European settlement. As Russia and China have discovered, the best way to play with America's strategic mind is to prod and irritate those insecurities. That is what has caused America to 'lose its mojo' and become rather less sure-footed now than it was for much of the twentieth century. From being a globally transformational power, it has slipped into a pattern of transactional behaviours that are both a cause and a consequence, in part at least, of its loss of strategic momentum.

In its dealings with China, for instance, America needs to do two things: act with considerably more self-confidence, and engage with its friends and partners. Instead of resorting to resonant but largely meaningless slogans like 'cooperate where we can, disagree where we must', as Australia's leaders do, America and Australia need to design a considerably more nuanced and comprehensive approach to managing extremely intricate and complex relationships with a nation that is itself of enormous complexity and cultural influence. Goal setting is critical. Ryan Haas puts this well:

The absence of a compelling vision of success for the United States' strategy with China is dangerous. First, if the American people do not know the purpose of their country's strategy, they will be less likely to support U.S. policy or make sacrifices in service of it. The absence of a vision also creates a vacuum in which American demagogues can frame the competition in ethnic terms, sowing the seeds of xenophobia and racism and tearing at the country's social fabric. Likewise, framing the contest in existential terms pushes the United States to pursue policies that seek China's collapse, while airbrushing the danger and self-harm that such a strategy would invite.[25]

For much of the past two decades, it has been stuck in a festering war in Afghanistan and the intractable instability of the Middle East – in important respects the unintended consequence of its own actions. President Trump certainly took his country down roads that were hitherto prudently unexplored. And, as he did, America's diplomatic capabilities were either discarded or allowed to atrophy. President Biden certainly moved to remedy America's loss of power and status, though they are more difficult to recover than they are to lose. It is as though America has lost sight of the critical role of diplomacy in its realising of its national power, and the fact that effective foreign policy is always an artefact of sound domestic policy.

America is endowed with a superabundance of the elements that together create national power. And as we saw in Chapter 3, diplomacy integrates the elements of national power to give them direction and weight. Military force, on the other hand, provides the brawn. While a nation's military capabilities are an important element of national power, they should never be the tool of first resort. It would appear that America has yet to take heed of the warning Eisenhower delivered at the end of his presidency, a warning that was as prescient as it was timely:

> In the councils of government, we must guard against the acquisition of unwarranted influence, whether sought or unsought, by the military-industrial complex. The potential for the disastrous rise of misplaced power exists and will persist. We must never let the weight

of this combination endanger our liberties or democratic processes. We should take nothing for granted. Only an alert and knowledgeable citizenry can compel the proper meshing of the huge industrial and military machinery of defense with our peaceful methods and goals, so that security and liberty may prosper together.[26]

Eisenhower's warning continues to go unheeded. The Pentagon and the military-industrial corporations continue to expand their parasitic relationship. Senior military officers retire into lucrative positions in the very industries that provide America's military capability, smoothing the way for industry carpetbaggers while providing eventual sinecures for those who buy their products and their services. And in a world of emerging, exciting and frightening technologies actively seeking military applications, such as AI, voices calling for even easier access to the public purse are growing louder. The retired generals are now flocking to venture capital firms to negotiate the cash investments needed to develop and exploit new applications. As *The New York Times* reported in December 2023:

> Retiring generals and departing top Pentagon officials once migrated regularly to the big established weapons makers like Lockheed Martin and Boeing. Now they are increasingly flocking to venture capital firms that have collectively pumped billions of dollars into Silicon Valley–style startups offering the Pentagon new war-fighting tools like autonomous killer drones, hypersonic jets and space surveillance equipment. This new route to the private sector is one indicator of the ways in which the United States is trying to become more agile in harnessing technological advances to maintain military superiority over China and other rivals. But the close ties between venture capital firms and Defense Department decision makers have also put a new twist on long-running questions about industry access and influence at a time when the Pentagon is under pressure to rethink how it allocates its huge procurement budget … The New York Times has identified at least 50 former Pentagon and national security officials, most of whom left the federal government in the last five years, who are now working in defense-related venture capital or private equity as executives or advisers. In many cases, The

Times confirmed that they continued to interact regularly with Pentagon officials or members of Congress to push for policy changes or increases in military spending that could benefit firms they have invested in.[27]

This opens up new and alarming avenues for the subjugation of national security policy to the extortionate demands of the military-industrial complex. Pork barrelling and its insatiable appetite for the defence budget has new and even more surreptitious channels for insider manipulation, mutual back-scratching and corruption. This undermines any credibility that America might have as an agent of peace.

Nor can Australia be complacent. Former prime minister Scott Morrison has decided to join the AUKUS gravy train in North America, while retired American generals and admirals on inflated stipends are now populating the upper echelons of the Australian defence department as 'consultants' imbued with little care and even less responsibility. They are essentially unaccountable.

It seems frequently to be the case that nations with significant military power want to use it, whether to signal their displeasure by deploying warships for strategic display or despatching gunboats to threaten countries directly. And, as David Vine has argued, the more bases a country has overseas, the more likely it is to use them.[28] Australia grants access to a few US military groups at various Australian defence bases. But whether that access or the bases America operates abroad truly help it to address the emergent problems of the twenty-first century is doubtful.

In all of this, Australia and America share convergent national interests and a history of bringing them to fruition. It is now time to examine how this odd couple should go about managing their unusual partnership.

# 9.
## Coupledom

If Australia and America were a couple that recognised that they had a problem and were trying to make a go of their relationship, they would probably be undergoing couples counselling, and the therapist would be asking hard questions. The disparity between the parties in terms of self-image and self-worth would be apparent – America, the indispensable nation, as Secretary of State Madeleine Albright put it, forever seeking to control the fortunes of its friends as much as its foes, and Australia, the perpetual acolyte, a permanent adoptee of the cringe, as Prime Minister Paul Keating had it.[1] America, overconfident yet curiously hesitant and tentative – until it is not – and Australia, underconfident yet curiously brash and strident, both harbour deep insecurities that impact on their agency and identity. America, long accustomed to acting with a jaunty disregard for international opinion, seems now to experience a kind of decision paralysis as it searches for self-affirmation in its own deeply divided society. And Australia, so afraid of putting a foot wrong that it cannot summon up the courage to put a foot right. So, while America faces the world with the smile of the overwhelmed, Australia is in a state of semi-permanent rictus, the carrion-eater's smile a sign of chronic dithering.

Both parties are under stress, and neither is coping well. At this point, America is coping less well than Australia, as we saw in Chapter 3. However, Australia's great failing, smug complacency, will take us in the same direction unless steps are taken to reinforce the communi-ty's support for transparent democratic practice and its respect for the rule of law. And both parties need to address serious flaws in their national character that, in combination, limit their agency as promoters and protectors of democracy and their credibility as advocates for a moral compass in the conduct of international relationships.

Australia's failure to adopt the constitutional amendments that would have recognised prior occupation of the continent by the First Peoples and their right to a constitutional voice indicate that racism is not even subcutaneous. Whatever some might say about the lack of detail and the discriminatory nature of singling out one ethnicity for special constitutional recognition, these claims are little more than code for preserving historical race-based discrimination. And the now entrenched habit of talking big but walking small when deploying forces in support of American military adventurism does nothing to build American confidence in Australia as a committed ally.

To take an example: America's GDP is about twenty times that of Australia, and its population about thirteen times Australia's. Yet during eight years of war in Iraq, America spent over a thousand times more than Australia (upwards of US 3 trillion compared with Australia's $2.4 billion) and sustained over two thousand times the number of casualties (4,431 GIs compared with two diggers – yes, two, and neither of them in combat).[2] And it is not that the Americans do not notice these things, as President Trump reminded his NATO partners.[3] Now this cautionary tale is not to suggest that Australia must saddle up for massive hits to its treasury or filling more body bags. Far from it. What it does suggest is that confidence comes from a frank discussion of risks, costs and strategic benefits, and from the ability to dissuade an ally from strategic folly rather than simply going along for the ride, which is the preserve of flunkeys.

Unevaluated assumptions as the basis for any relationship are dangerous. In the conduct of international relationships, unevaluated assumptions are harbingers of failure because the environment in which the relationship is conducted is so chaotic, fast-moving and volatile. When the global dynamics are so fluid, it is critical that the underpinnings of bilateral and multilateral relationships are rock solid, and not themselves subject to catastrophic collapse. And for those underpinnings to remain stable, they must be identified, evaluated and discussed. The reason for this is clear: the drivers of stable, long-term international relationships are values on which the parties agree and which they constantly refresh. The preamble to the UN Charter, for example, lists a set of values on which the negotiating parties were able to agree in 1945, and upon which the United Nations has operated (with declining success, perhaps) for three quarters of a century. This begs the question whether those values remain contemporary and operable. Values are not static – they evolve over time, just as societies evolve. So, periodically, they need to be reviewed and renegotiated. National leaders, senior politicians and 'international relations experts' constantly proclaim 'shared values' as the ties that bind. Australia, for instance, not only 'shares' values with America and Britain, but with India, Indonesia and Japan, massive cultural differences notwithstanding. But those national leaders, senior politicians and experts are well-practised employers of doover-words and platitudes to create the meaningless verbal blancmange that soothes the ear while it dulls the brain. One such expert announced in mid-2023 that the relationship between Australia and Vietnam was 'based on shared values, including independence, equality and the rule of law'.[4] With that kind of imprecision and laziness, anything is possible.

While these leaders and experts talk about 'values', they never define what they mean. 'Democracy', 'education' and 'prosperity' are casually thrown into the mix, with the public usually none the wiser. But these are not values, because they are not the drivers of how a society behaves. Democracy is a political practice, while education and prosperity are what sound government delivers. Just because a society values such things does not transform them into 'values'. Polysemy is such a beguiling thing: it's evident to most of us that 'book', 'chair' and 'man' have multiple meanings, yet so many fail to identify what exactly they mean by 'values'.

If, during their couples counselling, America's and Australia's therapist were to give them some homework, the therapist would probably direct them to explore the indicators of a strong relationship – the values that determine effective relationship behaviours. What is the power dynamic, and how is power shared? What is the nature and extent of trust? What generates confidence? How honest is the relationship, and how is honesty measured? Are there any common interests? How are burdens shared? How committed are the two parties? How do they rate their self-esteem and self-confidence? Is there mutual respect, and how does each party see the other? Are they 'compatible'?

## The indicators of a strong relationship

It would be surprising were any American or Australian leaders to have conducted a serious discussion about the intrinsic nature of the relationship and what gives it meaning, continuity and relevance. Apart from the roughly biennial pilgrimage to Washington by the Australian prime minister (who is occasionally rewarded with a state dinner and/or an opportunity to address the US Congress) and the sometimes annual AUSMIN talks (involving only the foreign and defence ministers on both sides), the Australia–America relationship has surprisingly few points of structured political contact.

AUSMIN has settled into a formalised reciprocal visit schedule where the Australian side always appears only too happy to take up the time of their rather busier counterparts, and the American side either seems reluctant to have travelled halfway around the world or to be relieved to have escaped Washington, or both. If the meetings are a set piece, the resultant communiqués are even more so, tiresome in their generality and bland superficiality. Everything is for the best in the best of AUSMIN worlds. The more or less empty theatre, however, is emblematic of a rather soulless formalism that masks its intrinsic banality. The ministers conduct a review of world events without ever addressing the more intriguing question of the institution's raison d'être – except as a sop to Australia's enduring sense of insecurity. And that in turn reflects Australia's inability to understand or to come to terms with its national power.

*Power* is one indicator of relationship strength that neither America nor Australia lacks. Of course, their power evidently differs in extent and in character. America is twenty times richer and thirteen times more populous. Australia's power is arguably more integrated than America's, with Australians enjoying a higher standard of living and considerably greater public and social amenity at the individual level. Americans, for instance, are over thirteen times more likely to kill each other in a gunfight than Australians,[5] and five times more likely to die of a drug overdose.[6] Remember, power is not just a scalar concept – brawn. It is also a vector concept – brains.

As we saw in Chapter 3, the elements of national power are well distributed in both America and Australia. Australia's principal deficiency is the size of its population. Rather than continually apologising for its perceived impotence, and fawning in the face of perceptions of American power, Australia would do well to engage with America on how both nations' power is complementary, and how it could work to mutual advantage, especially in Asia and the Pacific, and on the existential questions raised by global warming. Recalling Hans Morgenthau's injunction that diplomacy is what gives cohesion to the elements of national power, Australia and America would be particularly smart to align their diplomatic efforts and to establish much closer links between their diplomatic institutions, as already happens between their defence institutions. Trans-Pacific diplomatic secondments between Foggy Bottom and the Casey Building in Canberra would be a novel initiative with enormous potential. It would certainly build trust. And as the previous chapter demonstrated, when America and Australia combine in the exercise of diplomacy, they can exert considerable power.

*Trust* is so often declaratory rather than innate. Heads of government can, and often do, aver eternal trust and award 'no closer friend' status to international partners. But everyone knows that is a fiction, a statement of convenience when there is not much else to be said. Trust between America and Australia is often seen through the lens of the defence relationship, as though other domains that demand trust – trade, investment, scientific cooperation, copyright and patents, relations between law-enforcement agencies, to name just a few – are irrelevant. Yet in any buoyant relationship, trust needs to operate across the board.

As Simon Jackman and Shaun Ratcliff found in their 2018 study, Americans are intrinsically less trusting than Australians.[7] So it would come as no surprise were Americans less inclined to trust Australia than Australians to trust America. During President Trump's incumbency, 'Australians' trust and confidence in the United States as a responsible global actor' plummeted from a high of 83 per cent in 2011 to 55 per cent in 2018.[8] Yet by October 2022, polling ahead of the US midterm elections indicated that the alliance with Australia made Americans feel more secure, charting a rise from 44 per cent in December 2021 to 58 per cent in September 2022. Trust in this instance was security-driven; perhaps the truth here is that the lonelier you are, the more friends you need and the easier it is to confer trust.

On the other hand, during the height of the COVID-19 pandemic, Americans generally considered Australia's movement controls draconian and dystopian, expressing greater outrage than did most of the Australians who were living through them. One of the Republican Presidential candidates, Florida's Ron DeSantis, even questioned whether the relationship between America and Australia should continue.[9]

When fundamental differences on matters such as entrenched state and individual rights, a profound aversion to public goods (such as government-funded education and healthcare) and the absence of a universal safety nets are taken into account, it is difficult to establish common ground on what exactly constitutes trust. The point is that trust is fragile, it infuses the entire relationship, it cannot be assumed and it needs to be worked on. This is a key task for political leaders on both sides of the Pacific, including in Florida, which boasts a population almost as big as Australia's.

Perceptions aired for political effect notwithstanding, America and Australia do demonstrate high levels of mutual trust at the political and popular levels. There is nothing affected in the way that American and Australian leaders at all levels deal with each other. Lyndon Johnson and Harold Holt evidently enjoyed each other's company, as did Barack Obama and Julia Gillard almost fifty years later. And various American Pacific commanders-in-chief have not been backward in offering frank appraisals of Australia's under-gunned and under-prepared military capabilities – usually delivered more in sorrow than in anger as they commiserate with how much Australia's military leaders are expected to do with such small and underfunded forces.[10] In practice, mutual trust has less to do with shared history and shared personal values, though these may be relevant, than it does with social mores, urban amenity, public hospitality and convergent cultural underpinnings, as outlined in Chapter 6.

*Confidence* is always elusive. As noted earlier, America's seemingly boundless self-belief – its exceptionalism – and Australia's preference for a brasher kind of larrikinism betray a much deeper insecurity born of a shared inability to 'belong to' – as distinct from 'to own' – the continents on which they live. Americans and Australians have yet to develop a deeply rooted sense of place or a deep respect for the social and cultural authority of their First Peoples. Confidence is more evident in poise than in volubility, and on both counts America and Australia are quite well matched: they would do well to increase their poise and reduce their volubility.

Perhaps it is recognition of their similar problems with self-confidence that lends high levels of mutual confidence in their bilateral relationship. America is always confident that Australia will 'step up to the plate', doubts about commitment aside (see below), just as Australia is always confident that it will be asked to do so. Australia is always keen to pay what Prime Minister Robert Menzies called its 'insurance premiums' – its 'alliance dues', as Graeme Dobell describes them[11] – though whether America will pay out on the day a claim is made remains untested and therefore moot.

Part of the reason that confidence is elusive is that perceptions differ. America seems always prepared to dedicate treasure and blood to what it deems to be in its own interests – demonstrations of its exceptionalism, power and will – and less prepared perhaps to do the same in the interests of others. It was as reluctant to come to Britain's aid in 1939 as it was in 1914, for example, just as it is reluctant to do much to resolve the economic causes of the immigration pressures on its southern borders. Australia, on the other hand, had no option but to go to Britain's aid in both 1914 and in 1939, and perceives its support for American adventurism to be in its own strategic interests. So Australia mitigates its support by minimising the risks, as far as it can.

Hence, Australia seeks to engender American confidence in its reliability as an ally while keeping the costs, political and economic, as low as possible. American confidence in Australia remains high while Australia remains dependent on its security guarantees. This is yet another case of unbalanced mutuality in the management of bilateral relations.

*Honesty* has long been a core value in Australian and American diplomacy. President James Madison, for instance, took great exception to being duped by George III. In the lead-up to the War of 1812, Madison eagerly awaited news of Mad King George's demise in the hope – vain, as it turned out – that the regent would support an opportunity to negotiate the Ordinances of Council without necessitating resort to war.[12] While some US agencies with a predilection for a bit of diplomatic freelancing on the side – the CIA comes to mind – do seem to manipulate the truth somewhat, America's diplomacy values its reputation for honesty.

There are two principal vectors here, the White House (the President) and the State Department (the Secretary of State), which have different but convergent roles to play. The honesty of the President's promises and statements are always contingent upon their domestic political acceptability, while those of the Secretary of State and the State Department focus on policy formulations rather than political effect. The importance of this distinction became clear during *Konfrontasi*, the 1963 'non-war' between Indonesia and the British Commonwealth forces, including Australia, which supported Malaysia's independence.

The Menzies government believed that the ANZUS Treaty would necessarily deliver American support for Australia, were Indonesia to attack Australian forces or Australia. President Kennedy thought otherwise, more ambiguous indications from the State Department notwithstanding. And as the previous chapter acknowledged, America had other clandestine irons in the Jakarta fire at the time. To Menzies' disappointment, there was no American blank cheque.[13] Nor was there any lack of honesty and transparency, the 'need to know' principle notwithstanding. Indeed, the character of official relations between America and Australia, even in periods of relative coolness between political leaders (such as distinguished Prime Minister Whitlam's relationship with President Nixon in the early 1970s[14]), has always been based on honesty and trust.

The same spirit of openness obtains across the many levels of unofficial relations between Australia and America. Except for the rare occasions on which they want to punch each other's lights out – as they did in 'the Battle of Brisbane' on 26 and 27 November 1942[15] – fair dealing and easy familiarity are generally typical of the manner in which the two communities deal with each other across the Pacific. Whether it's in the America's Cup, tennis or swimming, where the two countries are fiercely competitive, sportsmanship generally defines the relationship. And although, to Australians travelling in the US, American honesty can appear homespun and reminiscent of Dagwood Bumstead or Li'l Abner, Americans travelling in Australia inevitably bump into bumpkins like Bluey and Curley or city slickers like Fatty Finn or Bazza McKenzie. The insouciance of which both Americans and Australians are frequently accused is often more a symptom of honesty and openness than of naivety or simple-mindedness. It is actually rather endearing.

*Common interests* abound. As citizens of affluent, highly urbanised first-world countries, Americans and Australians both place a premium on family, economic security, personal freedoms and a minimum of government intrusion into private matters – differing points of interpretation and weightings notwithstanding. As enduring democracies, there is extensive political alignment, together with the cultural, economic and social alignment discussed in earlier chapters. There are, of course, significant differences in emphasis. Americans attach a higher premium to authority, to social structures with assertive leadership styles and to individualism, whereas Australians are more inclined to egalitarianism, communalism and building a sense of 'we're all in it together'. Australians also tend to be less demonstrative, to be more reticent emotionally and much less outwardly religious, if they are religious at all. Australia's is a more secular society, America's a more ideologically driven one, especially in the political domain, as we saw in Chapter 3. Yet, putting these differences aside, Australians and Americans share core interests in freedom of political participation and practice, in individual rights, and in the fundamental freedoms of association, speech and religious affiliation. Support for democracy, too often declared by political leaders to be a 'value' as distinct from a basic tool for uniting the governed and those who govern, is an interest that both share, promoting it and protecting it where they can. Both nations sign up for peace and prosperity, and are committed to development assistance for those nations that are under-resourced or otherwise stressed.

*Burden sharing* only goes so far, at least in the minds of many in Trump-affected America, and especially when American ambition is itself part of the burden. As post–World War II America aspired to realise its exceptionalism and its manifest destiny – its 'indispensability', to use Madeleine Albright's term again – it was not concerned about how much its military dominance and the primacy that followed actually cost. A massive defence budget and a correspondingly massive global footprint was the price America seemed prepared to pay for its position as global leader and policeman. The procession of military misadventures, however, beginning with the Korean War and ending with Afghanistan, has dented America's self-confidence. It now promotes its global deployments as actions taken in the security interests of others – for which they should pay – and not simply in pursuit of its own security interests. So its European deployments have been rebranded as defence of NATO members, not constraint on Russia, and its Japanese and Korean deployments and military support for Taiwan are now promoted as defence assistance to deter

Chinese aggression, rather than to muscle up to China for America's own great-power purposes.[16] America's tactical withdrawal from funding, however, would almost certainly have strategic consequences: if America were no longer willing to pay for its membership of the single-member club it owns – the superpower club – it would forfeit its claim to be the leader of the free world. It remains to be seen whether that is a consequence America is willing to bear. We should hope that it is not.

America nonetheless remains sensitive to issues relating to burden-sharing – or 'free-riding', as some senior American leaders call it. So, to assess Australia's track record, it is important to look briefly at how America deals with its European allies.

As Fareed Zakaria argues in his excellent essay 'The Self-Doubting Superpower: America Shouldn't Give Up on the World It Made', America is a global heavyweight by any measure.[17] Its economy drives its power. Its military spending dwarfs that of its nearest competitor, China, by a factor of almost three to one, and accounts for nearly 40 per cent of global expenditure on armaments. The most recently available figures indicate that, in a global spend of around US$2.2 trillion, America commits over US$875 billion.[18] China spends just over US$290 billion. Personnel costs differ substantially, of course, so China may well get a better bang for its buck than does America. At the same time, America's technical know-how remains superior to China's, so the equation may be better balanced than it might appear at first blush.

Australia, at just over US$32 billion, spends almost thirty times less than America and around nine times less than China on its defence budget, but more than twice Taiwan. America fields just under 175,000 uniformed military personnel in approximately 140 countries, around 100,000 of them in Europe. Because the American force-in-being is designed for war anywhere in the world, it is impossible to determine the exact cost of America's European presence. A 2018 International Institute for Strategic Studies (London) study, however, estimated that direct US expenditure in Europe is between 5 and 6 per cent of the total US defence budget.[19] While the war in Ukraine has certainly led to additional expenditure by most NATO members, it is probably reasonable to estimate that America's contribution to European defence is around US$48 billion, or about 50 per cent more than Australia's defence budget.

Against these numbers – and bearing in mind America's preoccupation with its own funding pressures – Australia is most certainly not a freeloader. Not only has it historically carried the costs, financial and political, of its support for American military deployments in various parts of the world, but it has also been more than willing to meet its 'insurance premiums', as noted above, by signing up in the first place. And when it comes to other American international initiatives, Australia has a solid record as the indispensable backer. That is what epigones do.

*Commitment* is not a problem for either America or Australia when it comes to foreign adventures. 'All the way with the USA' is a generalised trope for Australian leaders, just as 'we have no closer friend than Australia' is the approbation of choice for US presidents.[20] But commitment is not really about the pursuit of shared objectives, important though that may be. Prime Minister Morrison's 'bacon and eggs principle' – the chicken is involved but the pig is committed – acerbically illustrated that commitment is an existential feature defining relationships, not activities.[21] So the question is: just how committed are America and Australia to each other? As former New South Wales premier Jack Lang said, 'Always back the horse named self-interest, son – it'll be the only one trying.'

For America, self-interest will always dominate, as it should (but does not always) for Australia. Self-interest, however, is what drives America to commit to allies and second parties: it sees strategic advantage in its core relationships, as it should. Sceptics will always doubt America's intentions, and at the very least its intentions should always be evaluated. For Australia, America's historical record of commitment to its allies, whether in Europe, Asia or the antipodes, is encouraging: within the practical realities of strategic management, it keeps its word. As does Australia. Perhaps the day will come when more thoughtful leaders avoid the sentimentality of 'friendship' and employ a more telling expression: 'there are no two countries more committed to each other than America and Australia'.

*Self-image and mutual respect* are critical determinants of any enduring international relationship because they bring the national psyche to bear on commitment and trust. Elements of deep insecurity notwithstanding, America enjoys a robust and confident self-image where respect for others is a function of its ability to control relationships. That is not the case for Australia, which prefers a more apologetic posture – Prime Minister Keating's 'cringe' – that reflects a longstanding sense of inequality and inferiority. America is considerably more self-affirming than is Australia, and hence more inclined to take the initiative and to represent itself as the more powerful party. But, as we saw in Chapter 2 and Chapter 8, Australia has considerable national power, and little to apologise for. The key to its power relationship with America is that the mix of elements that make up its national power means that its power is qualitatively different. It brings quite different things to the bilateral table, and for that reason (among others) it enjoys a high level of equality with America.

Naively, commentators often regard mass and quantity as the key determinants of national power. They are wrong: as the history of species extinction demonstrates, brains beat brawn every time. One simply needs to watch the Scandinavians on the international stage to see how apparent power differences are generally irrelevant. For example, and at the risk of using exaggerated stereotypes, America is a country with a remarkable capacity for discovery and invention, while Australia has a clearer instinct for innovation and adaptation – finding new applications for things that already exist. As the cliché has it, Australian farmers can do almost anything with a piece of wire. Australians do invent things, of course, aviation black boxes and wi-fi being just two instances. But Americans commercialise their inventions, whereas Australians sell theirs to Americans. The point is that there is an enormous complementarity between Australia and America. That is what needs to drive both self-image and mutual respect.

*Compatibility* is a strong bond between America and Australia, for reasons of culture, history and shared endeavour. Australia and America 'get on', because compatibility is ultimately a function of how both sides bring their strengths together to forge common destinies and resolve common problems. And this includes resolving differences between capability, capacity and what they bring to the table to generate synergy in cooperative and collaborative endeavour. Least of all is compatibility a function of equality, similarity or reliance on the conventional trope 'this is the way we have always done it'. Far from being a necessary co-dependency, as some suggest, enduring compatibility lies at the very centre of the Australia–America relationship. As this book has demonstrated, there are no two countries more alike than America and Australia, differences of culture, geography and history notwithstanding.

This compatibility really matters, because it is the foundation on which both parties can align self-interest with mutual interest. In the chaotic world of international affairs, such alignment is difficult at the best of times. But it is much easier when the basic cultural, economic, political, social and strategic sympathies are in sync. In a world of power shift – an emerging continental power (China), a declining continental power (Russia) and a very strong but quite separate continental power maintaining both power and influence (America) – the ability of any one of them to build and maintain enduring alliance networks is the game-changer. Since the end of World War II, America's 'free world' coalition has expanded beyond NATO, Japan, South Korea, the Manila Treaty countries and ANZUS to include almost every country in Europe, plus a number of other states. As Zakaria puts it starkly, 'the "West Plus" encompasses about 60 percent of the world's GDP and 65 percent of global military spending'.[22] And when one of those allies is itself a continental state (Australia), global leadership becomes more easily and effectively exercised. Compatibility facilitates the fulfilment of need: America needs Australia, just as Australia needs America. Compatibility is what makes that a statement of strength.

## The tools of institutional and structural alignment

The principal tool of interests and issues management is human inter-action – the agency exercised by national leaders and those delegated to conduct business on their behalf. Organisations and formal consultative bodies are all very well, and the fact that they exist, are staffed and need something to do is helpful. But their effectiveness and the quality of their performance is deeply dependent on the quality of the personnel assigned to them, and the quality of the national leadership that directs them.

Heads of government meetings are of the greatest importance. Political leaders give authority, credibility and legitimacy to the bilateral conversation. The quality of the conversation, both behind closed doors and in the public communiqués, is what really matters, however. To judge from the set-piece public media performances, the interactions often appear to be banal, not least because the individuals conducting them are themselves banal. Presidents and prime ministers, whether meeting in the Oval Office or in the PM's suite, need to appreciate that their agenda must always be substantive and strategic. They are not there for their good looks. They are there to conduct the peak business of a critical relationship. They must be as frank about their perceptions of each other's country and its performance as they should be about their mutual interests. That means both honest appraisal and identifying ways to address mutual problems, whether they are problems of social inequality, community and ethnic relations or political management. Australia and America have much to talk about, to teach each other and to learn from each other. The default setting – a concentration on what might be happening everywhere else in the world – is to trivialise the principal avenue for the management of convergent aspects of the national interest. Of course it is hard to do that. But that is the president's and the prime minister's job, and to the extent that they avoid it, they fail each other and themselves.

America and Australia have the established and valuable AUSMIN vehicle for annual consultations involving the defence and foreign ministers from both sides of the Pacific. These have, unfortunately, become rather ritualised in recent years, taking on the character of advertising shoots for toothpaste and costume jewellery, with plenty of gold braid and ribbons lurking in the background, rather than substantive discussions (as the lightweight communiqués show). But more than that, the media attention paid to AUSMIN blows its significance in the bilateral relationship out of all proportion. The defence relationship between Australia and America is important, and has an interesting history. But it is not a determinant in the bilateral relationship. It is an artefact of Australia's unhappiness with a 'soft' post–World War II treaty with Japan. As the price America had to pay for Australia's support, it is not in fact a security guarantee, but an agreement to consult. America was deft. Australia was dependent. In a sense, then, AUSMIN is the premium America pays for Australia's ongoing compliance.

A sound defence relationship is more a consequence of the strength of the economic, political and social relationship between the two countries. In contemporary global circumstances, structured dialogue between our treasurers, finance ministers and Reserve Bank principals is of greater import than discussions about things lying outside our mutual ability to affect – such as the war in Ukraine or Israel's military operations in Gaza. Ministerial counterpart discussions are really important, yet they are neither frequent enough nor sufficiently publicised and commented upon.

The same consideration applies to other very high-level contacts. The media love meetings between chiefs of defence forces: there is plenty of sound and movement, and, if the public is unlucky enough, a brass band or two with plenty of bunting and gold braid. Meetings between chief justices, vice-chancellors, premiers and governors and the plethora of engagement managers, opinion formers and 'influencers' (in a less trivial sense) pass unnoticed. Yet they are what put the flesh and sinews on the bones of a critically important relationship. They require much greater investment.

If the quality of the bilateral Australia–America relationship is as crucial as this book argues, the relationship needs careful husbanding. That, in turn, suggests the need for an institutional framework to ensure that so important an endeavour is managed strategically and not simply left to chance or individual enthusiasms. The Department of Foreign Affairs and Trade supports a number of bilateral foundations, councils and institutes that encourage broad consultation on key relationships. The Australia–Indonesia Institute, the Centre for Australia–India Relations (formerly the Australia–India Council), the National Foundation for Australia–China Relations (formerly the Australia–China Council), the Australia–Japan and Australia–Korea Foundations, the Council for Australian–Arab Relations, the Council on Australia–Latin America Relations and the Advisory Group on Australia–Africa Relations provide instructive examples.

These are all worthy enterprises, run by worthy people pursuing worthy aims under the direction of DFAT. As the various name changes and decommissionings indicate, however, they have not escaped their share of internal and party-political tensions. They are desperately underfunded. Consequently, they are largely tokenistic and ineffectual. Who from the Republic of South Africa, for instance, wants their cultural identity lumped in with that of Dahomey in the broader consideration of how Australia and South Africa connect? Senior departmental officers, or perhaps the Minister for Foreign Affairs, will (usually reluctantly) meet with these institutions' boards once a year, then happily ignore them and their suggestions for the rest of the time. That is exactly what is not needed in dealing with America.

Nor should a relationship as important as this be consigned to private initiatives representing private agendas. In Australia there are several private organisations that impinge on the broader Australia–America relationship. The American Chamber of Commerce in Australia (known affectionately to its supporters as 'AmCham') is a worldwide network-building association, creating links between American businesspeople working in Australia and between American and Australian businesses. It is extremely good at its job, bringing together the charm and ease at which Americans excel with generosity and hospitality. In commercial facilitation, it is without peer. Part of its success is due to the fact that it 'sticks to its knitting'.

A much more broadly based model is the Global Foundation, an Australian not-for-profit association that brings together 'prominent citizens from many walks of life and many parts of the world to align and work together in a coherent way to help shape the global common good'. With a conservative, idealistic and religiously informed charter, it convenes broad-based and non-threatening conversations attended by well-meaning, well-heeled international invitees to consider important global issues. Few comparable associations are able – or perhaps would wish – to run a letter from the Vatican Secretary of State on their website.[23] The Global Foundation is very dependent on the energy, enthusiasm and the motivational and organisation skills of its founder, Steve Howard. The risk that the Global Foundation faces, however, is twofold: its dependence on the highly motivated initiator, and confirmation bias among the membership.

The withdrawal of the founder, for whatever reason, often sounds the death knell for such associations. And with or without that person, the highly motivated and well-intentioned concerns of highly motivated and well-intentioned people can be mutually reinforcing without generating any appreciable change or material outcome. Inertia brings its own rigor mortis. This is the risk that all such associations face, though none more so than the Australian American Leadership Dialogue (AALD).

The AALD is a very private association, operating completely below the radar of public awareness or scrutiny. Its membership is not published, and attendance at its meetings and events has always been by invitation only. It would appear that attendees at its conferences and seminars meet their own expenses, paying a kind of conference fee or subscription to meet the costs of organisation, venue and event management, including hospitality. It is intentionally elitist, operating under the assumption that the best way to safeguard the durability and survivability of the relationship between Australia and America is to concentrate responsibility in the hands of trusted members of the political elite – mostly members of the Liberal Party and the right wing of the Australian Labor Party, with similar alignments among the US Democrats and Republicans – and their military and policy minions.

And who determines the membership of the elite, and whether they are trustworthy? The founder, Phil Scanlan, of course. Scanlan has been the AALD's driving force since its inception over thirty years ago, when the association was founded not by government design but as a result of Scanlan's personal concerns that the bilateral relationship risked going to the dogs and needed some high-placed support. Fortuitously, Scanlan found himself able to articulate his views directly to President George H. Bush, eliciting Bush's support and that of Prime Minister John Howard. Scanlan had considerable experience in the corporate world as a senior executive at Coca-Cola Amatil. His earlier experience was in the tobacco industry, where he defended the industry against medical claims of its ill-health consequences, especially lung cancer. He was influenced by neoliberal thinking and libertarianism, and was an early member of the now-defunct Crossroads Group and the Institute of Public Affairs, an ultra-conservative lobby group that subsequently morphed into the Sydney Institute.

Private-sector interests, such as the Visy Group, have been able to leverage their participation in and financial support for the AALD for their commercial purposes. This is the forum that successive Australian governments have endorsed as a principal vehicle for the conduct of informal, high-level and private interactions between Australian and American celebrities. With its complement of former politicians, the AUKUS Forum is headed the same way.

The elitist and privileged aspirations of the AALD found expression in its 'primary aim': '[To] help ensure that Australian policy makers and leaders in the broader community have knowledge of United States decision makers and real time understanding of their views on issues that we, as Australians, determine to be most important for Australia's national interests'.[24] The arrogance of this 'aim' is breathtaking, as evidenced by the demand that 'we' (the policymakers and leaders in the broader community) should determine Australia's national interests. Does it matter what a critic or a sceptic might think? Not to the AALD. As Vince Scappatura, a leading academic commentator on the role of the AALD, has written:

> When considered as a whole, the agenda of the AALD is not surprising given it accords with the long-standing bipartisan commitment among Australian foreign policy-makers and strategic elite to support and strengthen the US alliance and remain committed to a regional security and economic framework underpinned by US hegemony. In terms of ideology, the AALD clearly embodies the conventional alliance orthodoxy. The salient point is that the AALD's overriding objective is not to challenge this traditional thinking but to protect, strengthen and legitimise it.[25]

As a foreign policy clearing house, the AALD has largely supplanted the American Australian Association (AAA), founded in 1948 by Sir Keith Murdoch, father of Rupert Murdoch. The AAA was involved in the establishment of the United States Study Centre at Sydney University, and still promotes 'G'Day USA', a fiesta for the glitterati, as both a fundraiser and its major annual promotional event. It is evidently good fun. How it serves to build and strengthen a critical relationship, however, is uncertain. But what is certain is that a key diplomatic instrument is in the hands of entrepreneurs who have been able to take government along for the ride for over half a century.

That governments have been prepared to condone a form of diplomatic privateering for so long is remarkable. Whether the AALD's new CEO, the Hon. Tony Smith, former Speaker of the Australian House of Representatives, has the networking skills or the energy of his predecessor remains to be seen. And whether he has the personal authority, the diplomatic craft and the strategic foresight to transform the AALD from a jolly bunch of foreign policy hobbyists into a critical diplomatic asset is yet to be demonstrated. The danger is that consigning the future of Australia's most critical relationship – the Australia/America partnership – to self-appointed and self-directing enthusiasts is to substitute broad-based diplomacy with self-indulgent entrepreneurship. It takes foreign policy franchising to a new level.

## Another way: A conversation in the mutual interest

The management of Australia's most important international relationship must be reimagined and re-engineered. Of course there is a place for private initiatives, but they have to be situated within a strategic framework, the control and management of which is central to the constitutional role of the national government. While the engagement between presidents and prime ministers has enjoyed centrality in the theatre of the bilateral relationship since Prime Minister Curtin's speeches and editorials in 1941–42, the complexities and uncertainties that dominate the present-day global stage make it even more important that interaction at the top sets the pace for the entire relationship.

For the critical fact is that the heavy lifting in the American–Australian relationship is done at the political and strategic level. The heads of government lead, and they delegate. This is where AUSMIN and other set-piece ministerial meetings are also top priorities. AUSMIN needs to have new life breathed into it, becoming more political and less military, more substantive and less braid-festooned. And Australian ministers need to applaud their American counterparts' pronouncements less and advocate Australian strategic preoccupations more – especially concerning America's leadership and global role. If the international rules-based order matters – and it does – then Australia has a deep interest in how that order is constructed and how it is run. To return to Fareed Zakaria:

> The most worrying challenge to the rules-based international order does not come from China, Russia, or Iran. It comes from the United States. If America, consumed by exaggerated fears of its own decline, retreats from its leading role in world affairs, it will open up power vacuums across the globe and encourage a variety of powers and players to try to step into the disarray.[26]

For Australia, this is what really matters, not the shimmering distractions across the global firmament as America struggles with the consequences of its inability to see a way forward and to lead. On both sides of the Pacific, executive governments need face up to this inconvenient truth.

But it is not simply a task for the executive, critical though their role is. It is also a task for the national political institutions, especially the Australian Parliament and the US Congress, and for the members/representatives and senators who work there. Australia, employing parliamentary/congressional liaison structures that are well supported by the embassies in Washington and Canberra, needs to conduct a long-term influence campaign to work with America to deliver a better democratic deal for its citizens; Australian MPs need to do the same. Israel and Taiwan are brilliant at working Congress, manoeuvring legislation and resolutions that serve their strategic, political and economic interests even when those interests do not coincide with America's.

Australia's task is not to manipulate American political institutions in Australia's interests. It is to manipulate American political interests in America's interests, and therefore in Australia's interests. And for those who cringe at the thought of adopting a more assertive profile around Congress – 'they won't want to listen to us, and we won't get away with it' – the question is: what happens if we do not? With or without the re-election of Donald Trump, America is already in crisis: a crisis of confidence, a crisis of democracy, a crisis of equality, a crisis of leadership. These are crises that truly matter, to America and to Australia. It is in the interests of both nations to work together to resolve them. To sit idly by, worrying interminably and pointlessly about the threat from China when the threat of America's political and social collapse is infinitely more serious, would be a tragedy from which Australia would find it difficult to recover. For neither America nor Australia is helplessness an option.

Australia needs to move quickly to establish a properly led and funded campaign targeted at persuading America to act in its own interests, and in Australia's interests, to restore its authority, credibility and legitimacy as the leader of global democratic community. Even if America is not on a path to self-destruction, it is certainly moving towards self-absorbed irrelevancy. That would be a catastrophe for America and Australia. It is a catastrophe that can be avoided. If Australia is prepared to stump up a notional $400 billion or so on the AUKUS nuclear-powered submarine program to deal with an undemonstrated threat from China, what might it be prepared to spend on mitigating the greatest risk it currently faces: America's social and political collapse?

Let us imagine for a moment that the Australian government were to allocate an additional $40 million per annum to enable the Department of Foreign Affairs and Trade to mount an effective relationship-management campaign in America focused on Congress and some twenty or so state legislatures. Even if such a campaign were to run for a century, its cost would be one-hundredth of the notional submarine spend, and would represent infinitely better value for money.

The Doubting Thomases and naysayers will wring their hands and claim that Australia will never be able to cut through: our voice is too small and the Americans too stubborn. The reality, however, is that our voice is as large as we want it to be, and America will always act in its own interest. For Australia, it is not question of capacity. It is a question of agency. If Australia fails at this, Australia too faces failure as a state.

# Afterword

The dystopian world in which Australia would plough its own lonely furrow in the aftermath of an American collapse into itself is hard to imagine. So much would depend on the nature of that collapse and how quickly it occurred. America has endured parallels to the Trump phenomenon in earlier decades, perhaps most recently during the campaign that saw Richard Nixon elected in 1972. In his confronting reflection *Fear and Loathing: On the Campaign Trail '72*, the self-appointed dean of gonzo journalism, Hunter S. Thompson, offered a scathing assessment of Nixon and a wistful picture of what American might have been like:

> This maybe the year when we finally come face to face with our-selves; finally just lay back and say it – that we are really just a nation of 220 million used car salesmen with all the money we need to buy guns, and no qualms at all about killing anybody else in the world who tries to make us uncomfortable.

> The tragedy of all this is that George McGovern, for all his mistakes and all his imprecise talk about 'new politics' and 'honesty in gov-ernment,' is one of the few men who've run for President of the United States in this century who really understands what a fantas-tic monument to all the best instincts of the human race this country might have been, if we could have kept it out of the hands of greedy little hustlers like Richard Nixon.[1]

Nixon did not so much serve the interests of the people who elected him as he did those of the people who backed him: the military-industrial complex (of which Eisenhower warned), corporate America and moneyed individuals. His resignation in the face of impeachment left a broken America behind him, with the consequences of Vietnam weighing on a generation. America is resilient, however, as the Clinton, Bush and Obama presidencies showed, and as the Biden presidency has shown once again.

The Trump phenomenon fills many Americans, and many people who admire and look up to America, with a deep sense of foreboding. Those who might elect Trump are not mad. Nor are they 'deplorables'. They are voters who feel that they have nothing to lose, and that their protest justifies the consequences, especially for those who could lose even more than angry and alienated Republican voters might. There is a profound fatalism at play. That is what does not bode well, because it is so likely to be self-fulfilling.

With its manifest insecurities, Australia has a sense of dependency that America has filled for over eighty years. On whom would Australia depend, however, if it could not depend on America? That is the question that Australia cannot answer, and that it cannot bring itself to contemplate. Without America, Australia would be alone, adrift on its continent in a region that it does not understand and with which it has no affinity. And those infected with dystopian paranoia would imagine an Australia totally dominated and enslaved by 'communist China'. The renewed expressions of deep affection on Britain's part will last only as long as AUKUS holds out prospects of significant capital flows from Australia to Britain. Britain simply no longer has the power to manage a serious relationship across more than half the globe, even if it had the wish or intention so to do. Australia would be left with little more than its own helplessness.

Australia's habitual dependence on and deference to America renders it practically impossible to imagine what an isolated Australia would look like and how we might act. Would we become even more insecure and introverted as a nation, self-absorbed and self-preoccupied? Would we become even more remote – as if that were possible – from our neighbours, or, even worse, project onto them the fear of the 'other' that our sense of abandonment would generate? Would we become like Nietzsche's Last Man, anaesthetic, apathetic, bereft of agency, impotent, inert and unable even to dream? Would we hunker down, becoming ever more fearful and racked with uncertainty, building our defences and distrustful of effective (and affective) relationships?

Or would we see America's self-absorption as the trigger for constructing and participating in a different community operating under different rules? It is important to remember that when Prime Minister Whitlam foreshadowed a different Australia–America relationship in a different Asian community after the 1972 election, he was met with a fiercely negative reaction from President Nixon and Henry Kissinger. They resorted to threats and bullying. But in a state of decline rather than defeat, America would probably not care enough even to threaten. It would simply ignore us. Suddenly, we would feel even smaller than we do already.

There is, of course, a glimmer of hope. A Saturday afternoon visit to any Costco outlet in Australia, with its vibrancy and the multicultural faces of the new Australia, is a palpable reminder of the truth of L.P. Hartley's observation that 'the past is a foreign country'.

To comprehend the sense of desolation and isolation that Australia might confront, it would be salutary for all members of the Australian Parliament, and perhaps all members of the Australian public, to settle down at the cinema one Saturday afternoon and watch a screening of *On the Beach*, a post-apocalypse film starring Ava Gardner, Gregory Peck and Anthony Perkins. After a nuclear holocaust, Melbourne is the last city in the world to succumb; as Gardner is alleged to have said, '*On the Beach* is a story about the end of the world, and Melbourne sure is the right place to film it.'[2] But what infuses the film more than the inevitability of death is the pervading sense of helplessness. In the last scene, a Salvation Army banner flaps its final message: 'There is still time, Brother.'

Australia is not helpless, however, or at least not yet. Let us see if governments can rise to this challenge while there is still time.

# Notes

## Prologue

1   Like his predecessors and successors, President Theodore Roosevelt was not remotely interested in generating admiration, adulation and affection in the Australian community. A hard-nosed defender of American self-interest, Roosevelt was determined to deter Japanese strategic ambition through a show of naval power with a global reach. So Rear Admiral Sperry, the fleet commander, was instructed to gather intelligence to help fashion plans for the capture of Australian ports, should war with Japan eventuate. Gary Brown and Laura Rayner commented on this in their *Current Issues Brief* to celebrate the first fifty years of ANZUS: 'When the fleet arrived in each Australian port to a tumultuous welcome, its intelligence team went to work compiling detailed reports on the defences and infrastructure of each city as part of invasion plans. The hospitality of the local population undoubtedly made it easier for the fleet's officers to gain insight into Australia's strengths and weaknesses, and probably direct access to the information necessary to prepare plans to capture the new nation's major cities.' (Gary Brown & Laura Rayner, 'Upside, Downside: ANZUS After Fifty Years', *Current Issues Brief*, no. 3, 2001–02, p. 2.) Oblivious to all this, the citizens of Sydney, Melbourne and Albany fawned and feted. Australians still do.

2   Defence Strategic Review (2023), Executive Summary and paragraph 6.3, www.defence.gov.au/about/reviews-inquiries/defence-strategic-review.

3   Abraham Lincoln, "The perpetuation of our political institutions: Address before the young men's Lyceum of Springfield", Springfield, Illinois, 27 January 1838.

4   Emma Lazarus, *The New Colossus*, reproduced on a casting found on the inner wall of the pedestal on which stands the Statue of Liberty in New York Harbor.

5   Abraham Lincoln, Springfield Address, 1838.

6   Prime Minister Robert G. Menzies, 'Wartime broadcast', 3 September 1939, www.awm.gov.au/articles/encyclopedia/prime_ministers/menzies.

7   John Curtin, 'The task ahead', *The Herald*, 27 December 1941, https://john.curtin.edu.au/pmportal/text/00468.html.

8       For the transcript and audio file of this remarkable speech, see John Curtin's 'Speech to America', 14 March 1942, https://john.curtin.edu.au/audio/00434.html.

9       Richard Marles, 'Address: Center for Strategic and International Studies', 12 July 2022, www.minister.defence.gov.au/speeches/2022-07-12/address-center-strategic-and-international-studies-csis.

10      Clinton Fernandes, *Sub-Imperial Power: Australia in the international arena* (Melbourne: Melbourne University Press, 2022), p. 21.

11      See Troy Bramston, 'Defending Taiwan against Beijing is a must, says Peter Dutton', *The Australian*, 12 November 2021; and Peter Hartcher, 'Dutton raises stakes over Taiwan with talk of war', *The Sydney Morning Herald*, 16 November 2021.

12      See https://data.worldbank.org/country.

13      See H.S. Jones & J.E. Powell, *Oxford Classical Texts, Thucydidis: Historiae, Vol. 1: Tomus Prior* (revised edition) (Oxford: Oxford University Press, 1942), chapter 1. Anyone exploring this reference will enjoy Enoch Powell's elegant introduction, though to do so will require a familiarity with Latin at least comparable with the ability to read Thucydides' angular Greek.

## Chapter 1. Beginnings

1       For an entertaining account of crime in early seventeenth-century England, see Cara Swinden, 'Crime and the common law in England, 1580–1640', Honors thesis, University of Richmond, 1992, https://scholarship.richmond.edu/honors-theses/769.

2       For an overview of the British justice system in the seventeenth century, see the informative website *Proceedings of the Old Bailey, 1674–1913* at www.oldbaileyonline.org/index.jsp. Synoptic coverage of justice in the sixteenth century is difficult to find and access. For a comprehensive general coverage of the subject from medieval times, see John Briggs et al., *Crime and Punishment in England: An introductory history* (London: Routledge, 1996); and Andrew Barrett & Chris Harrison, *Crime and Punishment in England: A sourcebook* (London: Routledge, 1998).

3       See the History Press's amusing note 'The land of the "free": Criminal transportation to America', at www.thehistorypress.co.uk/articles/the-land-of-the-free-criminal-transportation-to-america.

4       For a useful summary, see the National Archives (UK) website entry 'Criminal transportation', at www.nationalarchives.gov.uk/help-with-your-research/research-guides/criminal-transportation.

5       See Jean Fitzsimmons, *The Transportation of Convicts to New South Wales, Australia, 1787–1840: Could free men and bondsmen exist together?*, MA thesis, University of Windsor, 1970, https://scholar.uwindsor.ca/cgi/viewcontent.cgi?article=7853&context=etd.

6      John Dunmore Lang, *Transportation and Colonization; or, The causes of the comparative failure of the transportation system in the Australian colonies: with suggestions for ensuring its future efficiency in subserviency to extensive colonization* (London: 1837), pp. 38–39, https://repository. wellesley.edu/object/wellesley30868.

7      Thomas Keneally, *A Commonwealth of Thieves: The improbable birth of Australia* (Sydney: Random House Australia, 2005). See Keneally's summary at www.penguinrandomhouse.ca/books/91467/a-commonwealth -of-thieves-by-thomas-keneally/9781400079568/excerpt.

8      Lang, *Transportation and Colonization*, pp. 38–39.

9      For an informative commentary on how New South Wales was chosen over its African competitors, see John Gascoigne, 'From Captain Cook to the First Fleet: How Botany Bay was chosen over Africa as a new British penal colony', *The Conversation*, 29 April 2020, https://theconversation. com/from-captain-cook-to-the-first-fleet-how-botany-bay-was-chosen -over-africa-as-a-new-british-penal-colony-128002.

10     Smyth's journal is held in the Mitchell Library, State Library of New South Wales. A transcription is available at https://acms.sl.nsw.gov.au/_ transcript/2015/D36405/a1085.html.

11     See Kieran Sheedy, *The Tellicherry Five: The transportation of Michael Dwyer & the Wicklow Rebels* (Dublin: The Woodfield Press, 1997). This author is a direct descendent of Hugh Byrne.

12     George Tanham, a former vice-president of the RAND Corporation, was a gifted strategist and an amusing raconteur. This gem was uttered during a dinner conversation with the author at the Cosmos Club, Washington, in September 1989.

13     See Alan Frost's cautionary entry 'Matra, James Mario (Maria) (1746– 1806)', *Australian Dictionary of Biography* (Melbourne: Melbourne University Press, 2005), https://adb.anu.edu.au/biography/matra-james- mario-maria-13084. Frost's article 'James Mario Matra: Voyager with Cook' (http://commonplace.online/article/james-mario-matra) is also informative, and leaves the impression that Matra was a 'thruster' with little enough to recommend him.

14     A.W. Greig published an informative note, 'Who was James Maria Matra?', in *The Argus* on 28 April 1917 https://trove.nla.gov.au/newspaper/ article/1613867.

15     E. Daniel Potts & Annette Potts, 'The Negro and the Australian Gold Rushes, 1852-1857', *Pacific Historical Review*, vol. 37, no. 4, 1968, pp. 381–99.

16     'John Martin', *People Australia* (Canberra: ANU, National Centre of Biography), https://peopleaustralia.anu.edu.au/biography/martin- john-30316/text37596.

17    See Mollie Gillen, 'John Martin (1757–1837)', *The Founders of Australia: A biographical dictionary of the First Fleet* (1989), p. 239, https://peopleaustralia.anu.edu.au/biography/martin-john-30316; and 'John Randall (1764–1822)', *People Australia* (Canberra: ANU, National Centre of Biography) https://peopleaustralia.anu.edu.au/biography/randall-john-30314.

18    'John Randall (1764–1822)', *People Australia* (Canberra: ANU, National Centre of Biography) https://peopleaustralia.anu.edu.au/biography/randall-john-30314.

19    Margaret Park, 'Blue, William (Billy) (c.1767–1834)', *Australian Dictionary of Biography, Supplement* (Melbourne: Melbourne University Press, 2005), https://adb.anu.edu.au/biography/blue-william-billy-12804.

20    See John S. Cumpston, 'Bunker, Eber (1761–1836)', *Australian Dictionary of Biography* (Melbourne: Melbourne University Press, 1966), vol. 1, https://adb.anu.edu.au/biography/bunker-eber-1849.

21    See Benjamin Wilson Mountford and Stephen Tuffnell, 'How gold rushes helped the modern world', *The Conversation*, 4 April 2018, https://theconversation.com/how-gold-rushes-helped-make-the-modern-world-91746.

22    For a short historical overview of the abuse of Native American land rights, see 'Removing Native Americans from Their Land', Library of Congress presentation, www.loc.gov/classroom-materials/immigration/native-american/removing-native-americans-from-their-land.

23    For a kinder and more sympathetic comment on Longfellow and his poetry, see James Marcus, 'What is there to love about Longfellow?', *The New Yorker*, 1 June 2020, www.newyorker.com/magazine/2020/06/08/what-is-there-to-love-about-longfellow.

24    Barsha Roy, 'How is Edward Norton related to Pocahontas? Ancestral family tree explored amid Finding Your Roots revelations', 3 January 2023, www.sportskeeda.com/amp/pop-culture/how-edward-norton-related-pocahontas-ancestral-family-tree-explored-amid-finding-your-roots-revelations.

25    'By the United States in Congress assembled. August 7, 1786: An ordinance for the regulation of Indian affairs', Library of Congress, www.loc.gov/resource/bdsdcc.19601/?st=pdf&pdfPage=1.

26    *Ibid*.

27    President James Munroe, 'Second inaugural speech', 6 March 1821, https://avalon.law.yale.edu/19th_century/monroe2.asp.

28    President Andrew Jackson, 'First inaugural speech', 4 March 1829, https://avalon.law.yale.edu/19th_century/jackson1.asp.

29    'An Act to provide for an exchange of lands with the Indians residing in any of the states or territories, and for their removal west of the river

Mississippi', 28 May 1830, https://memory.loc.gov/cgi-bin/ampage?collId=llsl&fileName=004/llsl004.db&recNum=458 et seq.

30    See David Grann, *Killers of the Flower Moon: The Osage murders and the birth of the FBI* (New York: Doubleday, 2017). This is a compelling and moving account of a conspiracy to dispossess native Americans. The State of Oklahoma has effectively legislated to proscribe the book.

31    King George the Third, 'Instructions for Our Trusty George R [*sic*] and well beloved Arthur Phillip Esq. Our Captain General and Governor in Chief, in and over (LS.) Our Territory of New South Wales and its Dependencies', 25 April 1787, www.foundingdocs.gov.au/resources/transcripts/nsw2_doc_1787.pdf (with very slight editorial amendments to the text by the author for clarity).

32    Peter Dowling, *Fatal Contact: How epidemics nearly wiped out Australia's First Peoples* (Melbourne: Monash University Press, 2021).

33    Raymond Evans & Robert Ørsted-Jensen, '"I cannot say the numbers that were killed": Assessing violent mortality on the Queensland frontier', paper presented at the 'Conflict in History' Conference, 7–11 July 2014, p. 4.

34    Lyndall Ryan et al., *Colonial Frontier Massacres in Australia, 1788–1930*, website, University of Newcastle, 2018, https://c21ch.newcastle.edu.au/colonialmassacres.

35    See Paul Daley, 'Why a Hann Highway could be a monument to Indigenous genocide', *The Guardian*, 27 September 2019, www.theguardian.com/australia-news/postcolonial-blog/2019/sep/27/why-a-hann-highway-could-be-a-monument-to-indigenous-genocide.

36    David Marr, *Killing for Country* (Melbourne: Black Inc., 2023).

37    See Mark McKenna, 'Follow the Sheep', *Australian Book Review*, no. 458, October 2023.

38    See Paul Daley, 'As the toll of Australia's frontier brutality keeps climbing, truth telling is long overdue', *The Guardian*, 4 March 2019, www.theguardian.com/australia-news/2019/mar/04/as-the-toll-of-australias-frontier-brutality-keeps-climbing-truth-telling-is-long-overdue.

39    See Paul Daley, 'Fault lines at the Australian War Memorial', *Meanjin*, Autumn 2021, https://meanjin.com.au/essays/fault-lines.

40    W.M. Hughes, 'Honouring the states', *The Sydney Morning Herald*, 13 March 1913.

## Chapter 2. Australia

1    Donald Horne, *The Lucky Country* (Melbourne: Penguin Books, 5th ed., 2009), 'Introduction to the fifth edition', p. xi. In the first edition, Horne saves this blast until the final chapter (p. 233 in the 2009 printing). Curiously, the fifth edition interpolates the definite article between the third and fourth words in the second sentence – reducing its immediacy.

2     See Joanna Walters, '"Shithole" remark by Trump makes global
      headlines – but it doesn't quite translate', *The Guardian*, 13 January 2018.
3     Winston Churchill, BBC Broadcast, 1 October 1939, https://ww2memories.
      wordpress.com/2011/09/24/
      churchills-ww2-speech-to-the-nation-october-1939.
4     Julianne Schultz, *The Idea of Australia: A search for the soul of the nation*
      (Sydney: Allen & Unwin, 2022), pp. 1–2.
5     For an analysis of the origins of Australia's extraordinary early labour
      input per capita and its higher labour productivity, see Ian McLean, 'Why
      was Australia so rich?', School of Economics, University of Adelaide, 2005,
      https://media.adelaide.edu.au/economics/papers/doc/wp2005-11.pdf.
6     Clare Wright, '"A Splendid Object Lesson": A transnational perspective on
      the birth of the Australian nation', *Journal of Women's History*, vol. 26,
      no. 4, 2014, p. 17. See also her outstanding book *You Daughters of
      Freedom: The Australians who won the vote and inspired the world*
      (Melbourne: Text Publishing Company, 2018).
7     Marilyn Lake, *Progressive New World: How settler colonialism and
      Transpacific exchange shaped American reform* (Cambridge, MA: Harvard
      University Press, 2018), especially chapter 1.
8     Lake, p. 68.
9     Christopher Mayes, 'Cultivating a nation: Why the mythos of the
      Australian farmer is problematic', *The Conversation*, 11 January 2019,
      https://theconversation.com/cultivating-a-nation-why-the-mythos-of-
      the-australian-farmer-is-problematic-106517.
10    Mayes, 'Cultivating a nation'.
11    Australian Government, 'Job Outlook and the Labour Market Information
      Portal', 2022, https://labourmarketinsights.gov.au/industries/industry-
      details?industryCode=B#:~:text=Mining%20is%20a%20small%20
      employing,of%20minerals%2C%20oil%20and%20gas.
12    Alfred Korzybski, 'A Non-Aristotelian System and its Necessity for Rigour
      in Mathematics and Physics', Paper presented before the American
      Mathematical Society at the New Orleans, Louisiana Meeting of the
      American Association for the Advancement of Science, 28 December 1931,
      http://esgs.free.fr/uk/art/sands-sup3.pdf.
13    Jim Stanford, 'Surging mining sector profits are distorting Australia's
      economy', The Australia Institute, Canberra, 8 May 2023, https://
      australiainstitute.org.au/post/surging-mining-sector-profits-are-
      distorting-australias-economy.
14    Miriam Cosic, 'How we wanted to be seen', *The Australian*, 1 January
      2008.
15    Matron Elsie Grant (1889–1927) is the author's great-aunt.
16    Quoted by Rob Harris, 'How John Howard stepped in to protect Don
      Bradman's name', *The Sydney Morning Herald*, 1 January 2021.

17    Corporations Regulations 2001, Schedule 6, Part 2 'Names unacceptable for registration', rule 6203, (i-v) and Part 3 'Restricted words and phrases', rule 6317 and 6317A and Part 4, 'Consent required to use restricted words and phrases', rule 6401.

18    Tony Abbott, 'Now is a good time to reassess what it means for us to be Australian', *The Australian*, 16 July 2020.

19    Francis Fukuyama, *Identity* (London: Profile Books, 2019), pp. 9–10.

20    See the document prepared by the Department of Prime Minister and Cabinet in advance of the 2023 Quad Leaders' Summit: www.pmc.gov.au/sites/default/files/resource/download/2023-quad-leaders-summit_0.pdf.

21    Australian Government, Department of Prime Minister and Cabinet, *The Sydney Declaration*, 18 March 2018, https://aseanaustralia.pmc.gov.au/Declaration.html.

22    Scott Morrison, Transcript of a virtual summit meeting with Prime Minister Narendra Modi, 4 June 2020, https://pmtranscripts.pmc.gov.au/release/transcript-42843.

23    Penny Wong, 'Australian Values in a Time of Disruption – Griffith Asia Institute's "Perspectives: Asia" Lecture', Griffith University, 3 August 2017, www.pennywong.com.au/media-hub/speeches/australian-values-in-a-time-of-disruption-griffith-asia-institute-s-perspectives-asia-lecture-griffith-university-brisbane-03-08-2017.

24    Joseph S. Nye, 'Redefining the National Interest', *Foreign Affairs*, 1 July 1999, pp. 22–35, www.foreignaffairs.com/articles/united-states/1999-07-01/redefining-national-interest.

25    Commonwealth of Australia, Department of Foreign Affairs and Trade, *In the National Interest*, 20 August 1997, https://apo.org.au/node/74891.

26    Commonwealth of Australia, Department of Foreign Affairs and Trade, *Advancing the National Interest*, 10 February 2003, https://apo.org.au/node/74888.

27    Catherine King & Laura Tingle, *7.30*, ABC TV, 8 September 2023.

28    Jeremy Bentham, *Introduction to the Principles of Morals and Legislation* (Oxford: The Clarendon Press, 1907), p. 3, https://oll-resources.s3.us-east-2.amazonaws.com/oll3/store/titles/278/0175_Bk.pdf.

29    Bentham, *Introduction to the Principles of Morals and Legislation*, p. 1.

30    Bentham, *Introduction to the Principles of Morals and Legislation*, p. 2.

31    Hans J. Morgenthau, 'Six Principles of Political Realism', *Politics Among Nations: The struggle for power and peace* (New York: Alfred A. Knopf, 1978), pp. 4–15.

32    Joseph S. Nye, 'Get Smart: Combining hard and soft power', *Foreign Affairs*, 1 July 2009, www.foreignaffairs.com/united-states/get-smart.

33    Morgenthau, *Politics Among Nations*, p.105.

34    Department of Foreign Affairs and Trade, 'Australia is a top 20 country', August 2022, www.dfat.gov.au/sites/default/files/australia-is-a-top-20-country-all-topics.pdf.

35    QS World University Rankings 2024, www.topuniversities.com/university-rankings-articles/world-university-rankings/top-universities-australia-2024.

36    Gavin Haines, 'Revealed: The world's "most liveable" cities in 2023', *Positive News*, 3 July 2023, www.positive.news/society/the-best-cities-to-live-in-2023.

37    Michael Fullilove, *The Boyer Lectures*, Australian Broadcasting Commission, 27 September–18 October 2015, www.abc.net.au/radionational/programs/boyerlectures/2015-boyer-lectures/6668786.

38    See Allan Behm, *No Enemies, No Friends* (Perth: Upswell, 2022), pp. 224–27.

## Chapter 3. America

1     Nick Bryant, *When America Stopped Being Great: A history of the present* (London: Bloomsbury, 2021), p. 334.

2     The Editorial Board, 'America can have democracy or political violence. Not both', *The New York Times*, 3 November 2022.

3     Vera Bergengruen, 'The united states of political violence', *Time*, 4 November 2022.

4     'These are conditions ripe for political violence: How close is the US to civil war?', *The Guardian*, 6 November 2022.

5     Andrew Daniller, 'Americans take a dim view of the nation's future, look more positively at the past', *Pew Research Center* report, 24 April 2023, www.pewresearch.org/short-reads/2023/04/24/americans-take-a-dim-view-of-the-nations-future-look-more-positively-at-the-past.

6     Charles King, 'The antiliberal revolution: Reading the philosophers of the new right', *Foreign Affairs*, July/August 2023, www.foreignaffairs.com/reviews/antiliberal-revolution.

7     King, 'The antiliberal revolution'.

8     Ian Bremmer, 'The U.S. capital riot was years in the making. Here's why America is so divided', *Time*, 16 January 2021.

9     The US Library of Congress has prepared a remarkable collection of publications documenting Jim Crow and segregation, along with accessible explanatory material: see www.loc.gov/classroom-materials/jim-crow-segregation.

10    See GAO, 'Featured topic: Race in America', 25 October 2022, www.gao.gov/race-america.

11    This remarkable collection has been reissued by Project Gutenberg at www.gutenberg.org/files/15041/15041-h/15041-h.htm.

12    W.E.B. Du Bois, 'The Talented Tenth', in Booker T. Washington (ed.), *The Negro Problem: A Series of Articles by Representative American Negroes of Today* (United States: J. Pott, 1903), pp. 74–75. For an insightful and sympathetic analysis of Du Bois and his work, see Zachariah Mampilly, 'The Du Bois doctrine', *Foreign Affairs*, Sept/Oct 2022, www. foreignaffairs.com/united-states/web-du-bois-doctrine-race-america-century.

13    See Henry Louis Gates Jr, 'Black America and the class divide', *The New York Times*, 1 February 2016.

14    See the moving memorial by Rev. William Barber and Jonathan Wilson-Hartgrove, 'Yes, Black officers killed Tyre Nichols. What is the correct response to that?', *The Guardian*, 7 February 2023.

15    Benjamin Francis-Fallon, 'Political divisions among Latinos are actually decades old', *The Washington Post*, 25 November 2020.

16    Joseph E. Stiglitz, *People, Power and Profits: Progressive capitalism for an age of discontent* (New York: W.W. Norton & Co, 2019), p. 243.

17    Stiglitz, *People, Power and Profits*, p. 243.

18    Gary Gerstle, 'The age of neoliberalism is ending in America. What will replace it?', *The Guardian*, 28 June 2021.

19    Adam Grundy, 'Service annual survey shows continuing decline in print publishing revenue', United States Census Bureau, 7 June 2022, www. census.gov/library/stories/2022/06/internet-crushes-traditional-media. html.

20    Ruth Ben-Ghiat, 'Being Trump's mouthpiece is risky for Fox News – and democracy', *Think* (NBC News), 6 November 2017.

21    This media event would have been extraordinary had it not become so commonplace during the Trump administration. See Eric Bradner, 'Conway: Trump White House offered "alternative facts" on crowd size', *CNN Politics*, 23 January 2017.

22    See Katharine Murphy, 'Former US intelligence director backs Turnbull and Rudd's call for Murdoch media inquiry', *The Guardian*, 21 April 2021.

23    'Political Polarization in the American Public', Pew Research Center, 12 June 2014, www.pewresearch.org/politics/2014/06/12/political-polarization-in-the-american-public.

24    'As Partisan Hostility Grows, Signs of Frustration With the Two-Party System', Pew Research Center, 9 August 2022, www.pewresearch.org/ politics/2022/08/09/as-partisan-hostility-grows-signs-of-frustration-with-the-two-party-system.

25    Drew DeSilver, 'The polarization in today's Congress has roots that go back decades', Pew Research Center, 10 March 2022, www.pewresearch.org/ short-reads/2022/03/10/the-polarization-in-todays-congress-has-roots-that-go-back-decades.

26    Jennifer McCoy & Benjamin Press, 'What Happens when Democracies Become Perniciously Polarized?', The Carnegie Endowment for International Peace, 18 January 2022, https://carnegieendowment.org/2022/01/18/what-happens-when-democracies-become-perniciously-polarized-pub-86190.
27    McCoy & Press, 'What Happens when Democracies Become Perniciously Polarized?'
28    Francis Fukuyama, 'Against identity politics: The new tribalism and the crisis of democracy', Foreign Affairs, 14 August 2018, www.foreignaffairs.com/articles/americas/2018-08-14/against-identity-politics-tribalism-francis-fukuyama.
29    President Joseph Biden, 'State of the Union Address', 1 March 2022, www.whitehouse.gov/briefing-room/speeches-remarks/2022/03/01/remarks-of-president-joe-biden-state-of-the-union-address-as-delivered.
30    For a brief and disturbing portrait of the Proud Boys, see the University of Maryland Research Brief 'Proud Boys Crimes and Characteristics', January 2022, www.start.umd.edu/sites/default/files/publications/local_attachments/Proud%20Boy%20Crimes%20and%20Characteristics%20January%202022%20FINAL.pdf.
31    See Kevin Roose, 'What is QAnon, the viral pro-Trump conspiracy theory?', The New York Times, 3 September 2021.
32    David Brooks, 'America is having a moral convulsion', The Atlantic, 5 October 2020.
33    Ruth Bader Ginsburg, 'Ruth Bader Ginsburg's advice for living', The New York Times, 1 October 2016.
34    Global Gender Gap Report 2022, World Economic Forum, Geneva, 2022, p. 10, https://www3.weforum.org/docs/WEF_GGGR_2022.pdf.
35    Rebecca Leppert and Drew DeSilver, '118th Congress has a record number of women', Pew Research Center, 3 January 2023, www.pewresearch.org/short-reads/2023/01/03/118th-congress-has-a-record-number-of-women.
36    See 'Women in the U.S. Congress 2022', Center for American Women and Politics, Eagleton Institute of Politics, Rutgers University, https://cawp.rutgers.edu/facts/levels-office/congress/women-us-congress-2022.
37    Carolina Aragão, 'Gender pay gap in U.S. hasn't changed much in two decades', Pew Research Center, 1 March 2023, www.pewresearch.org/short-reads/2023/03/01/gender-pay-gap-facts.
38    See 'The Gender Gap in Educational Attainment in the United States', Women in Academia Report, 1 March 2023, www.wiareport.com/2023/03/the-gender-gap-in-educational-attainment-in-the-united-states.
39    See Australian Parliament, Parliamentary Debates, House of Representatives, 9 October 2012, pp. 11581–85.
40    Alexandria Ocasio-Cortes, 'I am someone's daughter too', speech transcribed in The Independent, 24 July 2020.

41    Bruce Stokes, 'The decline of the city upon a hill', *Foreign Affairs*, 17 October 2022, www.foreignaffairs.com/united-states/decline-city-upon-hill.

42    This is also borne out in international surveys. See Caroline Gray, Lucas Robinson, Mark Hannah & Zuri Linetsky, 'Democracy's Promise', Institute for Global Affairs, 15 June 2022, https://instituteforglobalaffairs. org/2022/06/modeling-democracy-democracys-promise.

43    Stokes, 'The decline of the city upon a hill'.

**Chapter 4. Law**

1     James Madison, *Federalist No. 10*, 23 November 1787, Library of Congress Research Guides, https://guides.loc.gov/federalist-papers/ text-1-10#s-lg-box-wrapper-25493273.

2     Alexander Hamilton, *Federalist No. 78*, 28 May 1788, Library of Congress Research Guides, https://guides.loc.gov/federalist-papers/text-71-80. Hamilton's view was not uncontested, of course. The Anti-Federalists, represented by 'Brutus', mounted cogent arguments addressing the unspecified powers of the judiciary and the possibility of judicial 'creep'. For an accessible commentary, see Schlomo Slonim, 'Federalist No. 78 and Brutus' neglected thesis on judicial supremacy', Constitutional Commentary 1000, 2006, https://scholarship.law.umn.edu/cgi/ viewcontent.cgi?article=2010&context=concomm.

3     Harry Evans, 'The Other Metropolis: The Australian founders' knowledge of America', *Papers on Parliament*, No. 52, December 2009, www.aph.gov. au/About_Parliament/Senate/Powers_practice_n_procedures/pops/ pop52/11theothermetropolis.

4     See Harry Hobbs & Andrew Trotter, 'The Constitutional Conventions and Constitutional Change: Making sense of multiple intentions', *Adelaide Law Review*, vol. 38, 2017, p. 66, n. 130.

5     James Warden, *Federalism and the Design of the Australian Constitution* (Canberra: ANU Federalism Research Centre, 1992), p. 5.

6     Stephen Gageler, 'James Bryce and the Australian Constitution', an expanded version of the 'Sir Anthony Mason Lecture in Constitutional Law', delivered in the Banco Court of the Supreme Court of New South Wales, Sydney, 12 February 2015, *Federal Law Review*, vol. 43, pp. 177–200, published on the website of the High Court of Australia, www.hcourt. gov.au/assets/publications/speeches/current-justices/gagelerj/James_ Bryce_article_Vol_43_Federal_Law_Review.pdf.

7     Commonwealth of Australia, *Parliamentary Debates*, House of Representatives, 18 March 1902, 10967 (Alfred Deakin) in Stephen Gageler, 'James Bryce and the Australian Constitution', p. 196.

8     Commonwealth of Australia, *Parliamentary Debates*, Senate, 29 July 1903, 2693–94 (Richard O'Connor) at Stephen Gageler, 'James Bryce and the Australian Constitution'.

9     The Hon Robert French AC, 'United States Influence on the Australian Legal System', *University of Western Australia Law Review*, vol. 43, no. 1, 2018, p. 16.

10    French, 'United States Influence on the Australian Legal System', p. 11.

11    *Magna Carta* translation, clause 29, US National Archives text, www.archives.gov/files/press/press-kits/magna-carta/magna-carta-translation.pdf.

12    Robert French, 'Rights and Freedoms and the Rule of Law', Victorian Law Foundation Oration, 9 February 2017, https://a.storyblok.com/f/139306/x/3fed969f23/rights_and_freedoms_and_the_rule_of_law_-_victorian_law_foundation_2017_oration.pdf.

13    For a sombre commentary on the possible Americanisation of Australian race relations in the aftermath of the 2023 constitutional referendum, see Nick Bryant, 'Brexit-Britain. Trump in the US. Now it's Australia's turn to split in two', *The Sydney Morning Herald*, 26 September 2023.

14    French, 'Rights and Freedoms and the Rule of Law'.

15    UN Charter, Preamble, clause 2, www.un.org/en/about-us/un-charter/full-text.

16    Senator Penny Wong, 'Australian Values in a Time of Disruption', Griffith University, 3 August 2017, www.pennywong.com.au/media-hub/speeches/australian-values-in-a-time-of-disruption-griffith-asia-institute-s-perspectives-asia-lecture-griffith-university-brisbane-03-08-2017.

17    Anne Twomey, 'The Application of the Implied Freedom of Political Communication to State Electoral Funding Laws', *UNSW Law Journal*, vol. 35, no. 3, 2012, pp. 625–47.

18    French, 'United States Influence on the Australian Legal System', pp. 12–17.

19    George Williams, *A Bill of Rights for Australia* (Kensington: UNSW Press, 2000).

20    George Williams, 'Legislating for a Bill of Rights Now', *Papers on Parliament*, no. 36, June 2001, www.aph.gov.au/About_Parliament/Senate/Powers_practice_n_procedures/pops/pop36/williams.

**Chapter 5. Money**

1     See 'Australia's Trade in Goods and Services by Top 15 Partners', Department of Foreign Affairs and Trade, 2023, www.dfat.gov.au/sites/default/files/australias-goods-services-by-top-15-partners-2021-22.pdf. The $2.2-trillion value is the combined value of the bilateral trade and investment relationships.

2   See Lachlan Grant, 'The Fighting Gunditjmara', Australian War Memorial blog, 3 July 2021, www.awm.gov.au/articles/blog/the-fighting-gunditjmara.

3   'Start of Whaling', National Museum of Australia, 1922, www.nma.gov.au/defining-moments/resources/start-of-whaling. See also Martin Gibbs, 'Conflict and Commerce: American Whalers and the Western Australian colonies 1826–1888', *The Great Circle*, vol. 22, no. 2, 2000, pp. 3–5, 20.

4   J.C.H. Gill, 'Genesis of the Australian Whaling Industry: Its development up to 1850', *Journal of the Royal Historical Society of Queensland*, vol. 8, no. 1, pp. 111–36. See also Gibbs, 'Conflict and Commerce'. For an interesting account of the impact of whaling on Indigenous cultures and peoples, see Alistair Paterson et al., 'So Ends This Day: American whaler in Yaburara country, Dampier Archipelago', *Antiquity*, vol. 93, no. 367, 2019, pp. 218–35.

5   Gibbs, 'Conflict and Commerce'.

6   Bruce Mitchell, 'Edward Hammond Hargreaves (1816–1891)', *Australian Dictionary of Biography* (Canberra: ANU Press, 1972), vol. 4, https://adb.anu.edu.au/biography/hargraves-edward-hammond-3719.

7   Jerome O. Steffen, 'The Mining Frontiers of California and Australia: A study in comparative political change and continuity', *Pacific Historical Review*, 1983, p. 429.

8   Jeff Powell, 'How big was the leviathan "monster coach"?', *Queensland Museum Network*, 13 September 2017, https://blog.qm.qld.gov.au/2017/09/13/how-big-was-the-leviathan-monster-coach.

9   Robert Green, 'Australia's first electric tram: The Box Hill to Doncaster tramway', Melbourne Tram Museum, 1989, www.hawthorntramdepot.org.au/papers/boxhill.htm.

10  'Herbert C Hoover', Kalgoorlie Boulder Visitor Centre, www.kalgoorlietourism.com/herbert-hoover.

11  Joan Beaumont, *Broken Nation: Australians in the Great War* (Sydney: Allen & Unwin, 2013).

12  See 'Australia's Trade since Federation', Department of Foreign Affairs and Trade, 2016, www.dfat.gov.au/sites/default/files/australias-trade-since-federation.pdf.

13  Mark Clayton, 'Cutting the Gordian Knot: Reassessing Australia's Lend-Lease settlement', *Australian Journal of Politics and History*, 2023, p. 1.

14  Clayton, 'Cutting the Gordian Knot', p. 8.

15  Greg Baker, 'Gold! Gold to Australia! Gold! Australian gold statistics', Parliament of Australia Research Note, 6 December 2005, https://parlinfo.aph.gov.au/parlInfo/download/library/prspub/YV8I6/upload_binary/yv8i63.pdf.

16    The Australian APEC Study Centre at Monash University, *An Australia–USA Free Trade Agreement: Issues and Implications*, August 2001, www.dfat.gov.au/sites/default/files/aus_us_fta_mon.pdf.

17    See Richard Pomfret, 'Reorientation of Trade, Investment and Migration', in Simon Ville & Glenn Withers, *The Cambridge Economic History of Australia, Part 5: Building the Modern Economy* (Cambridge: Cambridge University Press, 2014, p. 405.

18    Kevin Rudd, 'How we staved off recession and the GFC', *Australian Financial Review*, 13 September 2018. Some textbook theoreticians disagree with Rudd's claims; see Tony Makin, 'Kevin Rudd did not save the economy in 2008', *Australian Financial Review*, 15 October 2018. It is well that Rudd relied on the economic policy skills of Ken Henry and Ben Bernanke instead of textbook theoreticians.

19    President Woodrow Wilson, Speech to the US Congress, 8 January 1918, www.archives.gov/milestone-documents/president-woodrow-wilsons-14-points.

20    The FIRB's threshold for US FDI in sensitive sectors was raised from $50 million to $100 million (see Stephen Kirchner, 'Foreign Direct Investment in Australia Following the Australia-US Free Trade Agreement', *The Australian Economic Review*, vol. 45, no. 4, 2012, pp. 410–12). See also David Uren 'Enduring Partners: The US–Australia investment relationship', United States Study Centre, 16 July 2020, p. 13. On the implications for the FIRB, see *Foreign Investment Review Board Annual Report 2003–04*, p. 35, https://firb.gov.au/sites/firb.gov.au/files/2016/01/FIRB-Annual-Report-2003-04_Chapter_3.pdf. For a summary of the US understanding of the implications of the AUSFTA, see United States Trade Representative, *2022 National Trade Estimate Report on Foreign Trade Barriers*, pp. 35–38, https://ustr.gov/sites/default/files/2022%20National%20Trade%20Estimate%20Report%20on%20Foreign%20Trade%20Barriers.pdf.

21    Philippa Dee, 'The Australia–US Free Trade Agreement: An assessment', Parliament of Australia, Senate Select Committee on the Free Trade Agreement between Australia and the United States of America, June 2004, pp. 39–40, www.aph.gov.au/~/media/wopapub/senate/committee/freetrade_ctte/rel_links/dee_fta_report_pdf.ashx.

22    See Ann Capling, *All the Way with the USA: Australia, the US and free trade* (Sydney: University of New South Wales Press, 2004).

23    Linda Weiss, Elizabeth Thurbon & John Mathews, *How to Kill a Country: Australia's devastating trade deal with the United States* (Crows Nest: Allen & Unwin, 2004).

24    Shiro Armstrong, 'The costs of Australia's "free trade" agreement with America', East Asia Forum, 8 February 2015, www.eastasiaforum.

org/2015/02/08/the-costs-of-australias-free-trade-agreement-with-america.

25    Australian Bureau of Statistics, *International Investment Position, Australia: Supplementary Statistics (2022)*, released 3 May 2023, www.abs.gov.au/statistics/economy/international-trade/international-investment-position-australia-supplementary-statistics/2022.

26    See Uren, 'Enduring Partners', pp. 4–5, 9, 13–14.

27    See Australian Bureau of Statistics, *International Investment Position, Australia*.

28    See Joey Herlihy, *Money Talks: The Australia–America economic relationship: Where from and where to* (Canberra: The Australia Institute, 4 August 2023), https://australiainstitute.org.au/report/money-talks-the-australia-america-economic-relationship-where-from-and-where-to.

29    See, for example, 'Trade and Investment', Embassy of Australia in the USA, 2023, https://usa.embassy.gov.au/trade-and-investment.

30    See Deloitte and the American Chamber of Commerce, *Building Prosperity: The importance of the United States to the Australian Economy*, 23 July 2020, https://amcham.informz.net/amcham/data/images/Building%20Prosperity_The%20importance%20of%20the%20United%20States%20to%20the%20Australian%20economy_web.pdf.

31    For a detailed analysis of the strategic limitations of the ANZUS Treaty and its contemporary utility as a basis for security planning, see Allan Behm, *ANZUS and Australia's Security* (Canberra: The Australia Institute, 28 July 2020), https://australiainstitute.org.au/wp-content/uploads/2020/12/200107-ANZUS-and-Australia-WEB.pdf.

32    See Kyla Tienhaara & Patricia Ranald, 'Australia's rejection of Investor-State Dispute Settlement: Four potential contributing factors', International Institute for Sustainable Development, *Investment Treaty News*, 12 July 2011, www.iisd.org/itn/en/2011/07/12/australias-rejection-of-investor-state-dispute-settlement-four-potential-contributing-factors.

33    For an overview of how the ISDS system works, see the short paper prepared by the UK-based action group Global Justice Now, 'The case against corporate courts', February 2019 www.globaljustice.org.uk/wp-content/uploads/2019/01/isds_briefing_web.pdf. See also Claire Provost & Matt Kennard, 'The obscure legal system that lets corporations sue countries', *The Guardian*, 10 June 2015.

34    Australian Productivity Commission, *Bilateral and Regional Trade Agreements*, Research Report, November 2010, p. 84 *et passim*, www.pc.gov.au/inquiries/completed/trade-agreements/report/trade-agreements-report.pdf.

35    Parliament of Australia, Select Committee on the Free Trade Agreement between Australia and the United States of America, August 2004, p. 7,

www.aph.gov.au/~/media/wopapub/senate/committee/freetrade_ctte/
report/final/report_pdf.ashx.

36    Thomas Faunce, 'How the US trade deal undermined Australia's PBS', *The Conversation*, 24 October 2014, https://theconversation.com/
how-the-us-trade-deal-undermined-australias-pbs-32573.

37    See Julia Kollewe, 'Covid-19 vaccines: The contracts, prices and profits', *The Guardian*, 12 August 2021.

38    Parliament of Australia, *Comprehensive and Progressive Agreement for Trans-Pacific Partnership*, Joint Standing Committee on Treaties, August 2018, https://parlinfo.aph.gov.au/parlInfo/download/committees/
reportjnt/024179/toc_pdf/Report181.pdf;fileType=application%2Fpdf.

39    Parliament of Australia, *Comprehensive and Progressive Agreement for Trans-Pacific Partnership*, p. 40.

## Chapter 6. Culture

1    Fintan O'Toole, 'Eldest Statesman', *New York Review of Books*, 18 January 2024, www.nybooks.com/articles/2024/01/18/eldest-statesmen-fintan-otoole.

2    'We should be ashamed (says Dr Benson)', *The Argus*, 13 February 1956.

3    Entire libraries have been written on the impact of Senator Joseph McCarthy on American politics and public intellectuals. For a comprehensive analysis of McCarthy's destructive impact on America, see Stanley Kutler, *The American Inquisition: Justice and injustice in the Cold War* (New York: Hill & Wang, 1982), and Ellen Schrecker, *The Age of McCarthyism: A brief history with documents* (Bedford: St Martin's, 2001).

4    For a summary of the *Communist Party Dissolution Act* 1950 and its aftermath, see 'Communist Party Dissolution Act 1950', part of the *Prime Facts Series* of the Museum of Australian Democracy, Canberra, http://static.moadoph.gov.au/ophgovau/media/images/apmc/docs/82-Communist-Party-ban.pdf.

5    Roger Scruton, 'The Great Swindle', *Aeon*, 17 December 2012, https://aeon.co/essays/a-cult-of-fakery-has-taken-over-what-s-left-of-high-culture.

6    Scruton, 'The Great Swindle'. To find such an Aristotelian take on the life of the mind is oddly refreshing.

7    See, for example, *The Sydney Morning Herald*, 2 July 1947, p. 5.

8    For an amusing account of the growth of suburbanism in Sydney, for example, see Paul Ashton, 'Suburban Sydney', *Dictionary of Sydney* (State Library of New South Wales, 2008), archived in 2021, https://
dictionaryofsydney.org/entry/suburban_sydney.

9    Jonathan Mahler & Jim Rutenberg, 'How Rupert Murdoch's empire of influence remade the world', *The New York Times*, 3 April 2019.

10    See, for instance, John Menadue, 'What Rupert Murdoch told the US Ambassador about the pending Whitlam dismissal – 12 months

beforehand in November 1974? Yes 1974', *Pearls and Irritations*, 21 May 2013, https://johnmenadue.com/what-rupert-murdoch-told-the-us-ambassador-about-the-pending-whitlam-dismissal-12-months-beforehand-in-november-1974-yes-1974-john-menadue, and Jon Stanford, 'Cold War imperatives: Whitlam and the US National Security Council', *Pearls and Irritations*, 10 November 2023, https://johnmenadue.com/cold-war-imperatives-whitlam-and-the-us-national-security-council-part-3-pic-pine-gap.

11    Robert Milliken, 'A man of selfish loyalties: Rupert Murdoch's apparent overture to Tony Blair strikes a chilling chord among Australian politicians he has supported', *The Independent*, 14 August 1994.

12    See Dan Sabbagh, Leveson inquiry: Tessa Jowell quizzed Tony Blair over Murdoch deal', *The Guardian*, 21 May 2012, and Robert Thompson et al., 'Rupert Murdoch made his own rules – what is the media mogul's real legacy?', *The Guardian*, 24 September 2023.

13    See Hannah Ritchie, 'Rupert Murdoch: How magnate transformed Australia's media', BBC News, 22 September 2023, www.bbc.com/news/world-australia-66875222.

14    See Zoe Samios, 'How much influence does the Murdoch media have in Australia?', *The Sydney Morning Herald*, 15 October 2020, and RMIT ABC Fact Check, 'How large is Rupert Murdoch's reach through News Corp in Australian media, old and new?', ABC News, 14 April 2021, www.abc.net.au/news/2021-04-14/fact-file-rupert-murdoch-media-reach-in-australia/100056660.

15    Niall Stanage, 'The Memo: How Murdoch changed American politics', *The Hill*, 22 September 2023, https://thehill.com/homenews/media/4217532-the-memo-how-murdoch-changed-american-politics.

16    See 'International Education and Research', Australian Embassy to the USA, Department of Foreign Affairs and Trade, https://usa.embassy.gov.au/international-education-and-research.

17    Group of Eight Australia, 'Go8 Media release', 31 January 2017, https://go8.edu.au/go8-media-release-go8-washington-meetings-lobby-to-continue-valuable-us-australia-research-collaboration.

18    See Milanda Rout, 'The most successful Aussie in Hollywood you've never heard of', *The Australian*, 5 June 2023.

19    For more detailed and expert coverage than can be delivered here, see *Rolling Stone*, Special Collector's Edition 003, 7 December 2020, https://au.rollingstone.com/50-greatest-australian-artists/.

## Chapter 7. War

1    See *The Smithsonian Magazine*, 'Special Issue on America at War', January 2019 www.smithsonianmag.com/history/america-at-war-introduction-180971014.

2 Fletcher Center for Strategic Studies, 'MIP Research', 2023, https://sites.tufts.edu/css/mip-research.

3 See Catwhipple, 'America's real longest war was against Indigenous Indians', *The Circle (Native American News and Arts)*, 2 September 2021, https://thecirclenews.org/opinion/americas-real-longest-war-was-against-indigenous-americans.

4 The Veterans Museum, 'Revolutionary War (War for Independence) 1775–1783', https://veteranmuseum.net/research-revolutionary-war/#:~:text=Between%2025%2C000%20and%2070%2C000%20American,least%2017%2C000%20died%20from%20disease.

5 Bob Zeller, 'How many died in the American Civil War?', *History*, 23 August 2023, www.history.com/news/american-civil-war-deaths.

6 David Michael Smith, 'Counting the Dead: Estimating the loss of life in the Indigenous holocaust, 1492–present', in Mark B. Spenser (ed.), *Proceedings of the Twelfth Native American Symposium* (Durant: Southeastern Oklahoma State University, 2018), pp. 7–17.

7 Smith, 'Counting the Dead'; see in particular p. 13.

8 See Samuel J. Cox, 'The Battle of the Pearl River Forts, China, 1856', *Naval History and Heritage Command*, July 2021, www.history.navy.mil/about-us/leadership/director/directors-corner/h-grams/h-gram-063/h-063-1.html

9 See H.G. Rickover, *How the Battleship Maine was Destroyed* (Washington DC: Naval History division, 1976).

10 Rickover, *How the Battleship Maine was Destroyed*, p. vii–viii.

11 See 'Louisiana Purchase, 1803', Office of the Historian, US State Department, https://history.state.gov/milestones/1801-1829/louisiana-purchase.

12 See 'Purchase of Alaska, 1867', Office of the Historian, US State Department, https://history.state.gov/milestones/1866-1898/alaska-purchase.

13 Theodore Roosevelt, 'Fourth Annual Message to the Congress', 6 December 1904, https://millercenter.org/the-presidency/presidential-speeches/december-6-1904-fourth-annual-message.

14 David Vine, *The United States of War* (Oakland: University of California Press, 2020), p. 6.

15 See Carlo D'Este, *Patton: A genius for war* (New York: HarperCollins, 1995), and Peter FitzSimons, *Monash's Masterpiece: The Battle of Le Hamel and the 93 minutes that changed the world* (Sydney: Hachette Australia, 2018).

16 See 'American War and Military Operations Casualties: Lists and statistics', US Library of Congress, 29 July 2020, https://crsreports.congress.gov/product/pdf/RL/RL32492, and 'The American Expeditionary Forces', US Library of Congress, www.loc.gov/collections/

stars-and-stripes/articles-and-essays/a-world-at-war/american-expeditionary-forces.

17    See Christopher Clark, *The Sleepwalkers: How Europe went to war in 1914* (London: Penguin Books, 2013).

18    For a brief synopsis of the key dynamics of the Japanese Greater East Asia Co-Prosperity Sphere and the principal reasons for its ultimate failure (apart from Japan's abject defeat at America's hands in 1945) see Nathaniel W. Giles, *The Great East Asia Co-Prosperity Sphere: The failure of Japan's 'Monroe Doctrine for Asia'*, Honours thesis, East Tennessee State University, 2015.

19    Speech by Franklin D. Roosevelt, 'The President Requests War Declaration (December 7, 1941, a date which will live in infamy)', Library of Congress, www.loc.gov/resource/afc1986022.afc1986022_ms2201/?st=pdf&pdfPage=1.

20    For a penetrating insight into the drafting of the text, see *Our Heritage in Documents*, 'FDR's "Day of Infamy" Speech: Crafting a call to arms', National Archives, Washington, 2001, www.archives.gov/publications/prologue/2001/winter/crafting-day-of-infamy-speech.html.

21    Clausewitz prescribes two qualities above everything else that the commander needs: 'an intellect that … retains some glimmerings of the inner light which leads to truth; and second, the courage to follow this faint light wherever it may lead … *Coup d'oeil* [and] *determination*'. MacArthur certainly had these. See Michael Howard & Peter Paret, *On War* (Princeton: Princeton University Press, 8th printing, 1984), p. 102.

22    In summary terms, the underlying political and strategic tension of the Korean War is described in 'The Firing of MacArthur', National Archives, Harry S. Truman Library and Museum, www.trumanlibrary.gov/education/presidential-inquiries/firing-macarthur.

23    For a synopsis of MacArthur's *in camera* repudiation by his senior military peers, see H.W. Brands, 'The redacted testimony that fully explains why General MacArthur was fired', *The Smithsonian Magazine*, 28 September 2016, www.smithsonianmag.com/history/redacted-testimony-fully-explains-why-general-macarthur-was-fired-180960622.

24    The Pentagon Papers constitute one of the most damning archives of deceit and incompetence ever revealed. As a whistleblower, Daniel Ellsberg risked life imprisonment by bringing these documents to public notice. They are available on the US National Archives website at www.archives.gov/research/pentagon-papers.

25    See Australian War Memorial, 'Vietnam War 1962–75', last updated 30 October 2023, www.awm.gov.au/articles/event/vietnam.

26    See David Halberstam, *The Best and the Brightest* (New York: Random House, 1972). Halberstam offers a penetrating commentary on how

intellectual elitism and academic privilege can led to hyper-confidence and delusion. This is a must-read account of the Vietnam War.

27    See Robert McNamara & Brian VanDeMark, *In Retrospect: The tragedy and lessons of Vietnam* (New York: Vintage Books, 1996).

28    Lewis Sorley, *Westmoreland: The general who lost Vietnam* (Boston: Houghton Mifflin Harcourt, 2011). See also Thomas E. Ricks, 'Today's list: The top ten reasons Gen. Westmoreland lost the war in Vietnam', *Foreign Policy*, 11 October 2011, https://foreignpolicy.com/2011/10/11/todays-list-the-top-ten-reasons-gen-westmoreland-lost-the-war-in-vietnam.

29    Central Intelligence Agency Report, *Implications of an Unfavorable Outcome in Vietnam*, 11 September 1967, released January 2005, p. 2, www.cia.gov/readingroom/docs/DOC_0001166443.pdf.

30    The then Secretary of State, James Baker, provided a sound comment on the US response strategy in 'Why the U.S. didn't march to Baghdad', *The Los Angeles Times*, 8 September 1996, www.latimes.com/archives/la-xpm-1996-09-08-op-41778-story.html.

31    See 9/11 Commission Report, www.9-11commission.gov/report/911Report.pdf, p. xvi.

32    Susan Neiman, *Left Is Not Woke* (Cambridge: Polity Press, 2023), p. 59.

33    See Julian Borger, 'From Bush to Blix: What happened to key figures in the Iraq war?', *The Guardian*, 23 March 2023.

34    Bobbi Nodell, 'Study: Nearly 500,000 perished in Iraq War', University of Washington, 15 October 2013, www.washington.edu/news/2013/10/15/study-nearly-500000-perished-in-iraq-war.

35    For a relatively simple schema, see Peter Brecke, 'An Aid to Finding the Causes of Conflict: A taxonomy of violent conflicts', Georgia Institute of Technology, Sam Nunn School of International Affairs, Atlanta, n.d., https://bpb-us-w2.wpmucdn.com/sites.gatech.edu/dist/1/19/files/2018/09/Brecke-Taxonomy-of-Violent-Conflicts.pdf.

36    Raphael S. Cohen & Gian Gentile, 'America's dangerous short war fixation', *Commentary (The RAND Blog)*, 31 March 2023, www.rand.org/pubs/commentary/2023/03/americas-dangerous-short-war-fixation.html.

## Chapter 8. Peace

1    C. Suetonius Tranquillus, *The Lives of the Twelve Caesars*, 'The Life of Titus' (Chicago: Loeb Classical Library, 1914), para. 3, my translation. In the original, Suetonius writes *'docilitas ad omnis fere tum belli tum pacis artes … ac saepe profiteri maximum falsarium esse potuisse'* (https://penelope.uchicago.edu/Thayer/L/Roman/Texts/Suetonius/12Caesars/Titus*.html#2).

2       George Washington, 'First Annual Address to Congress', 8 January 1790, *The American Presidency Project*, University of California Santa Barbara, www.presidency.ucsb.edu/documents/first-annual-address-congress-0.

3       See Allan Behm, 'Talk us through AUKUS … and Australia's dream submarine', The Australia Institute, February 2023, https://australiainstitute.org.au/wp-content/uploads/2023/02/P1364-Talk-us-through-AUKUS-final-pdf.pdf.

4       ABC TV programs aired in January–February 2024, https://iview.abc.net.au/show/nemesis/series/1/video/NS2412H003S00.

5       Hugh White, 'Fatal Shores: AUKUS is a grave mistake', *Australian Foreign Affairs*, no. 20, 2024, p. 37.

6       Philip Bobbitt, *The Shield of Achilles: War, peace and the course of history* (London: Penguin Books, 2002).

7       See Jeffrey D. Sachs & Guillaume LaFortune, 'Adhering to the UN Charter: Barbados first, and the United States last', *Common Dreams*, 13 November 2023, www.commondreams.org/opinion/multilateralism-index-united-nations.

8       For an elegant analysis of how the international community responds to blatant disdain for important global rules, such as are implemented by the WTO, see Kristen Hopewell, 'When the Hegemon Goes Rogue: Leadership amid the US assault on the liberal trading order', *International Affairs*, vol. 97, no. 4, 2021.

9       President Woodrow Wilson, 'A World League for Peace', Address to the US Senate, 22 January 1917, www.presidency.ucsb.edu/documents/address-the-senate-the-united-states-world-league-for-peace.

10      President Woodrow Wilson, 'Fourteen Points', Address to the US Congress, 8 January 1918, https://millercenter.org/the-presidency/presidential-speeches/january-8-1918-wilsons-fourteen-points.

11      Bobbitt, *The Shield of Achilles*, p. 477.

12      Walter Russell Mead, 'The End of the Wilsonian Era: Why Liberal internationalism failed', *Foreign Affairs*, January/February 2021, www.foreignaffairs.com/articles/united-states/2020-12-08/end-wilsonian-era.

13      Philip Bobbitt devotes over forty pages of his titanic book to House and his influence. It contains fascinating insights into the diplomatic manoeuvres in Paris. See Bobbitt, *The Shield of Achilles*, pp. 367–410.

14      Bobbitt, *The Shield of Achilles*, p. 362.

15      Harry S. Truman, 'Address to the United Nations Conference in San Francisco', 25 April 1945, The American Presidency Project, University of California Santa Barbara, www.presidency.ucsb.edu/documents/address-the-united-nations-conference-san-francisco.

16      See the excellent short paper by Dr Moreen Dee, 'Dr H.V. Evatt and the Negotiation of the United Nations Charter', n.d., www.diplomatie.gouv.fr/IMG/pdf/ONU_moreen_dee.pdf.

17    For a compelling account of American involvement and interference in this critical transition period in Indonesia's political development, see Vincent Bevins, *The Jakarta Method: Washington's anti-communist crusade and mass murder program that shaped our world* (Sydney: Hachette, 2021).

18    President Dwight D. Eisenhower, 'Atoms for Peace', Address to the UN General Assembly, 8 December 1953, www.iaea.org/about/history/atoms-for-peace-speech.

19    President Ronald Reagan, 'Tear Down This Wall', Address at the Brandenburg Gate, Berlin, 12 June 1987, www.historyplace.com/speeches/reagan-tear-down.htm.

20    For a very brief summary of the Dayton Accords, see the NATO media release, '15 Years Ago, Dayton Peace Accords: A milestone for NATO and the Balkans',14 December 2010, www.nato.int/cps/en/natolive/news_69290.htm.

21    For an interesting American response to Macron's comment, see James Dobbins, 'Is NATO Brain Dead?', *Commentary (The RAND Blog)*, 3 December 2019, www.rand.org/pubs/commentary/2019/12/is-nato-brain-dead.html.

22    Errol Morris, *The Fog of War*, documentary transcript, www.errolmorris.com/film/fow_transcript.html.

23    Gyngell, *Fear of Abandonment: Australia in the world since 1942* (Melbourne: La Trobe University Press, 2017), p. 304.

24    For a typically detailed discussion of the GFC and his role in the elevation of the G20, see Kevin Rudd, 'How we staved off recession and the GFC', *Australian Financial Review*, 13 September 2018.

25    Ryan Haas, 'What America Wants From China: A strategy to keep Beijing entangled in the world order', *Foreign Affairs*, November/December 2023, www.foreignaffairs.com/united-states/what-america-wants-china.

26    Dwight D. Eisenhower, 'Farewell Address', 17 January 1961, National Archives, www.archives.gov/milestone-documents/president-dwight-d-eisenhowers-farewell-address.

27    Eric Lipton, 'New spin on a revolving door: Pentagon officials turned venture capitalists', *The New York Times*, 30 December 2023, www.nytimes.com/2023/12/30/us/politics/pentagon-venture-capitalists.html.

28    Vine, *The United States of War*, p. 328.

## Chapter 9. Coupledom

1     See Madeleine K. Albright, 'The Today Show', NBC-TV Interview, 19 February 1998, https://1997-2001.state.gov/statements/1998/980219a.html, and Paul Keating, Response to a Parliamentary Question, *Parliamentary Debates*, House of Representatives Hansard, 27 February

1992, https://australianpolitics.com/1992/02/27/keating-blasts-liberal-party-fogies.html.

2   See Shane Wright, 'Ex-ASIO chief called in after 11th hour discovery of missing Iraq War secret papers', *The Sydney Morning Herald*, 1 January 2024.

3   Eric Lutz, 'Trump privately discussed destroying NATO alliance', *Vanity Fair*, 15 January 2019, www.vanityfair.com/news/2019/01/trump-privately-discussed-destroying-nato-alliance.

4   Layton Pike, 'Australian expert hails Vietnam's bamboo diplomacy', *Vietnam* (blogsite), 3 July 2023 https://en.vietnamplus.vn/australian-expert-hails-vietnams-bamboo-diplomacy/255636.vnp.

5   'By the numbers: Stark contrast in Australian, US gun deaths', United States Study Centre, University of Sydney, 1 June 2022, www.ussc.edu.au/by-the-numbers-stark-contrast-in-australian-us-gun-deaths.

6   See 'Drug Overdose Deaths', Centers for Disease Control and Prevention, Washington, 2021, www.cdc.gov/drugoverdose/deaths/index.html, and 'Alcohol, tobacco & other drugs in Australia', Australian Institute of Health and Welfare, December 2023, www.aihw.gov.au/reports/alcohol/alcohol-tobacco-other-drugs-australia/contents/impacts/health-impacts.

7   Simon Jackman & Shaun Ratcliff, 'America's trust deficit', United States Studies Centre, University of Sydney, 18 February 2018, www.ussc.edu.au/americas-trust-deficit.

8   Ben Doherty, 'Trump drives Australian trust in US to all-time low', *The Guardian*, 20 June 2018, quoting a Lowy Institute poll: www.lowyinstitute.org/publications/2018-lowy-institute-poll.

9   See Zoe Daniel, 'We live in a time when Americans think it's Australians who are the crazy ones', *The New Daily*, 21 October 2021, www.thenewdaily.com.au/opinion/2021/10/02/zoe-daniel-us-australia-crazy.

10  The Commander-in-Chief, Pacific Fleet (CINCPAC) Admiral Archie Clemins USN was a naval officer who did not mince his words. During a 1998 meeting with senior ADF and Defence officials in Canberra, Clemins advised his Australian counterparts not to raise expectations too high, since 'there's not much you guys are able to do' (author's recollection). Clemins was very fond of Australia and Australians, and his attitude was reciprocated.

11  See David Corbett, 'The Legacy of Menzies', *International Journal*, vol. 21, no. 3, 1966, p. 348, and Graeme Dobell, 'Cabinet papers reveal Australia was on path to war in 1998', *The Strategist*, 20 January 2020, www.aspistrategist.org.au/cabinet-papers-reveal-australia-was-on-path-to-war-in-iraq-in-1998.

12  For a highly technical and very well referenced analysis of diplomatic credibility and honesty in relation to power, resolve and strength, see Alexandra Guisinger & Alastair Smith, 'Honest Threats: The interaction of

reputation and political institutions in international crises', *Journal of Conflict Resolution*, vol. 46, no. 2, 2002, p. 197.

13    For more detail on this fascinating exchange, see Allan Behm, 'ANZUS and Australia's Security', The Australia Institute, 28 July 2020, https://australiainstitute.org.au/report/anzus-and-australias-security, p. 18.

14    With the benefit of hindsight, Whitlam was right to challenge the flabby assumptions on which Nixon and Kissinger had based their assessments of Australia's subservience to America's muddled strategic aims in Vietnam. See the excellent analysis by James Curran, *Unholy Fury: Whitlam and Nixon at war* (Melbourne: Melbourne University Publishing, 2015).

15    See 'United States forces in Australia', Australian War Memorial, https://australiainstitute.org.au/report/anzus-and-australias-security. See also the more colourful account 'The Battle of Brisbane – 26 & 27 November 1942' at www.ozatwar.com/ozatwar/bob.htm.

16    Stephen Wertheim, in his insightful essay 'Why America Can't Have It All' (*Foreign Affairs*, 14 February 2024, www.foreignaffairs.com/united-states/why-america-cant-have-it-all) skirts around the core issue in the American dilemma: in advocating an imperative for America to choose between primacy and prioritising, he neglects the role that buoyancy and self-confidence has played in traditional US strategic posture.

17    Fareed Zakaria, 'The Self-Doubting Superpower: America shouldn't give up on the world it made', *Foreign Affairs*, January/February 2024, 12 December 2023 www.foreignaffairs.com/united-states/self-doubting-superpower-america-fareed-zakaria.

18    See Einar Dyvik, 'Countries with the highest military spending 2022', *Statista*, 30 November 2023, www.statista.com/statistics/262742/countries-with-the-highest-military-spending.

19    See Lucie Béraud-Sudreau & Nick Childs, 'The US and its NATO allies: Costs and value', *Military Balance Blog*, International Institute for Strategic Studies, London, 2018, www.iiss.org/online-analysis//military-balance/2018/07/us-and-nato-allies-costs-and-value.

20    See, for instance, President Barack Obama, 'Remarks by President Obama and Prime Minister Abbott of Australia after bilateral meeting', The White House: Speeches and Remarks, 12 June 2014 https://obamawhitehouse.archives.gov/the-press-office/2014/06/12/remarks-president-obama-and-prime-minister-abbott-australia-after-bilate.

21    See Michelle Grattan, 'Scott Morrison tells public servants: Keep in mind the "bacon and eggs" principle', *The Conversation*, 18 August 2019, https://theconversation.com/scott-morrison-tells-public-servants-keep-in-mind-the-bacon-and-eggs-principle-122021.

22    Zakaria, 'The Self-Doubting Superpower'.

23    See the Global Foundation website, https://globalfoundation.org.au/wp-content/uploads/2022/12/Letter-from-Vatican-Secretary-State.pdf.

24    Phillip Scanlan, 'Australia and the United States, towards a deeper relationship', Speech to the Australian Institute of International Affairs (WA Branch), 26 July 2005, quoted in Vince Scappatura, *The US Lobby and Australian Defence Policy* (Melbourne: Monash University Publishing, 2019), p. 129. See also Diane Stone, 'The informal diplomacy of the Australian American leadership dialogue', *Australian Journal of International Affairs*, 2015, www.academia.edu/16743728/The_informal_diplomacy_of_the_Australian_American_leadership_dialogue.

25    Vince Scappatura, *The US Lobby and Australian Defence Policy*, p. 135. Scappatura's work offers a forensic examination of how a private, unaccountable organisation, operating *sub limina*, can posture as a significantly more authoritative and credible organisation than any serious due diligence might substantiate.

26    Zakaria, 'The Self-Doubting Superpower'.

**Afterword**

1     Hunter S. Thompson, *Fear and Loathing: On the Campaign Trail '72* (San Francisco: Straight Arrow Books, 1973), p. 415.

2     Jake Wilson, 'On the Beach, 60 years on, still makes a mark at the bottom of the world', *The Sydney Morning Herald*, 14 January 2019. It was actually Neil Jillett who created the aphorism, but who cares?

# Acknowledgements

Many literary offspring are conceived in haste and born after prolonged labour. *The Odd Couple* could not be more different. It took almost a year for the team at the Australia Institute to decide whether the absurdities of the Trump administration (America's revenge on itself), the 6 January 2021 assault on the US Capitol and the prospect of a second Trump presidency warranted yet another study on the Australia–America relationship. The answer was a resounding 'yes'. From go to whoa, it took just over six months to complete. Less time for conception and more time for creation and crafting would have been ideal. But we did want to mark Independence Day 2024 by releasing this book on 4 July. We hope that policymakers on both sides of the Pacific appreciate the gesture.

Books such as this never appear in a vacuum. In 2016, Melbourne University Press published *Australia's American Alliance*. It is a particularly useful book, bringing together a collection of essays that provide a remarkable insight into the self-absorbed, self-reinforcing and self-referential character of Australia's 'official' ANZUS policymaking. Confirmation bias is rampant, and there is Kool-Aid galore as the inhabitants of the echo chamber amplify each other's opinions. It is all so safe and bipartisan. It is all so uncritical of Australian deference and complacency and American hauteur and disdain. It was necessary reading for this book, and I am grateful to the authors for their faithful conformity to the 'received wisdom'. It is emblematic of the intellectual consequences of strategic subjugation. A measure of heterodoxy would have been so welcome.

Fortunately, over the past few years there have also been critical commentaries on the dynamics and nature of the Australia–America relationship. James Curran's stimulating 2016 Lowy Institute paper, *Fighting with America*, asked whether Australia had become too reliable as an American partner, and advocated greater independence and single-mindedness on Australia's part in managing the alliance. Vince Scappatura, in his investigation into how a private, self-directing and unaccountable foreign policy franchise could manipulate and manoeuvre bilateral relationship management for its own purposes, delivered an entirely different critique of Australia's complacency. His 2019 study, *The US Lobby and Australian Defence Policy*, is an eye-opening and eye-watering account of how entrepreneurs captured the policy high ground. Emma Shortis challenged foreign and strategic policymakers to examine the high cost of 'sharing' with America and the flimsiness of the myths on which that sharing is based. Her 2021 book, *Our Exceptional Friend*, is a confronting journey into the real costs of dependence and its potentially fatal consequences. Nick Bryant, with his journalist's eye for colour, movement and danger, chronicles the missteps and self-delusion that have dragged America towards atrophy, impotence and possible self-destruction. His 2021 page-turner, *When America Stopped Being Great: A History of the Present*, is a latter-day jeremiad, as electrifying as it is terrifying. It is the necessary companion piece to Michael Pembroke's 2021 *America in Retreat: The Decline of US Leadership from WW2 to Covid-19*, a relentless trip through American bullying and sanctimonious cant. And in his 2022 volume, *Sub-Imperial Power: Australia in the International Arena*, Clinton Fernandes details how Australia constantly pulls its punches in its dealings with the United States, highlighting once again the dangers of complacency and subservience.

I am deeply indebted to each of these scholars for their provocative portraits of a dystopian future. They galvanised me into considering whether we had any credible alternative to a partnership with America and, if not – that is my conclusion – how we might save our mutual hides.

*The Odd Couple* is the result. It is in important respects a sequel to *No Enemies No Friends: Restoring Australia's Global Relevance*, published by Upswell in mid-2022. The anti-Chinese sentiment that appeared during the global COVID-19 pandemic found expression, in both Australia and America, in alarmist academic and political commentary claiming that China was on a path to war. Academics, commentators claiming connection to the intelligence communities, journalists, politicians and some prominent public-sector leaders offered alarmist assessments that Australia and America had little time in which to prepare for annihilation. The stridency of their claims was inversely proportional to the actual threat – not that a lack of evidence is ever a barrier to an outbreak of hysteria. While the risk of war is properly a subject of government policy deliberation, informing as it does considerable expenditures on defence equipment, the threat of armed conflict is an unsatisfactory basis for force planning. Threats emerge quickly. Military systems – especially in Australia, it seems – take decades to materialise. That is why disciplined defence planning is based on the objective characteristics and dynamics of armed conflict – conducted in space and time, on the land, at sea and in the air – and the risk assessments that quantify the shape and cost of strategic prudence. Risk is the assessment of possible negative outcomes. Threat is the articulation of fear, which is never a sound basis for planning.

And as the team at the Australia Institute discussed risk, it dawned on us that the risk of a social and political collapse on America's part was a significantly more consequential spectre than the 'threat' of an armed attack by China. Ben Oquist, director at the time, was an early advocate for a deep dive into Australia's transpacific partnership. Richard Denniss, the current director, also offered enthusiastic support and provided in-depth feedback on the text. I am grateful to both for their confidence and for providing a convivial workplace for my practice of the writer's craft. My colleagues at the Australia Institute were characteristically helpful and supportive, with a constant stream of ideas and suggestions that invariably found their way into the text. Jack Thrower, one of the institute's economists, dreamed up the cover. They are a wonderful group of clever young people. It is a privilege to work with them.

It is our practice at the Australia Institute, as we develop our ideas and test our solutions, to engage with thought leaders and opinion formers across the Australian policy community. The late Allan Gyngell was an early advocate of the need for a close and sympathetic examination of the quality of the bilateral relationship and was characteristically generous in articulating his ideas. His groundedness, modesty and wisdom are missed by everyone in the foreign policy community. My long-time friends Ross Buckley, James Renwick and Patrick Walters were unstinting sounding boards, reinforcing logic and constraining fancy. They bring a depth of knowledge to which I can only aspire, and as conversationalists they are without peer.

I have a particular debt to the participants at our July 2023 Colloquium, held in Canberra. Indeed, this book is both a distillation and a winnowing of the many gripes, hopes and ideas that were ventilated during a day's conversation. Chris Barrie, Victoria Cooper, James Curran, John McCarthy, Beejay Silcox (whose subsequent comments on the cultural affinities between Australia and America were invaluable), Deborah Snow, Anne Twomey, Terri-ann White – along with my Australia Institute colleagues – deeply influenced both its structure and content. Andrew Farran and Clare Wright were, as always, generous with their time and their insights. I am especially grateful to Emma Shortis, whose wonderful book *Our Exceptional Friend* was an early inspiration for this enterprise, as I mentioned above. And I am also indebted to Joey Herlihy, a master's program student at Georgetown University's

Walsh School of Foreign Service, who spent his Northern Hemisphere summer vacation labouring through Canberra's Southern Hemisphere winter to provide the foundations and much of the superstructure of the chapter on the bilateral economic relationship. If cheerfulness, energy and intelligence are reliable indicators, Joey has a brilliant future before him.

The ideas in this book have many progenitors, and I thank all of them wholeheartedly. But how they have come together – well, that is entirely my responsibility, and any errors of fact or interpretation are entirely mine.

Channelling T.S. Eliot to some extent, the renowned critic F.R. Leavis had a point when he claimed that literary texts do not simply stand on their own, but are embedded in the cultures, societies and traditions that sustain them. Publishing embeds culture, society and tradition in the literary texts on which the national conversation depends. It is a labour of love, bringing ideas and stories out of the shadows and into the light of public scrutiny and enjoyment. Eliot wrote:

> Between the conception
> And the creation
> Between the emotion
> And the response
> Falls the Shadow.

Terri-ann White and her imprint, Upswell, resolve the indecision of 'the shadow' and turn the whimper back into a bang – to strain the metaphor beyond its limit. Without Terri-ann's energy and enterprise, and Upswell's fabulous editor Julian Welch, this author would remain, like the hollow men, in 'death's dream kingdom'. And Jeanne Ryckmans, who brought Upswell into my life, remains a source of inspiration. She is an agent extraordinaire.

Writing is at once exhilarating and painful: exhilarating for authors and painful for those who endure their strange behaviours. My wife, Rhyan, has again put up with the silences and the staring into space that, in my case, pass for creativity. Without her love, care, encouragement and patience, *The Odd Couple* would have remained nothing more than an idea in search of words. Thank you.

**About Upswell**

Upswell Publishing was established in
2021 by Terri-ann White as a not-for-profit
press. A perceived gap in the market for
distinctive literary works in fiction, poetry
and narrative non-fiction was the motivation.
In her years as a bookseller, writer and then
publisher, Terri-ann has maintained a watch
on literary books and the way they insinuate
themselves into a cultural space and are
then located within our literary and cultural
inheritance. She is interested in making books
to last: books with the potential to still be
noticed, and noted, after decades and thus
be ripe to influence new literary histories.